The Goals of Higher Education

THE WILLIAM J. COOPER FOUNDATION LECTURES
AT SWARTHMORE COLLEGE

The Goals of Higher Education

HAROLD TAYLOR · JACOB KLEIN

RICHARD SULLIVAN · GORDON ALLPORT

BRAND BLANSHARD · ARTHUR MORGAN

WILLIS D. WEATHERFORD, JR., Editor

HARVARD UNIVERSITY PRESS
Cambridge, Massachusetts   1960

378.04
W 378

Library of Congress Catalog Card Number 60–8005
Printed in the United States of America

Contents

The Goals of Higher Education

Introduction

A rising ferment of public questioning has forced itself upon our educational system since the Second World War. But no educational system can remain vital unless it continually creates from within constructive criticism of itself. This series of lectures on the goals of higher education is dedicated to that task. They were delivered at Swarthmore College in the spring of 1958 under the auspices of the William J. Cooper Foundation. The foundation was established by a bequest from Mr. William J. Cooper to bring to the college outstanding statesmen, scholars, and business leaders.

Since the Second World War our most persistent educational question has been how to adapt our institutions of learning to the ever-growing numbers of students. On the lowest and quantitative plane, state legislatures have been concerned to maintain the flow of teachers and buildings commensurate with the increase of students. Important though this is, it is but part of the problem, since it side-steps the questions of quality and the persons to whom this education should be made available. The American people have not developed a consistent philosophy of who should be educated, unless "more and more education for more and more people" can be said to constitute such a philosophy. Some, viewing education quantitatively, have become fanatics in Santayana's terms by redoubling their efforts when they have lost sight of the goal. Some of the problems which we face because of the increasing numbers of college students are discussed by Dr. Richard Sullivan.

Beyond the question of numbers is the problem of quality, but to judge quality we must know the purpose of education. The educational philosopher's view of the goals of our learning institutions rests on his concept of the nature of man and the nature of knowledge, though most educators are willing to accept their goals without tracing them back to these philosophical presuppositions. Since the Second World War a renewed interest has intensified the running debate over the proper ends and means of education; at the extremes of this argument are the progressive educators and those who follow the classical view.

The classical tradition holds the chief end of education to be mental development. If one is a philosophical idealist and views man's distinguishing characteristic as rationality, he will likely adhere to this tradition, but many others would also agree regardless of their philosophical position. It is held that the best way to achieve this mental development is to acquaint the student with the best literature and thought which our culture has produced since the Greeks. Language is stressed, since it transmits culture, and mathematics is emphasized as the highest development of the rational faculties. Learning to think and evaluate is crucial; objective and universal values lie at the center of the classic curriculum, so the humanities form the core of study. Mental development thus involves not merely a study of rational analysis, but of values and virtue as well. Since men in their essential nature are alike, this type of education is the best basic discipline for everyone. The chief qualification for teaching should be scholarship. It is this education which has traditionally been known as "liberal," but today it is followed by very few schools and colleges, although many still hold to it as an ideal. Modifications of this view can be seen in the writing of Robert Hutchins, Arthur Bestor, Albert Lynd, Gilbert Highet, as well as President A. Whitney Griswold of Yale and former President Harold Dodds of Princeton, and are reflected in several of the lectures which follow.

If, on the other hand, one is a pragmatist believing that no great gulf separates mind and matter and that those ideas are true which give satisfactory results, he is likely to ally himself with progressive educators who hold that the chief end of education is to help the individual develop all his faculties to their full potentiality. Since thought has no object outside of experience, it is through experience that education must be achieved; but since experience is as broad as life itself, so education must also be all inclusive. Truth is found through experience, but experience is always subject to re-evaluation; thus no final truth nor objective universal values can exist. The progressive therefore does not seek to transmit our cultural heritage to the younger generation except to the extent that it illumines present experience. Education should aid our youth to evolve their own ideas and ideals; "good" values are those which permit us to make a satisfactory working relationship with our present surroundings, so an important aim of education is to help the student adjust to his surroundings and to himself. Since individual development is primary and individuals differ, it follows that many types of education must be provided; a vocational school serves just as basic a need as does a liberal college. Individual freedom and great latitude in the choice of curriculum to suit individual needs are essential; an effort is made to introduce the empirical or scientific approach to as many studies as possible. Since individual development is central, motivation to learn is crucial; a good teacher is one who can find a way of motivating each student, and good methods of teaching are at least as important as scholarship in a teacher. John Dewey stands as the pre-eminent exponent of this view, though he never carried it so far as some of his followers. Teachers College at Columbia has spread the progressive idea which now dominates most primary and secondary education throughout the land.

Although there are many intermediate positions, the two views above have been stated in their extreme form in order to help the reader place the present essays in the context of current educational discussion. One will recognize ideas from both these schools of thought in considerably modified form in several of the following lectures. In particular, the lectures by Dr. Jacob Klein and Dr. Harold Taylor show generous elements of these two contrasting views. But the refreshing thing about the whole series is that the authors have not allowed themselves to be bound by the traditional categories of educational thought but have ranged freely in finding a new synthesis of their own.

A partial result of the whole debate outlined above can be seen in two contrasting developments in American education during the last decade. In response to a resurgent statement of the classical position, many colleges and universities have decided that the old elective system permitted a student to graduate with almost no acquaintance with his great cultural heritage. Core curriculums have been instituted and required of all to provide a minimum of what "every educated person should know." In many institutions special general education studies have been introduced, with a heavy emphasis on reading from timeless authors. These programs have developed a second emphasis. In a world racked by crises, the ability to make sound value judgments has assumed renewed importance. It has been felt that pragmatism has invaded even the humanities and that in the name of objectivity faculties have been unwilling to discuss values, so that students do not gain experience in weighing conflicting claims. Yet this is an essential ability in the present or any age. General education programs stimulate this faculty, since the student reads the masters of the ages, who have in large measure discussed problems of value—intellectual, aesthetic, or moral. Dr Brand Blanshard discusses the place of values in higher education in the fifth lecture.

Concurrently, a very different trend, springing from the pragmatic thesis, is seen both at high school and college level in the expanded emphasis on science. To be sure, science has always been an important part of the liberal classical curriculum because it helps us understand nature. But the recent interest stems from a pragmatic and technological interest in controlling nature. It is study for results rather than for enlightenment; understanding becomes a means rather than an end in itself. No doubt both these trends will strengthen modern education, even though they are motivated by different philosophies. If this is true, it emphasizes that neither the classical thesis nor the progressive antithesis is an adequate educational philosophy for modern man. This series of lectures was designed to help evolve a more adequate statement of goals for higher education.

Until the First World War, college and even high school education was reserved for a privileged few. In America this was a privilege of income and leisure, but in Europe it more nearly resembled an elite of ability. The relative homogeneity of the student body made the classical idea of one education for all easy to maintain. But the vast increase in college students has inevitably broadened their diversity of ability as well as of vocational interests. Vocational and professional training has all but swamped liberal learning. High schools find it increasingly necessary to give special treatment to the retarded and gifted youth in order even to approximate the democratic ideal of equal opportunity for development. Colleges find the range of ability among students a continually more difficult problem; to what extent and in what manner should colleges provide special opportunities to match the special talent of the gifted? Research shows that students can also be separated into personality types and that these types of students may require different sorts of classes for optimum learning. Should colleges endeavor to create special programs for different personality types as well as for students of differing abilities? These are some of the questions to which Dr. Gordon Allport has addressed himself.

During the greater part of the nineteenth century, Oxford and Cambridge existed to produce good citizens; they gave a general liberal education to an elite who were expected to govern judiciously. They were not professional schools, nor did they think of the advancement of knowledge as primary. Much of this viewpoint was transplanted to the American liberal arts college. Do our colleges have a responsibility to make our youth ready for leadership in the community? How can such an end be accomplished? Dr. Arthur Morgan discusses these questions in the final lecture of the series.

This brief introduction has raised only a few of the questions discussed in the following essays and posed by current educational developments. Many others remain. How can the universities provide a liberal education and at the same time train the professional groups? How can we re-establish communication across departmental lines so that the university can be a *community* of scholars rather than an aggregation of specialists? Can the university have a unifying view of life which gives coherence to education, and if so, what can serve this high purpose? Can we afford to exclude religion, as a vital aspect of experience, from serious study in our educational institutions? All these questions can be satisfactorily answered only as we gain an adequate idea of the goals of education. It was the purpose of these lectures to help Swarthmore College in clarifying these goals. We make them available to a wider public hoping that others will be stimulated by them as we have been. In presenting these lectures to the public, the Cooper Foundation and Swarthmore College express their deep appreciation to the several authors for their creative insights and for their cooperation in making this series a unified whole.

Willis D. Weatherford
Chairman, William J. Cooper Foundation

INDIVIDUALISM AND
THE LIBERAL TRADITION

By Harold Taylor

The idea of liberalism and of liberal education is a fairly
recent one and a local one. It has its origin in the Western
world, in political and social changes which began in the
seventeenth century with the discovery of a new universe
and a new world, with a new mercantile class and the
growth of common law. Liberalism as a social philosophy
grew in the eighteenth century through the organization of
new political forms and social classes. It exploded the nineteenth century with a series of revolutions against the re-
gimes of church, royalty, aristocracy, and state. It emerged
into the twentieth century to face its greatest test in two
world wars, a world depression, and any number of minor
wars and current conflicts and revolutions. There are
those who look at this short history and say that liberalism
is now bankrupt, that individualism is dead, and that a
liberal democracy cannot stand up against authoritarian
systems, either in international affairs or in the development of internal strength. What is needed is said to be a
stronger and more ordered political doctrine and stronger
social controls, including the control of education.

Liberal education is the intellectual and cultural instrument through which the basic ideas of liberalism are transmitted and developed. This kind of education began with

the clusters of scholars and students who joined together to study, examine, and revise the known ideas of Greek society, religion, and classical thought. Throughout the history of Western society, liberal education has been both the institutional expression of liberalism as a philosophy and the intellectual force which helped to create the political and social changes of liberalized societies.

The central idea of liberal education is therefore the idea of individualism and individual freedom. Its tradition is that of the liberal revolt against state authority, religious dogma, and all the elements of the old regime. It is allied to the Protestant movement in its assertion of the individual conscience and the individual reason against church doctrines and church control. It is part of the tradition of the enlightenment and the age of reason. It is centrally concerned with the struggle of reason against ignorance, moral values against brute force, freedom against tyranny.

The tradition of liberalism and of liberal education does not lie solely within the arts and the humanities; it has to do with the doctrines of social progress and the disciplines of science. For it was the combination of liberal social theory and scientific thinking which infused Western society with a spirit of discovery and the idea of change. The universe itself had been considered a static entity; space was a local affair; society was fixed and unchangeable. The scientific spirit, with its insistence on rational proof and objective evidence, was the driving force in the seventeenth century which released intellectual and social energies into new dimensions of thought and action.

The characteristic of the modern movements in philosophy, the movements which began in the nineteenth century and set the framework for the twentieth, is the scientific basis on which they stand. In the nineteenth century, the scientific disciplines, when applied to the study of nature, society, and man, produced discoveries in all fields from physics to psychology. The idea of evolutionary change affected the concept of religion, of society, of art, of human nature; the philosophies of Bergson, Russell, Whitehead, Dewey, and Santayana, for example, are based on the facts of science and their interpretation by scientists and philosophers. The new emphasis on psychology as a science came from the application of philosophical theory and the scientific method to individual case studies of human nature, culminating in the work of Freud, Jung, and Adler, among others. New attitudes to the individual found their way into twentieth-century literature, poetry, painting, sculpture, and the arts. From Martha Graham to Dylan Thomas, from the surrealist poets to the experimental novelists, from Bauhaus design to Frank Lloyd Wright, new forms, new traditions, new philosophies emerged in the first half of this century. The central core of the new aesthetic was a philosophy of individualism.

On the other hand, the central idea of modern philosophy came to be that of a profusion of unfolding possibilities emerging from the development of the universe and everything in it through billions of years. If the world is a huge organism, alive, changing, moving toward an expanding goal whose ultimate point is unknown, then everything in it is in a state of change. Everything in it is in the process of becoming something else. The teeming birth of cells, the constant unfolding of new forms of life were all considered to be demonstrations of the creative energy which lies within nature.

William James, to come closer to our present world, accepted a philosophy of creative evolution and accepted the idea of creativity as a basic concept in his system of thought. The human mind, for William James, was continually creating its own knowledge out of the day-to-day run of human experience. "All the while," said James in his

Principles of Psychology, "the world *we* feel and live in will be that which our ancestors and we, by slow cumulative strokes of choice, have extricated out of this, like sculptors, by simply rejecting certain portions of the given stuff. Other sculptors, other statues from the same stone. Other minds, other worlds from the same monotonous and inexpressive chaos."

The essence of the modern movement in education is the idea of creative experience and its liberating effects on the individual. The modern movement is in fact a fundamental shift in attitude toward life itself. It refuses to accept the conventional forms in which life is presented to us and looks for fresh ways of interpreting facts, for new forms of art, of architecture, of scientific discovery, of literature, of society. It refuses to accept the fatalism of the classical philosophy, or the classical tone of reconciliation to things as they exist, or the warning to mankind that everything which is done has already been done before and that everything will pass away and return to nothingness. The modern movement believes in the reality of novelty and discovery; it believes in progress toward goals which man has made and which he can remake as he goes along.

For it is true that every society is in a state of equilibrium, brought about by the balance of opinion, both private and public, and by what we call political, economic, and social forces. But what we mean when we use these words is that people live together as they do, with certain laws, habits, customs, and privileges, because there are individual opinions held by all the members of a society about what should be done and what should not. Educational institutions transmit the habits of mind and the social customs of a given society from one generation to the next. They are essentially stabilizing forces where children are taught the point of view and the values of the older generation.

But I do not believe that schools and colleges should be

merely the agencies for transmitting American middle-class values. This is in fact what they usually are, when they should be agencies for transforming and re-creating the values of each generation and each individual within each generation.

Here is the point at which newer theories of education in this century have broken with conservative doctrine. Each generation of children is different from its predecessor; each child has a fresh start; and the institutions of education should be agencies of creative effort by children and teachers together for adding new insight and new ideas to the present fund of knowledge and custom. This demands a positive attitude by the teacher toward the student, one which looks toward the student expectantly for a fresh outlook and new truth.

The creative element in a society consists of the people in it who do not accept everything as it is but who question and probe to find new ways of improving whatever exists. Liberal education is concerned with the nurture of creative energy. The creative element in education, and therefore in society, is a thrust against convention and standardized opinion.

Creative thinking and imagination in politics and social issues, coupled with a will to act on ideas in which one believes, will change societies and whole civilizations. The radicals and the heretics are those to whom we owe the greatest social debt. Without them the social order becomes either rigid or flabby.

It is one of the characteristics of our age that we have no radicals and heretics. Salvador Dali is now a society painter. Norman Thomas is welcomed by the conservatives. Howard Fast is again respectable. *The Chicago Tribune* in some of its columns reads like a liberal weekly. In a democratic society in which authority and status are not centered in any one social group, the authority of a particular point of view held by a few cannot prevail. On the other hand, when majority opinion is reinforced by a common prosperity, the tensions within a society do not develop creative thinking with a cutting edge but rather generate a number of accommodations of one social group with another. Everything must be adjusted.

I would therefore conclude that, in societies as in the individual, creativity needs at its base a drive—a moral, aesthetic, and intellectual energy which will not rest content with the forms of life, art, or social order that presently exist. I would also conclude that in education, as in society and the individual, the way to evoke that energy is to give freedom, encouragement, and help to the individual, to create in him a sense of self-confidence, to trust him, to cherish him, and to give him that sense of expectancy for the excitement of the unforeseen which is the necessary condition of the creative act. It is the task of education to teach that sense of expectancy, and it is in the college of liberal arts that the task can best be carried out.

This task must now be undertaken in the face of a new attitude on the part of the present generation of Western youth. Having been brought up in the Western world to have no illusions, the present generation is not so much disillusioned, since it had none to start with, as unillusioned. It accepts the world as it finds it, having been taught to do so, having lacked the leadership of a previous generation which had lost faith in itself and its liberalism. The present generation has lived through its own private duration of time. We need to know what are the truths of this generation, what are its particular hopes, expectations, and needs.

At a conference held at Sarah Lawrence College, a cross section of three hundred college students from forty colleges met with eight discussion leaders, among whom were W. H. Whyte, Jr., author of *The Organization Man*, and Robert Hutchins. The conference undertook to consider the character of the present college generation. It was agreed among the students that this is an age of the security-minded and the conformist, an age of public relations in which the problem, Mr. Hutchins said, is not to be good but to look good. Mr. Hutchins commented further on the fact that the magazines are full of articles on dieting, a sign that we all have too much. He found the spirit of the age in an article in an issue of *Coronet* with the title "How to *Look* Ten Pounds Lighter."

The students said that this is the age of the safe man, the man who, right from his kindergarten to his college days, wants to be adjusted, well-liked, popular, noticed, and successful. One student said that the ideal is to be well-rounded—well-rounded, that is, in the sense that all the rough edges have been smoothed off until a man is perfectly round, like a tennis ball with a little friendly fuzz on top.

One student went on to say, "We've replaced the ideal of splendid excellence with a new ideal of competent decency." The speaker, who was a Princeton man, said, "The species currently inhabiting the Princeton campus resembles a lumbering armadillo, with the guts of a clam. . . . It is one thing to want the calm before the storm, it is quite another to want the calm itself, without the storm.

"Everywhere is blah, and when our own blah stops like a toy that has run down, we turn on television and the phonograph to stuff the void. Everywhere, in the subway, in the airport waiting room, in rest rooms even, the music plays and races through our veins like a file of ants—but only while the Wurlitzer whirls. When we run out of dimes, when the joint closes up for the night, not one beat remains in our bones. Only a pre-dawn inquietude. But, happy to report, we are slowly erasing this unpleasantness from our daily schedule: with the pocket-sized radio, we soon will never walk alone.

"We have no other-rooms, no private dens, we do not have the back-shops Montaigne advised all men to keep; our hearts are public houses. . . . Wine needs time and the darkness of a cellar. But the minute we receive any juice at all, we spill it out before it can assume an intoxicating dimension: hence the flatness of our speech and of our lives."

This young man and others at the conference went on to say that we had heard enough about how flattened out we all were, how conformist, how security-minded. The real question is, "How do we go beyond it? The students found one answer in a phrase quoted from Dylan Thomas' *Under Milk Wood*, a phrase whispered by a milkmaid to herself, "Oh, isn't life a terrible thing, thank God." Another answer came in the insistence that the individual must discover for himself his own identity, must press forward to his own conception of himself and his world, must learn to feel and to think for himself. To do otherwise is to accept easily the opinions of others, so that in the safety of the crowd one's own opinions and character will never be revealed. From another student came the answer that the individual must get outside himself into some effort in the service of humanity; one must escape beyond the limits of self-interest, self-concern.

There has been so much talk about the value of a liberal education for starting a commercial career that students and educators and the public have become confused about its true purpose. In most countries other than America, the student does not go to the university merely to increase his income in later life. In Burma, in Ceylon, in Indonesia, in Africa, to be a student is to accept the responsibility for becoming a leader of one's country, for being educated to bring one's gifts to the country's service at a time when education has not been able to catch up to the demand for educated men and women who can build new countries.

The student in America has the same responsibility, and it is through the college of liberal arts that he learns to fulfill it. A student is a person who is learning to fulfill his powers and to find ways of using them in the service of mankind. The student at his best has a purity of motive which is the mark of his true function. He wants to know the truth, to know what is good, not merely for his own or for other people's advantage but in order to achieve his maturity as a student. He is granted the priceless advantage of looking openly at the world to discover its secrets. He is given the rare privilege of withholding his assent to the claims the world makes for its own particular brand of truth, and he can decide what he thinks on the basis of the evidence, not on the basis of pressure, because this is in fact what it means to be a student, and what the world asks the student to be. For a little time before he begins a life which will gradually involve him in more and more commitment to tasks and duties which are not central to the concern with truth and ideals, the student lives in a world of discovery and of possibility, where nothing is yet completely settled, where everything, including the achievement of greatness, is still actively possible.

The student must make the most of this time, for it may never come again. If his life as a student does not possess the excitement, the innocence, and the hope of the true inquirer, he may never again experience a time for thoughtful and sensitive attention to the big issues of human life. If he possesses that quality in his life as a student, he can be sure it will remain with him as a way of thinking and acting for the rest of his days.

The real challenge to this country is not from the propaganda battle with the Soviets, nor from the science and missiles race, nor from anywhere outside the United States. The real challenge lies deep within American culture. It is simply: How can we give to our young people—those who will become scientists, artists, writers, intellectuals, teachers, lawyers, businessmen, doctors, and our future citizens—the educational support they need to carry out their mission as Americans? The outcry for more science drowns out the pleas for more art, more philosophy, more depth in our education, more depth in our culture.

It is a symbol of our present attitudes that we now find ourselves with huge expenditures of money and manpower for shooting rockets to the moon and exploring outer space, while we spend trivial amounts to handle the problems which lie on our educational doorsteps. If we can have a new committee of distinguished experts on outer space, why can we not have at least an equivalent committee on the deepest inward problem of all: the quality of our American education and American culture?

The true scientist, as is the case with any educated professional, depends for his achievement on the quality of his total education. The quality of his total education depends not only on the particular training he has had in science or any other field, but on the infusion of the passion for learning into his intellectual blood stream. If we are to have first-rate education, we must have first-rate teachers, and we will not get first-rate teachers until we bring into the teaching profession the very best among our young people.

I think we will gain little by continuing to condemn American high school education for the fact that it does not compare favorably with the European or the Soviet system. The Soviet system is itself a secondhand copy of some of the worst defects of the European system and is as rigidly organized as the nineteenth-century system which prevailed before new advances were made in this field in the Western world, particularly in America. There is no doubt that American youth could do more in high school and in college than they are now doing; they want to do more, can do more, and will do more if they are given the opportunity. But this is not to say that therefore we should select our youth for specific technical and professional potentials and then put them at the service of their country by training them to become specialists in assigned fields which are needed for America's military supremacy and prosperity. If we try to do that, we will destroy the most important values we already have in our high school system, which is strong, growing, and lacks only the support of the American people to gain its full maturity.

This is not a matter of increasing academic discipline by the administration of what are called hard subjects, but by enhancing the quality of the teaching of all subjects in every way. This can only be done when we develop in our students a sense of commitment about what they are doing and a sense of importance in being students. The young will never achieve this sense of importance until we treat them seriously and treat our educational needs as a far greater national crisis than those involved in our present state of military and scientific preparation.

Liberal education is the means by which the student achieves his selfhood. To gain the flavor of individuality, for a person or an institution, it is necessary to be oneself and not to be simply a cluster of approved characteristics. It is necessary to give up wanting to be liked and wanting to have everything smooth and easy. It is necessary to discover what truths are really true and really valuable, and to discover this by oneself. No one can make these discoveries except by individual effort, and life in the college of liberal arts must be organized in such a way that the student is continually thrust into situations from which he must extricate himself by his own efforts.

The educational destinies of the student and the teacher are in fact identical. Where teaching is cautious, noncommittal, and inhibited, learning is timid and ineffectual. Christopher Fry, when he writes of the effect of hostile criticism on the artist, is describing the teacher, the scholar, and the student. "The artist," says Fry, "at some level of himself, will respect an adverse criticism, if he can understand it; he has no wish to get away with anything, and he is so close to his work that he is, or should be, glad of a more distant eye. . . . But creative criticism—by which I mean criticism that takes as its starting place the individual talent it deals with and not some ready-made rule of thumb or personal preference—creative criticism has always been rare . . . much of the rest is as boring as a small child who insists on being looked at. And everywhere today can be heard the patter of tiny criticism, the busy sound of men continually knowing what they like. How anything manages to create itself at all is a wonder."

I should like to say that learning does not thrive in the situation in which the students are on one side facing a set of requirements, all the way from examinations and grades based on them to required texts, lectures, and particular subjects, with the faculty on the other, waiting with their criticisms to catch the man who has not done his work, or who has not read the right book, or who does not say what he is supposed to. In that situation, the intelligence and animal cunning of the student are used to beat the system rather than to learn, and teaching becomes a series of tiny punitive actions which keep the student constantly on his guard. He is then unable to let himself go in the enjoyment of the reading which he wants to do, reading which moves him into new insight or captures him as he reads or tells him things that he wants to know and needs to know in order to accomplish something important to him. Most good students can beat any system the educators put in front of him, and the "best" student, the one we used to admire when I was in college, was the man who could beat the system with no apparent effort, who was so clever at it and showed so much style and grace under stress that no one could have believed he had ever opened a book, attended a class, or listened to a word that was said.

It is therefore very important to change the system so that it is one you cannot beat because there is nothing to beat except yourself, a system which does not align the forces in opposite camps but which joins together the teacher and the student in a common endeavor to gain insight into truth and knowledge.

When we ask what is the greatest evil in the whole of education, the answer is boredom. A bore is a person who tells you things you do not need or want to know, and to be bored is to know ahead of time what is going to be said or done and to put up the natural defenses of the body and the mind against it. Freshness, spontaneity, joy, responsiveness, passion, commitment—these are the positive words which mark off the areas where learning and living happen. The freshness and spontaneity must come from within the lives and minds of the teachers and the students, and the great teacher is one who is a master in the art of starting fresh things moving, of evoking response, of putting things in new relations which have not been seen before, of creating the sense of importance. We all know that the particular materials of knowledge, whether they be science, poetry, or history, are irrelevant to the great teacher. If he is captured by the interest in the knowledge which is his, if he has a sense of commitment to the things he knows, the exact subject might be anything. But this is also true of the student. If he is captured by the ideas, information, values in an area of knowledge, whether this be contemporary politics in China, Greek drama, or the binomial theorem, the intellectual development which we seek as an end of liberal education will be achieved. On the other hand, a study of every subject in the college catalogue will fail to educate him in depth and liberally if the study is undertaken with a feeling of duty and obligation rather than with a feeling of excitement for the thing to be learned.

This is not to say that we should expect or even want everyone to be in a perpetual state of excitement, even if that were possible. There are long stretches in the process of education which involve disciplined attention to fact, necessary tasks to be carried out, simply in order that the student be informed and knowledgeable.

To be well educated, it is necessary to know at least a hundred times more than it is ever necessary to talk about, to have a grasp of so many details and ideas that some sense of comparison among them is possible. But, as is the case in football or tennis, the self-discipline of careful attention to detail, of endlessly taking pains, is essential to the achievement of the joy of the game. Achievement in any field has this same character: the sense of involvement, the willingness to commit oneself to the matter in hand for its own sake, and the satisfaction which comes from doing something difficult and ultimately useful.

The present system of higher education is built on the assumption that learning occurs in one dimension—the dimension of memory. It assumes that the rewards of learning are to be found not in the pleasure and joy of the knowing, not in achievement of belief, not in finding a sense of personal and intellectual identity, but in receiving academic credit, social status, a higher income, and exemption from the necessity of further study or intellectual development after college.

How does learning take place? By the effort of the individual to grasp the materials of knowledge. The process of learning is exactly like the process of creating a work of art. A wish to get at something important must precede the knowing, as hunger is a condition of eating. There is a latent power in the student which can be quickened into action, but only when certain conditions have been met. To move eternally through barren stretches of a subject matter whose relevance to human life and destiny he cannot see, confronted with objects of art, facts, theories, outlines, summaries, and explanations that he must remember rather than understand and use, treated as a sullen child who will be willing to learn only if we bribe him with honors or threaten him with a bad grade, leads the student to ignorance and cynicism. I suggest that we turn to the students themselves for insight into liberal education, that we first understand our students in their terms, that we listen to them in the way we listen to music—sympathetically and receptively—to catch the rhythms, the themes, the sounds of the individual instruments, and the combination of sounds they make together.

I turn to one such student for insight into the problem of learning and the meaning of liberal education. This is a statement from a college freshman who was asked for comment on his first year of college work: "My belief is that one of the principal causes of academic difficulty is not intellectual incapacity, but lack of real interest in the material presented for consumption, for which the student is only partially responsible and for which the instructor may be even less so. But because of the limitations imposed by schedules and time limitations of every sort, the instructor is obliged to present much more material to his students than they can profitably assimilate. Aware of this, he is constantly driving for simplification, for 'essences,' and for 'main ideas.' This, to be sure, can be stimulating. But most of his students, consciously or not, will be dissatisfied because there do not seem to be any problems to work out. All the interest is simplified out of the material, and the course becomes just another collection of facts for the notebook; and no fact, idea, or theory is interesting unless its acquisition has cost something."

I believe what this student has said. If the student is to pay the intellectual price for learning, he must feel that the learning is worth the price. He must be given time enough to read, to concentrate on a few things, without being shuttled from one subject to another throughout each day and from one semester to another throughout each year. He must be allowed to work at the things which interest him most at the time they interest him and not be put off by sequences of introductory, preliminary, and preparatory courses which have to be overcome before the forbidden fruit may be eaten. At least half the student momentum is lost, half his interest is destroyed by the mere fact that he must make his way through preliminary requirements merely in order to study what he wants to study. This is not only psychologically inept on the part of educators, but it is downright unfair to the subject being studied. How many times has the student heard his professor begin a course something like, "I know that you wouldn't be here unless you had to, but we're going to make the best of it together." In their anxiety to eliminate the elective system and to give every student what is called a common core of identical subjects, American educators have lost track of the student himself.

First, then, the content of the curriculum, particularly in the freshman year, should be drawn from original materials in the fields of politics, social science, philosophy, psychology, the arts, literature, and science, dealing with issues and questions which can evoke genuine concern in the students. Courses should be planned which are not summaries and outlines of fields of subject matter but which deal with fresh and interesting ideas about man and nature, society and the individual. The purpose of the course is not to cover ground but to plunge the student into a world of ideas with which he can become truly concerned. He will cover the ground once he becomes involved with the ideas. Give the freshman or the sophomore some room to move among fields of his choice; do not restrict him only to required courses; give him the largest chance he can have to work at the things he wants to know.

Secondly, the lecture system, the academic credit system, the conventional examination system must be replaced by a combination of discussion methods, independent study, tests of achievement, and a greater freedom and responsibility for the individual student.

Thirdly, programs of study should be planned to individual needs, allowing those with the ability to go as far and as fast as their capacities can take them in those areas to which their aims, motives, and interests drive them. This need not involve the complete rearrangement of present college structures but only a change in the attitude of educators toward their students by which their individual differences are respected in the development of educational programs.

Fourthly, the value of immediate experience must be recognized as a prime educational force. Such recognition would mean that students could paint, sculpt, compose, act; write plays, poetry, novels, short stories; carry out research projects and experiments as a regular part of their academic program. The whole life of the college campus is thereby enriched, and the spirit of the creative arts infuses the community with ideas and values which are simply not available from other academic sources.

These are the dimensions of an approach to learning which seeks to maintain the central tradition of liberal education—the tradition of individualism and humanism. It is an approach which gives promise of developing in the generations of the young an open and active mind, a capacity for further growth, and a concern for those ideals of liberalism which can transform a mass of human beings into a community of interesting citizens.

THE IDEA OF LIBERAL EDUCATION

By Jacob Klein

The volume of noise made about education all over the country for many years now has, in recent months, increased to such a crescendo that no man with a sane mind should try to add a note to it. Yet this is what I am doing. There is, of course, always some justification for talking about education: the desire to clarfy the problem itself and to outline certain principles of education that ought to underline all possible practical applications. The problem of education, and certainly of liberal education, has nothing to do with satellites, rocketry, the organization or disorganization of the Pentagon, or the Soviet Union. And yet it is not by chance, as we shall see, that these topics creep into all that educational talk. Nor can it be spoken about in the jargon of educational psychology that takes for granted a great many things and ignores even more. I shall use simple terms at the risk of being trite and saying things that everyone seems to know anyhow. All I want is to remind you of things that you do know.

I

Every one of us (that is, every human being on this earth, without exception) is in some way educated. By this I mean that everyone assimilates from his early childhood sets of customs, beliefs, opinions of all kind, ways of behavior, and even ways of feeling and reacting. Without this elemental kind of education we could not become members of our families, of clans, and of all the smaller or larger communities to which we belong. To be a human being means to be educated in this elemental way, to be educated in the elements of human life. Ours is a double growth, double nourishment, double ripening. Our maturity as human beings does not necessarily coincide with our maturity as living organisms, whereas no such discrepancy seems to exist in the case of our incomprehensible cousins, the animals. The nourishment that leads to our human maturity is provided for us by our parents, our friends, by the innumerable relations, associations, and hierarchies that bind us to the life of our communities; most of the time we are rather passive recipients of this kind of feeding, the lowest and yet perhaps most important level of what I have called elemental education. Most of the time we are not even aware of it.

We are much more aware of another level of elemental education, the one that takes place through what is loosely called "experience." When we invoke experience, we mean mainly the disappointments, difficulties, troubles, obstacles, sufferings, and catastrophes that we have encountered, succumbed to or overcome, and keep anticipating. We become wise (not all of us, to be sure) through such adverse experiences. An elemental generalization takes place, variously called ritual, or tradition, or "ways of doing things," or "the wisdom of the ages."

And at this point a new medium of education comes to the fore, the medium of deliberate reflection and of systematic procedure. In this medium the troubles and obstacles are lifted, by a process of conscious formalization, to a new level, the theoretical level. They become problems. How to solve them has to be learned: formal disciplines are required to bring a problem into focus; that is, to disentangle the kernel from the shell, to proceed methodically, to aid our memory, to make visible what is obscure. This cannot be done without effort and, just as experience is basically painful, formal learning is intrinsically difficult. What I am now describing is the way of formal education that grows out of our elemental education and remains rooted in it. We can dispense with it only at the expense of our winning clarity and greater skills and greater ease to cope with the necessities of life.

Have I now given a complete story of education? Obviously not. I hope of lifting the troubles and obstacles encountered in experience to a new level that I called theoretical, and I introduced the notion of formal disciplines that have to be mastered before theoretical problems can be solved. But how does this lifting take place? How is elemental education transformed into formal education? Did I not skip something crucial at this point? I did. I neglected to mention the lever of that lifting and transforming operation: our questioning. I have, therefore, to retrace my steps and to digress quite a bit in order to consider the phenomenon of questioning at some length.

II

There are many ways of questioning and as many, of course, of answering. Most of our questions are concerned with actions and the means to carry them out. Not only questions like these: "How do you do that?" or "How does one proceed to achieve this end?" but also ones like these: "Have you a pencil?" or "Where is Swarthmore Avenue?" For these latter questions mean that I need a pencil to write something down and that I have to go to that street for some definite purpose. Most questions are indeed of a practical nature; that is, they refer to our doing and acting. Another class of question is formed by queries of a gossipy nature, stemming from our passions—for example, from malice, grudge, vanity, or envy. I suspect that this class of questions is numerically as large as the first one, if not larger. And closely related to the gossipy class there exists a class of questions rooted in what may be called "idle curiosity." It is worth while to reflect for a moment upon the nature of idle curiosity, a curiosity, that is, not guided by any malevolent or benevolent feelings. All gossip has an element of curiosity in it, of wonderment, and that means some quest, however infinitesimal, however distorted, for knowledge. If we were to adopt the metaphor "body of knowledge," we might perhaps say, using a famous phrase from recent political and military history, that gossip constitutes the soft underbelly of knowledge. Gossip is the small tribute that our passionate and appetitive life pays—in very, very small coins—to intellectual life. And it may even reach a nobler part of the body of knowledge, if channeled in a proper direction. This brings us to still another class of questions, where idle curiosity is replaced by a kind of passionate or, if you please, serious curiosity. Questions raised out of idle curiosity are, strictly speaking, none of our business. But when we raise them because we attach very definite importance to the answers—that is, when we make it our business to know the answers—we deal with questions of a different nature. In a trial, where crucial facts have to be established, or in our travels, confronting unfamiliar customs, we ask questions in order to win certainty about things, situations, people and their character, and so forth. Such queries could be properly called exploratory questions. In raising them we want to know, either in order to base a judgment on the knowledge obtained or just simply in order to know. It must be granted that it is not always easy to draw the line between idle curiosity and this nobler kind of curiosity. And I should add, of course, that there are other kinds of questions that do not quite fall into the classes I have mentioned—for example, polite questions, affectionate questions, rhetorical questions—that we need not consider now.

Whatever the difference between these kinds of questions, the practical ones, the gossipy ones, the exploratory ones, and all the others, they all have something in common. They all originate within the horizon of our daily lives, a horizon that includes the familiar and the surprising, routine and novelty, that which has precedents and that which has not. The usual and the unusual are labels put on things and events within the frame of our common and conflicting experience. The unexpected is still woven out of the texture of the expected. And it is this frame of the fundamentally familiar that actually allows us to formulate our questions. That is: they can be put into words. Our questioning is guided by language itself, which is oriented toward the world around us as we know it, including those parts or elements or factors that in some way remain hidden to us. There are usually some dark corners behind or beneath pieces of furniture in a room full of light. The world has many such dark corners. Questions of the kind I have mentioned are like flashlights, the beam of which we direct towards those dark corners. This beam is our language. And it is not too difficult to see that the articulations of language correspond to the ways in which we raise questions and try to answer them. Aristotle, in his analysis of language, has shown how the various modes of being which determine the structure of what we call a world, our world, our not too hospitable home, are prefigured in the various forms of our questioning. The names of his categories are, for the most part, interrogatives.

Let me now consider another aspect of our questioning. In raising a question we expect an answer. A question, by its very nature, wants to be satisfied. Or, in other words, questions as such are possible (including the so-called impossible ones) only on the assumption that there is something which we do not know but which can be known. And this something is expected to appear in any answer. A question is indeed a state of mind (the state of mind of us as questioning beings) in which we want to know what we do not know. The phenomenon of questioning points to the possibility, at least, of knowledge. The answer that we get is, for the most part, an opinion. We live, for the most part, in holding and meeting opinions. But the important thing about opinions is precisely that they cannot avoid putting on the cloak of knowledge. The possibility of our having opinions rests on the possibility, at least, of our having truth. In our thoughtful moments—and there are not too many—we try to see whether our opinions, our answers to questions, are true or not.

Questioning, then, presupposes as unquestionable that there is something not known: the unknown. And it does that, it seems to me, in two fundamentally different ways. The unknown is understood either as something not yet known or as something once known but forgotten. Whatever the relation between time and the substance or state of knowledge, the temporal character of questioning compels us to envisage the way to knowledge in this double temporal perspective. The way to knowledge can be understood either as the pursuit of the not yet known (as discovery of the not yet known) or as the pursuit of the once known (as recovery of the once known). Prophecy and divining are the primordial forms of the first kind of pursuit, myth-making the primordial form of the second kind. Derivative forms (by this term I do not mean to imply any censure) are what we call science and history. Science is forever on the way to discover the not yet known; history is forever recovering the once known. Both embody the type of questioning that I have called the exploratory kind in its purest form. But both also depend on a quite different kind of questioning that I have, with some trepidation, to consider now.

I have said before that within the confines of our horizon there is the expected as well as the unexpected, the old and the new, the known and the unknown, the familiar and the unfamiliar. We do, however, experience a kind of question which, as it were, tends to smash the bounds that limit us. We do occasionally stop altogether and face the familiar as if for the first time—anything: a person, a street, the sky, a fly. The overwhelming impression on such occasions is the strangeness of the thing we contemplate. This state of mind requires detachment, and I am not at all certain to what extent we can contrive its presence. We suddenly do not feel at home in this world of ours. We take a deep look at things, at people, at words, with eyes blind to the familiar. We re-flect. Plato has a word for it: *metastrophē periagogē*, a turnabout, a conversion. We detach ourselves from all that is familiar to us; we change the direction of our inquiry; we do not explore the unknown any more; on the contrary, we convert the known into an unknown. We wonder. And we burst out with that inexorable question: Why is that so? To be sure, we have raised the question "why" before. I can certainly ask: Why did it snow yesterday and does not snow today? Why did Mr. X say this or that to Mr. Y? But this "why" I am talking about now is of a different kind. It does not lead to any discovery or recovery. It calls myself in question with all my questioning. It compels me to detach myself from myself, to transcend the limits of my horizon; that is, it educates me. It gives me the freedom to go to the roots of all my questioning. I can begin to understand that even our gossiping may ultimately rest on the transcendent power of this "why"; that even the children's "why," repeated endlessly to the disgust of their mothers and fathers, may ultimately derive from the human possibility of a total conversion.

III

It is time to revert to the point that prompted me to digress into a consideration of the phenomenon of questioning. The question was: How does elemental education transform itself into formal education? I can try to answer that now.

Elemental education that comes to us through experience, and mostly through adverse experiences, congeals into many kinds of habitual opinions and traditional beliefs. But human questioning never stops. In particular, there is the tendency to go to the roots of our experience, to explore the not yet known or the once known but forgotten. On the other hand, we are bound, at some point at least, to reflect, in wonderment and detachment, not only on all that offers itself to our exploration, on all the visible, the audible, and the intelligible about us, but also on our doing this questioning and exploring, on the means and tools that we use in this enterprise, on ourselves as questioning and exploring beings. This metastrophic reflection, in conjunction with our exporatory questioning, leads us to the establishment of those formal disciplines that I mentioned before. The phenomenon of language, for example (it is only an example, but a significant one), presents itself to us in all its strangeness. We reflect about it, about our speaking to each other. And in exploring this phenomenon this is what we see: we understand each other in speaking and, no doubt, we also misunderstand each other, the latter perhaps more easily than the former. But it is not difficult for us to see that all misunderstanding is based on some understanding. In our speaking, in our language, we convey to each other thoughts that we want to be understood, and we achieve this purpose in spite of all the failings that we may experience. This means that we know how to speak, even if our speech is imperfect. We know how to link words with each other, how to arrange a sequence of such assemblages of words, how to emphasize or de-emphasize some of them, how to make sense, how to tell what we mean, and how to conceal what we mean. Not only do we know how to speak—that is, to speak imperfectly—we also know about this very imperfection. This knowledge, if formalized and formulated, becomes the discipline of grammar. It is of little use in our actual speaking, and yet, upon reflection, we cannot fail to see how utterly dependent on grammatical forms we are in our actual speaking. A similar reflection upon speech leads us to the formal discipline of logic. And I should like, at the risk of being tiresome, to add another example derived from a continuing reflection upon our speech. The act of speaking presupposes the distinguishing of one word from another and the relating of one word to another. It presupposes, that is, counting. For counting is distinguishing and at the same time relating one thing to another. At all times, therefore, speaking and the thinking involved in it have been understood as a sort of computing. This does not mean that in speaking we have an explicit knowledge of numbers. But reflecting and pursuing our exploratory questioning, we arrive at the formal discipline of arithmetic; that is, the science of numbers and of their relations on which all our computing is based.

There is no limit to the further exploration of those formal disciplines. They get enlarged and refined, branch off into other disciplines, combine and support each other, and finally encompass whatever might be knowable in our world; they become all the scientific and historical disciplines taught and learned around the globe. Their acquisition is called *formal education*. And I can repeat now with somewhat greater clarity what I said earlier: formal education grows out of elemental education but remains rooted in it. The formal disciplines come into being as the result of our human ability to detach ourselves from our familiar and conflicting experiences, to turn about, to ask the radical question "why" and to persist in it, pursuing at the same time the exploratory questioning within the horizon in which we live. That is why the theoretical level thus reached always remains a two-sided one: the formal disciplines and sciences can also be applied disciplines and sciences; theoretical problems have or can have direct relation to our doing and making, to our practical life. It is only when we dedicate ourselves to the radical, metastrophic questioning, when we free ourselves from the ever-present concern that the burden of life imposes upon us, that formal education becomes *liberal education*, that the formal disciplines become liberal disciplines or liberal arts. Obviously, this is a precarious and even perilous kind of business. But I do not know of anything worth while that is not precarious and perilous.

IV

The idea of liberal education was conceived by the Greeks. For them it meant an education proper to the free and noble men in contradistinction to slaves and other people engaged in any kind of menial work. To be a free man meant to be a man enjoying leisure—that is, precisely, a man not under any necessity or compulsion to do servile work. But to have leisure in turn meant primarily dealing with affairs of the state, pursuing political ends, and also pursuing knowledge and wisdom. The Greek word for leisure, *scholē*, is significantly the root of the word "school" in Latin as well as in all our vernacular languages. Leisure meant schooling; that is, the opportunity to learn. The history of education is the history of the meaning of the term "school." Let me quote from Aristotle's *Politics* (VIII, 3): "Nature herself, as has often been said, requires that we should be able not only to work well, but to use leisure well; for, as I must repeat once and again, the first principle of all action [that is, the end for the sake of which any action is undertaken] is leisure . . . and therefore the question must be asked in good earnest, what

ought we to do when at leisure? Clearly we ought not to be
amusing ourselves, for then amusement would be the end
of life." And Aristotle goes on: "It is clear, then, that there
are branches of learning and education which we must
study with a view to the enjoyment of leisure, and these
are to be valued for their own sake." To study for the
enjoyment of leisure and in leisure means to be engaged
in liberal education. It is an arduous task. This kind of
education does not look for some goal or good beyond
itself. It is in itself its own end. Long before Aristotle and
long after him, even under totally different social conditions, this statement defined liberal learning and liberal
education. What this understanding of liberal education
assumes is that man's most proper and specific character
is his desire to know. Only in pursuing this goal is man
really man and really free. To acquire the various means
that enable man to persist in this pursuit is to cultivate the
arts of freedom.

The idea of liberal education, then, whether you accept or reject it, is not definable in terms of some peculiar
subject matter. Some applied sciences may well fall outside
its scope. But, by and large, any formal discipline may form
its vehicle and basis. It is not the subject matter that de-
termines the character of studies as liberal studies. It is
rather the way in which a formal discipline, a subject
matter, is taken up that is decisive; whenever it is being
studied for its own sake, whenever the metastrophic way
of questioning is upheld, whenever genuine wonderment
is present, liberal education is taking place.

Foremost among the formal liberal disciplines are, of
course, the mathematical disciplines, the physical sciences,
the science of life, the sciences of language—grammar,
rhetoric, and logic—and also the great works of literature,
those incomparable mirrors of man. But it is a rather fan-
tastic idea to equate liberal studies with the so-called hu-

manities; as if mathematical and scientific disciplines were less human than historical or poetic or philosophical studies. And do we not know that philosophy itself can be studied in the most illiberal way?

V

Liberal education is a precarious and even perilous kind of business. Let me show you the great obstacles that stand in its way. These obstacles are not external impediments, nor do they stem from nonrational sources in man. On the contrary, these obstacles are rooted in what is specifically human in man, and it is not possible not to meet them.

1. The first obstacle is the learning situation itself. What is the ideal learning situation? It is the more or less continuous contact between a student and his teacher, who is another student, more advanced in many ways, but still learning himself. This situation usually does not prevail; in fact, it is extremely rare. Since time immemorial, institutions of learning, especially higher learning, have been established, called "schools"—and the ambiguity of the term becomes immediately apparent. Institutionalization means ordering of activities into certain patterns; in the case of learning activities, into classes, schedules, courses, curriculums, examinations, degrees, and all the venerable and sometimes ridiculous paraphernalia of academic life. The point is that such institutionalization cannot be avoided: both the gregarious and the rational character of man compel him to impose upon himself laws and regulations. Moreover, the discipline of learning itself seems to require an orderly and planned procedure. And yet we all know how this scheduled routine can interfere with the spontaneity of questioning and of learning and the occurrence of genuine wonderment. A student may even never become aware that there is the possibility of spontaneous learning which depends merely on himself and on nobody and

nothing else. Once the institutional character of learning tends to prevail, the goal of liberal education may be completely lost sight of, whatever other goals may be successfully reached. And I repeat, this obstacle is not extraneous to learning. It is prefigured in the methodical and systematic character of exploratory questioning. It has to be faced over and over again.

2. The second obstacle to liberal education is our condition as heirs of intellectual traditions. Here again it is man's own rational nature that brings this obstacle about. Animals do not pass on their skills to their progeny in such a way that those skills can accumulate and grow. Man, and only man, does precisely that. His skills and knowledges are many-storied edifices. Each generation adds something to what had been previously built and preserved. We are proud of this fact and call it progress. And, indeed, such progress does exist in definite areas. But this very fact confronts us with the ever-present danger of sedimentation, fossilization, or petrification of our knowledge. We are fond of pointing to the European universities of the fifteenth and sixteenth centuries which exhibit those petrifying tendencies rather clearly and to exalt the fresh wind of the Renaissance and Humanism that blew all the accumulated dust away. But it behooves us to look at our own institutions of higher learning and to discern these same tendencies among us. We are not immune. This danger is inherent in all learning and all scholarship, and liberal education can never ignore it.

3. But the most serious obstacle is the relation of liberal education to the political community, the state. The Greeks, you remember, saw in leisure, in schooling, the source of a twofold activity: the pursuit of learning and of political ends. Greek thought, in fact, circles continuously about these two highest poles of human life. The relation of man to his citizenship, to the obligations that flow from his being

a citizen, a member of a political community—this relation is one of the great and standing themes of all classical philosophy. Man conceived as a political animal and man conceived as a being desirous to know are not necessarily identical. What complicates matters is the immediate and compelling interest that any state takes in the education of its children and youth. Plato's *Republic* is devoted to this theme. Aristotle says (*Politics*, V, 9): "Of all things I have mentioned, that which most contributes to the permanence of constitutions is the adaptation of education to the form of government," and (in VIII, 1): "No one will doubt that the legislator should direct his attention above all to the education of youth, or that the neglect of education does harm to states. The citizen should be moulded to suit the form of government under which he lives." And let us listen to champions of political doctrines differing sharply from the conservative and aristocratic views of Aristotle. We all know how decisive Jefferson considered education to be for the preservation of the republican form of government. In a letter to John Adams (October 28, 1813), for example, he speaks of a bill he had prepared but which was not adopted by the Virginia legislature: "It was a bill for the more general diffusion of learning. This proposed to divide every county into wards of five or six miles square, like your townships; to establish in each ward a free school for reading, writing, and common arithmetic; to provide for the annual selection of the best subjects from these schools, who might receive, at the public expense, a higher degree of education at a district school; and from these district schools to select a certain number of the most promising subjects, to be completed at an university, where all the useful sciences should be taught. Worth and genius would thus have been sought out from every condition of life and completely prepared by education for defeating the competition of wealth and birth for public trusts."

This educational scheme is conceived as a means to an end, a political end. And Horace Mann, in the middle of the nineteenth century, has this to say: "The establishment of a republican government without well-appointed and efficient means for the universal education of the people is the most rash and foolhardy experiment ever tried by man." How often is the phrase "education for citizenship" used in our schools today! I need not mention the present-day pressure for a change in the educational system of the country to be undertaken for the sake of political ends. The demands of the political community to which we belong are indeed inexorable. It is important to understand, however, that the idea of liberal education cannot be easily reconciled with those demands. It is important to see that there is a definite tension between the exigencies of political life and the self-sustained goal of liberal education. This tension is very great. Consider that ultimately the existence of a state (any state) involves the question of life and death for any of its members. But consider also that no less is at stake for a commitment to leisure in the true understanding of this word. I can hardly think of a better illustration of that tension than the story of Archimedes' death, which I shall recount by way of conclusion.

There are many versions of that story. It seems, at any rate, that Archimedes took an active and even decisive part in the defense of Syracuse, his home town, when it was besieged by the enemy, and he contrived, by means of ingenious machinery, to repel the attacker. He was fulfilling his civic duty. His end came when a Roman soldier stepped close to the place where he was drawing his figures on the sand. This is how Plutarch relates one of the versions: "A Roman soldier, running upon him with a drawn sword, offered to kill him . . . Archimedes, looking back, earnestly besought him to hold his hand a little while, that he might not leave what he was then at work upon inconclusive and imperfect; but the soldier, nothing moved by his entreaty, instantly killed him. The figures on the sand and the problem they represented were for Archimedes a question of life and death; or should we perhaps say a question of more than life and death. Whether this story be true or not, it makes us see the precarious position that is the lot of any genuine searching and questioning; it makes us see the ultimate incommensurability between this kind of searching and questioning, the basis of all liberal learning, and the implacable conditions of our existence. But what would the world be like if that searching and questioning were not possible at all?

WHO SHOULD GO TO COLLEGE?

By Richard H. Sullivan

Different interpretations of the meaning of our large question, "Who should go to college?" are both possible and probable. Let me postpone just a bit and start with a more limited question, "Who will go, or who is likely to go, to college?" This is indeed not just a quibble but a first attempt to limit our discussion and stay within the bounds of realism.

How, then, are decisions about college-going made, and how are they influenced? Sampling studies have disclosed a variety of factors that, in the past, have increased the chance that any one student would go to some college. Most of these are fairly obvious, but it may help to note them in passing. Living in a town, suburb, or city is much more conducive to college-going than living in a village or on the farm. Living near a college, almost any college, increases the chance that a boy or girl will go to some college, not necessarily that same one. The higher the educational level of the parents, the greater the odds favoring college attendance by the children. In general, the higher the socioeconomic level of the parents, again the greater the chance of college-going, with the exception that the type of parental occupation, notably work in such professions as teaching, law, and medicine, contaminates this finding, since these correlate imperfectly with economic rewards. (Sons and daughters of teachers tend, in high degree, to attend our colleges, but, sadly, such parents are not blessed with any excess of the world's riches.) Statistically, other factors that change the odds include the general geographic area and even state of residence, distance in years and generations from first immigration into this country, race, religious sect, age at time of leaving high school, proportion of classmates going on to college, number of books, magazines, and newspapers regularly in the home, and sex.

There is also a positive correlation between likelihood of college attendance and academic success in high school and level of verbal and mathematical aptitude, but it is by no means perfect, and I should like to leave these conditions until later.

The factors that I have mentioned—and I believe the list could be extended—are by no means pure, isolated, or unrelated. College graduates in professional occupations are likely to have respectable private libraries and to live in areas where their children are going to school with numbers of other children subject to the same home influences. Nor are the parents likely to change their aspirations readily. In New Jersey a few years ago all the friends of one such suburban father clucked most sympathetically when he denounced the school adviser for suggesting that his high school sophomore daughter should begin thinking about secretarial school rather than about college. The adviser had available a number of interest and aptitude tests and the girl's whole school record to date, and he had interviewed the girl extensively. He may still have been wrong, but the curious thing to me was that the father—who enrolled his daughter forthwith in an independent school—and all of his friends, including many who did not know the girl at all, were completely convinced. The adviser just *had* to be wrong, and there were no two ways about it! The girl might have escaped college only by a serious physical accident or by eloping and having children when still quite young.

Examples at the other extreme are perhaps even clearer. Students who otherwise would have the ability and motivation to succeed in college are often accustomed to the idea from early childhood that the only path for them that is acceptable to their parents, peers, community, or economic condition is to go to work as soon as possible.

It is not necessary to dwell longer on this general question of influence, but it has seemed desirable at the outset to make clear, in effect, that a great many individuals are very active in providing their own answers, positively and negatively, as to who will and even who should (from their respective points of view) go to college.

Under our American system the colleges have, in a sense, somewhat less to say about the matter, and what is said is almost always partially negative. Neither legislators nor educators make, or can make, positive requirements that certain individuals will go or must go to college. College officers can recruit, urge, and exhort prospective students and sell them on the idea of attending their college, and schoolteachers, counselors, and principals can urge students and their parents to consider some college, but none can require them to go. By my reference to the negative aspect of what we are in a position to do, I mean three things. First, the phrase, "You may not attend this college unless . . ." characterizes our procedure. Secondly, many colleges now have an excess of applicants who meet all formally stated minimum requirements, and while admitting some they are rejecting others. Thirdly, even in the publicly supported institutions which by state law are required to accept all high school graduates, the faculties say, "We may have to admit you but we do not have to keep you." The principle of automatic promotion has not so far reached the college level, although in our weakest colleges that may sometimes appear to be the case.

One can, with little imagination, visualize a gigantic placement agency which would theoretically solve the admissions puzzles. All colleges could be active subscribers to and beneficiaries of such a service. The choices of particular colleges by individual students; their academic (and perhaps someday even their emotional) fitness for such a college; their financial capacity and needs, including scholarship awards; their high school records, test scores, and occupational aspirations would all form one set of relevant data. To be matched with those would be the statements of each college on the number of new freshmen and transfer students it wished to have, the numbers it could admit as a maximum, the proportion of residential and commuting students it desired, the proportion of geniuses to others, the numbers of basketball players with high school varsity letters, the numbers of beautiful candidates for homecoming queen, the minimum acceptable level of academic aptitude, the proportion of probable science majors to other types of students, and a few similar desires, minima, and maxima. Our hypothetical service agency would then produce a "best fit" between the two sets of data; some funds would change hands between individuals and institutions; at least part of the office staffs of registrars and admissions officers would be assigned to other duties, such as fund raising; and all would be in readiness for the first day of classes. The further back this process could be pushed toward the freshman year in high school, the more chance there would be for us in the destined college of a student to pass down expert prescriptions for his high school study.

For a variety of overwhelmingly cogent reasons, and for some other invalid reasons, the individual colleges are most unlikely to give up their sovereign rights in these matters. The national decision as to who *will* attend college (the practical definition of who should attend college) will therefore remain the aggregate of a whole myriad of decisions by each student to enter a particular college and to stay there and by each college to allow him or her to enter and to stay. It is possible to generalize about the corpus of higher education, and it is possible to effect substantial changes over a long period in the composition of student bodies. Such generalizations and proposals for change should, however, be based on a common understanding of the decision-making process and what can affect it.

If the decisions about college attendance are likely to continue to be made more or less as I have described the process, what change is predictable, and what changes are under our own control? Two factors of very great importance have been much discussed, and I shall mention them rather briefly. The first is the sharp and continuing increase in the *proportion* of the available student supply that does in fact attend college. In 1900 the college enrollment equaled only 4 per cent of the number of youth aged 18–21. This has risen rather steadily, despite wars and depression, until now the national college enrollment is on the order of one third of the age group of 18–21 years. Enrollments are higher than ever before, despite the fact that sudents now of college age were born in the middle and late thirties, when the national birth rate was relatively low. A number of intermingled causes for this upward trend in college attendance include the long-range effects of child-labor laws, compulsory school attendance laws, the increasingly technological nature of our economy, the consequent demand for more men and women with both broad education and specialized professional competence, the prestige of college attendance, a relatively high level of prosperity extending over a long period, and the greater availability of post-high-school educational opportunities. I pose as no prophet, but I do not see any major reason for assuming a reversal of trend. If anything, an even higher proportion of young men and women will want to attend college five or ten years from now.

Secondly, the sheer numbers of high school graduates will increase markedly in the next few years. The national birth rate jumped during the war and postwar years and is continuing at a remarkably high level. The *demand* for college education is thus being compounded by the dual effect of expecting larger numbers and of anticipating a higher proportion of that supply with a desire for college work. What college doors, and what types of educational opportunity, will be open to these high school graduates will depend upon our responses.

What changes in college attendance are more or less under the control of educators, the public, and their combined agencies? Where will more students go? First, the establishment of new institutions will have its effect. These seem to me most likely to take the form of new two-year colleges, chiefly tax supported. My state of Oregon is sandwiched between two of the states, California and Washington, where such colleges have been in widest and most systematic use. I expect the trend to continue.

Secondly, some of the present and, later, some of the new two-year institutions will change to four-year colleges, and some four-year colleges will more and more resemble universities with increasing graduate and professional work.

Thirdly, existing colleges and universities without changing in pattern and type will expand capacity. In broad outline the largest change of this nature will occur in our tax-supported institutions. It would be a mistake to assume that such expansion will be restricted to the public institutions. A survey of the ten accredited private colleges in Oregon has indicated that, collectively, they would be willing nearly to double their aggregate enrollments by 1970. The history of some independent colleges during the postwar veterans' bulge, when some of them tripled and quadrupled in size almost overnight, is also illuminating. Nevertheless, after the effects of inflation, the serious problem of finding capital for physical expansion (over and above meeting needs for higher salaries and increased operating costs) will be a limitation on a great many independent colleges; for in fact they have a lot of catching up to accomplish after a quarter century during which depression, war, and sharply inflating costs of operation have seriously limited adequate plant replacement, let alone plant addition of acceptable quality.

Moreover, those independent colleges that have had high prestige and that have already become selective, in the face of excesses of applicants, show little disposition to expand at a rate anywhere near the rate of increase in student supply. At Reed College most of us are in agreement with the proposition that we should prefer to see the emergence of other Reeds than, by a large increase in our size, to risk the loss of the one Reed that now exists. Much expansion now would radically change the present character and, we think, lose many of the present advantages of today's Reed College. The revised institution might, in certain respects, not be a "worse" institution, but it would be essentially different. (Parenthetically, I might state my belief that the private college has a very difficult prospect whether it does or does not expand. Land, buildings, and so forth, requiring much new capital, are necessary in the first case. In the second, assuming long-run inflation, continued efforts to raise salaries without increased enrollment means inevitably higher unit costs per student.)

In any event, it does seem likely that the greatest impact

from increased numbers of students will come through expansion of our public colleges and universities of all types and, among the independent institutions, through expansion of those not primarily residential in character.

I suppose that most of us tend to think of "college" in terms of such institutions as Swarthmore and Reed: independent, four-year, selective colleges of liberal arts and science, somewhat limited in size, coeducational, and largely residential. It is not too hard to think also of the separate colleges for men or for women that otherwise have the same characteristics, or to think of church-related colleges, or of the undergraduate colleges within our independent universities. It is more of a leap to include various engineering institutions, the teachers' colleges, the more vocationally oriented divisions of state and urban universities. It is perhaps still more of a leap to consider the two-year institutions: normal schools (which are rapidly dying out), community colleges, and junior colleges; and the one-year technical institutes. Nor do we think automatically of the extension division, the evening students in all kinds of curriculums at our urban institutions, and the various methods of providing forms of adult education, often at the undergraduate college level. Yet we must recognize that the expanding apparatus of college education is more dependent upon all of these other types of institutions than upon our own.

It may therefore be somewhat presumptuous for the president of a college like Reed, speaking at a college like Swarthmore, to answer the question, "Who should go to college?" In terms of the quantities of students who will want an education, and in terms of the quantities of those who will obtain one, we are likely to be touching directly an ever-decreasing fraction of the total. Moreover, it is at least possible that we have already been contributing the basic influences that we can contribute.

Unless new predictive and descriptive means of judging student applicants are found, which are not now available to us, a number of colleges will have gone approximately as far as they can in the direction of selectivity. They are receiving more strong applicants now than they can admit without radical changes in size. This does not mean that such colleges will stop competing, five years or ten years from now, for the outstanding, well-rounded, brilliant, highly motivated young leader who is at once dedicated in purpose, generous, humble, poised, and blessed with a marvelous sense of humor and mature judgment. For such paragons, the decision to admit is not only obvious but is properly accompanied by prayers, incantations, and special witchcraft ceremonies in the full of the moon that they will accept.

Aside from them, the questions for such colleges are going to be relatively subtle. How far should we go in admitting the very bright but neurotic malcontent, at the cost of refusing admission to the slightly less brilliant but personally organized and effective individuals? As numbers of applicants increase, faculty admissions committees and admissions officers are going to have to struggle with these and similarly frustrating questions, but their responses even so will not in large degree affect the answer to our central question when viewed nationally.

In another way, the influence of a selective admissions policy on the part of colleges of high prestige has already begun to work, I think, in a salutary way. This is the impact (of the presumed difficulty of gaining admission to such colleges) on the high school student and on secondary educators. To have students striving for high grades in the earlier years through direct fear of failure to attain the later goal of college admission may not be the most ideal form of motivation, psychologically, but the result of more serious application in school on the part of more students is not one to be decried. It seems to operate in the direction of eliminating waste, and this is generally good.

With larger student supply in prospect, more colleges are going to be able to attain their optimum size and still be more selective. The influence of this situation on the schools should therefore be more pervasive. Greater selectivity should result, moreover, in an increase in the retention rate from entrance to graduation. There are, I think, three reasons for this. The first is direct and obvious: the opportunity of the college to select more carefully does in general bring about some elimination of those least likely to succeed in meeting the college's standards. Secondly, the more apparent difficulty of gaining admission will result in the students' placing a higher value on meeting those standards: we do value scarce and rare merchandise. Thirdly, as a compounding effect, with higher retention rates it will be more difficult for a student to transfer from one college to another of the same type and standards, and again there will be a higher value on the desirability of completing the college course, once started.

The dropout rates in American colleges have been very high, and to me they represent one of the most wasteful aspects of our system of higher education—wasteful for student, teacher, and institution. I shall therefore welcome what seems to me to be a likely and real improvement. I am not sure, however, that I would welcome the attainment of a perfect score, 100 per cent retention from admission to on-time graduation. There are too many human factors involved to make this likely or possible, to be sure, but reaching it would imply to me that an admissions committee was not taking chances. Our system and our means of prediction about college success, on grounds of academic preparation, intellectual ability, motivation, and personality, do not answer all questions in advance. The most brilliant students will, not as a rule but occasionally, be the most erratic; they nevertheless should have a door open to make a trial in a strong institution. Sometimes there will be failure, and the perfect retention rate is gone a-glimmering.

Let me return to the public institutions and the urban, nonresidential institutions, which are most likely to bear the brunt of expansion. They will have a splendid opportunity to raise standards—not for grading and retention after admission, where this is already somewhat operative, but before admission. That opportunity is tempered, of course, by political considerations and by one's social philosophy. As to the first, the present deep concern over the rate of Russian scientific and educational progress has, I think, created an unusual mood. The people are more prone to face real questions of the quality needed in teacher and student, to help provide conditions better to ensure the former and to begin a more persistent demand for the latter. If the degree-granting institutions are willing to set more rigorous admissions criteria and to use their influence to push for more solid and serious secondary school performance, they have been in a better position to do so only rarely—and perhaps never since the emergence of the modern, comprehensive high school.

As to the effect of social philosophy on the problems facing us, it has already been true that many states have been willing, in less propitious times, to eschew the notion that bare high school graduation should guarantee admission to a senior college. They are in an even stronger position now.

On the other hand, I do believe that rates of maturation vary quite widely among students in adolescent years, and I dislike the prospect of such a tight system that the boy or girl of ability who has wasted early opportunities should forever be disbarred. The two-year colleges and the whole panoply of evening and adult education programs do offer the possibility of keeping open a number of doors, and this I think should remain an important feature of the American educational scene.

Let us not only fervently hope but also assume for a moment that the public colleges move in the direction not of indiscriminate expansion and of automatic admission but of increased selectivity. Combine this with the present and future effects of similar attitudes among an increasing number of independent colleges. The influence on secondary and eventually on elementary school work could be very great indeed. In turn, consider what the resulting effect on the college teaching loads might become. Suppose that we could reduce, even by 50 per cent, the amount of elementary—or perhaps introductory—work now carried on by the colleges in the sciences, mathematics, foreign languages, and English writing. I can imagine few boons for the college teacher that would be equal in stimulation.

This reference to particular subjects discloses what has been, I am sure, no secret. My hidden reference, throughout all of these remarks, has been to the college curriculum that places at the center liberal studies in the humanities, social sciences, and natural sciences. Over the postwar years I have been viewing with much pleasure the movement of the engineering schools toward a more balanced and broader concept of the undergraduate curriculum; of the medical schools to influence premedical students to engage in a broad, rather than narrowly technical, set of courses; of the law schools and dental schools in a similar direction; of the agricultural and mechanical colleges toward more nearly university status, with some of the same effects.

I think, therefore, that I shall not be misunderstood if I suggest parenthetically that our postsecondary efforts at technical and vocational education, chiefly in other than degree-granting institutions, can stand both improvement and expansion. There are students who will not profit greatly from the baccalaureate program but who with increased technical competence can assume greater responsibilities as technicians in support of the graduate engineer, dentist, doctor, public accountant, and others, as well as in the factory and other places of production and of services. The population growth, through both higher birth rates and increased longevity, will impose these demands upon the economy in the next ten or twenty years, without question.

I have perhaps erred in tone in this paper, particularly at the beginning, in invoking an attitude of *Laissez faire* or even fatalism with respect to the decisions made by students voluntarily to attend or to apply to college. By that, I certainly did not mean to minimize the very great importance of inducing—by all the means in our power—those students of high ability who are now evading college to turn in our direction. Such inducements include early identification, better guidance, work with parents to remove blocks to motivation, and removal of economic barriers through scholarships, loans, and other forms of financial aid. Nor can the opportunities to attend college be so strongly conditioned as they have been by race, creed, color, and geographic factors. Intellectual power is not so common that we can squander, waste, or neglect it. It is perhaps unnecessary to extend my remarks on this theme, since so much has been and is being said elsewhere.

At the close, I feel constrained to offer one more answer, of a different type, to the central question, "Who should go to college?" In presenting it, I must express on the one hand a reaffirmation of my belief in liberal education and on the other some pessimism, for it may be feared that the pressures toward expansion, coupled with a highly possible failure to achieve true economic solutions for higher education soon enough, will make even less likely the proposition that those who go to college become educated.

It seems particularly clear that in liberal education learning is an individual matter, and such learning is likely to be affected by the possibility of intimacy between younger and older personalities, younger and more mature minds. If excellent teachers cannot be attracted and held, or if our undergraduate institutions expand and expand again, or if the pressures to finish up a college degree become more intense, then those possibilities become more remote.

President Barnaby Keeney of Brown University has observed that "education is a lengthy and complicated process that requires thought, contemplation, discussion, selecting, discarding, and selecting again. In the course of education, the student may become informed, as he is when he is trained, but, far more important, he becomes formed; he changes, he develops. There is no point in talking about education if you think of it as credit-hours. . . . But if you are thinking of it as an effort to develop a person who will live a life of 'usefulness and reputation,' if you are thinking of it as a means of developing all of a person's resources, then you are thinking of education and you have got to think of something that only begins in the undergraduate years and should continue as long as the person is capable of developing. It may be intensive, but it may not be short."

The atmosphere of a college has much to do with the response of students to teachers, and the attitude of students has much to do with determining that atmosphere within which teaching has to be performed, within which learning does not necessarily take place. One could then make out a case for the proposition that those students should go to college who are most likely to be "formed, changed, and developed" by that experience, who are most likely to achieve a strengthening and maturing of responsible attitudes, and who may help to create that atmosphere in which learning may flourish. The catch, however, is that we do not know very well how to identify and select such students. We may come closest by making sure that applicants know as much as possible about the facts as well as about the dreams of a college, and then by depending heavily on self-selection by the students. The question in any case is not an idle one, for in the composition and attitudes of our student bodies must lie a major part of the answer to President Keeney's fear that "education will progressively be thought of as a process that confers a label rather than as a development that makes a person."

I have strayed quite widely and perhaps disjointedly over the educational scene, touching briefly on the need for upgrading our educational efforts at all levels, on the need for discovering and encouraging hidden talent, on the desirability of marrying the opportunity to expand with the opportunity to select more judiciously, and on the kinds of places that will bear the brunt of our problems of quantity in the next decade. In recognizing the final point, I trust that I have not understated the continuing importance of the independent liberal arts colleges—the importance not only in terms of what they touch directly and of the particular students whom they change into alumni but also in terms of the pace that they must set. It is arrogant to assume that they have an overriding influence on American education, but it is blind to assume that they have little influence. More than most other colleges, they have the crucial responsibility. The key task which they must face and must accept is simply stated, although complex and difficult of attainment. This is to provide assurance that the *quest for excellence* will not be replaced by enforced acceptance of mediocrity. Whatever our dilemmas about quantity, none are so critical as our utter necessity for educational quality in the years ahead. This is a proposition that the largest bulk of our schools and colleges, and of the public, have tended to evade in this century. Today, it must be faced squarely.

UNIQUENESS IN STUDENTS

By Gordon W. Allport

May we start by drawing a distinction between the goals of *education* and the goals of *higher education?* Primary and secondary schools, we will agree, are dedicated to education; and universities, we hope, somehow serve higher education. But it seems that the position of the modern American college lies somewhere between. Unless I am mistaken, this ambiguous mid-position is responsible for much of our current perplexity concerning the functions of the American college.

The goal of education is the transmission of culture. The stupendous cultural cumulation that has piled up through the centuries must somehow be passed on from parent to child, from teacher to pupil, so that the structure of civilization may persist. Your life and mine are transitory, but our culture continues. The goal of higher education, on the other hand, is to inspect and criticize, to improve and increase this cultural cumulation. Higher education seeks newer and better solutions to the physical, intellectual, and moral predicaments of mankind.

Too often we blur this distinction and slip into the belief that by multiplying our hordes of college graduates, our "educated" citizens, we shall thereby strengthen our way of life. We do not realize that the only way to ensure what we have is to keep it advancing.

This fallacy enters into almost all of our contemporary

discussions of education—and these, we know, have become legion in number since the launching of Sputnik in October 1957. An avalanche of congressional bills is one token of the confusion. These have to do with the building of schools, but not with improving the competence of teachers; they offer scholarship aid, but no relief to colleges; they have to do with training in scientific skills, but not with the advancement of democracy; they safeguard America's physical safety, but not its spiritual leadership in an anxious world.

It would be too much to expect any act of Congress to recognize the somewhat subtle distinction I am drawing, but it is not too much to expect those of us who are partisans of higher education to keep our own thinking straight and to fight for the conservation and extension of the values of freedom, criticism, and inventiveness. Our model is to be found not in the stampede for more and more education. We do better to look to those observant loiterers and unacademic seers who throughout the ages have examined nature and society with greater penetration. The prophets of the human race and most of its inventors were not members of schools, colleges, or universities. But they had, nonetheless, the quality of excellence that we aim to produce through higher education.

College: the bridge between education and higher education. Present-day American colleges, as I have suggested, embrace in part the goals of education and in part the goals of higher education. Students entering college do not have nearly enough of languages, history, mathematics, or philosophy to act as cultural doorkeepers. Nor can they profitably criticize or invent until they have such a store in hand. In our graduate schools we sometimes encounter wretched nonsense produced by students who have come from colleges where they had no discipline, no drill, few examinations, and no orderly arrangement of knowledge. They burst with self-expression, but have little or nothing to express. To them the ideals of spontaneity and freedom from restraint were offered prematurely. They would have done well in their younger years to rebel as did a little girl who entered her too progressive school one morning and said to her teacher, "Do we *have* to do what we want to do today?"

We grant, then, that the American college has the duty to transmit codified knowledge. But it is our ambition that it serve also the goal of higher education, so that a fair proportion of its graduates, properly prepared, may join the ranks of creators and benefactors. A few of our best colleges keep this dual aim in view, but many, I fear, are in danger of losing it.

It is only within the last two generations that college education has been sought by more than a small minority of our young people. The earlier seekers, for the most part, were rare souls who were interested in pure scholarship or in preparing for one of the professions. Those who took this road, it was soon discovered, got ahead. They became important people in the professions and acquired unmistakable prestige. Before long the result was that in order to get ahead, and to enjoy prestige, and to acquire the self-assurance allegedly provided by college, and to keep up with the Joneses, millions of young people fell in with the fashion. As mobility motives increased, the longing for knowledge decreased. It is no wonder that many institutions of so-called higher learning came to accommodate themselves to the trend. Jane and John were offered courses in cheerleading and fudge-making, and perhaps a course on how to feed fudge to a cheerleader—all of them good for self-assurance and prestige, but distressingly remote from the original purpose of scholarly communities.

To make the point in a different way: until recently

nearly all scientific research was motivated by intellectual curiosity. But soon the scientific truth thus discovered led to spectacular technological advance. Whereupon new demands for technological advance began to guide and direct the course of scholarly research. And now in mid-century we face the imminent possibility that scientific research in our colleges and universities will be motivated and guided chiefly by the demand for military weapons, one of whose gruesome objectives may be to wipe out scholarly communities in other lands.

Please do not misunderstand me. I would not deny college education to the majority of youth now seeking it; nor am I arguing against the useful application of knowledge. My point is simply that the ideal of higher education is in jeopardy. A century ago Cardinal Newman conceived the university as a free atmosphere where the intellect may safely range and speculate, encountering wholesome antagonism and exposing its own error in the collision of mind with mind; where teachers aflame with wisdom somehow implant their fire in the breasts of their students.[1] The ideal seems still valid, but the portrait scarcely fits the American college of today. Nor does the happy image of Mark Hopkins on a log with a youthful partner, the two of them rhythmically inhaling and exhaling Socratic wisdom. At mid-century there are too many students who aspire only to social ease, to skill in salesmanship, or to a high salary in engineering, and who regard anything else college may offer as so much intellectual chewing gum.

Two elites. We have no right to be snobbish in the matter. Since so many youth now attend college, we must expect a large proportion of them to seek only basic skills and the cumulations of culture in their own fields of interest. We should do our best for them. They will, we hope, constitute what Bergson has called an *élite de l'action.* It would be a grave error, however, if we were to neglect the second, smaller elite, the *élite de la pensée*.[2] The creation of the second elite is far more vital for the future of our nation, and will be accomplished only if some colleges and universities fight with vigor to keep alive the goals of higher education in the face of the depreciating forces at work today.

In principle the distinction I am drawing is clear enough, but in practice no sharp separation is possible. As teachers and as students, our lives are concerned with the transmission of culture, and we are scarcely aware of the moments when we cease transmission and engage in creative reflection. The precise point where the young student is successfully wooed from potential membership in an elite of action to potential membership in an elite of thought is not ascertainable. In the college routine the difference between education and higher education turns out to be a mere matter of accent. But by employing the right accent we hope to foster self-development wherein inert ideas will become alive, cultural cumulations will become cultural challenges, and scraps of information will enter a state of creative agitation.

The growing edge. But when we speak of self-development, we are focusing attention no longer on the culture but on the individual student. Our colleges are geared to the transmission of culture en masse, whereas the creativity we seek in higher education is the precious and volatile possession of single individuals. In the mass somewhere are sparks that can be fanned into flame, and sparks also that can be easily extinguished. Seldom can we tell in advance which students are authentic candidates for higher education and which will be content with the cultural cumulations offered by ordinary education. The board of admissions to the college, the teachers, and even the student himself have no sure way of predicting.

Recently I had occasion to lecture to a mass of six

hundred and fifty students—the entire senior class of a neighboring college. The course, compulsory for all, dealt with the principal social problems confronting the nation today. My subject was race prejudice. Some students, I noted, were eager, alert, attentive, sitting on the edge of their seats. Others were hostile, bored, or somnolent; a few were totally unconscious. What can the devotee of higher education do under such circumstances? What can the head of the course do? What can the administration do? Is there any conceivable way to ensure the utilization of knowledge in such a course by all of the students so that it may lead to their self-development? Poor students— they will have to take an examination on my lecture. For many of them the experience is merely a clutter of inert ideas; ideas that are unutilized, untested, and unassimilated to the growing edge of their personalities. This episode makes me question sharply the practice of compulsion at the college level. Compulsion often engenders resent-ment, and resentment closes the mind against novel ideas. We may lay it down as a law that unless college students elect their programs of study or, at the very least, concur willingly in what is prescribed, their achievement at best will be inert knowledge. (Here I am arguing against compulsion, whereas earlier I argued for discipline. This contradiction—more apparent than real—is one that good teaching can overcome. Good teaching builds on such relevant motives and willing acquiescence as exist and tries to win the student to the stage of precision, discipline, and adequacy without which he cannot enter the gates of higher learning.)

It is easy to say that a class of six hundred and fifty is too large. The instructor cannot hope to individualize his ef-forts in the face of such an educational stampede. True, numbers are an important factor, but they are not all im-portant. A class (or tutorial session) with only one student poses the same basic problem. The student comes to the conference. He has a growing edge, but this growing edge is almost surely hidden from the instructor. It may even be hidden from the student himself, though in most cases, I suspect, the student knows his intimate aspirations and gropings, but finds them too sensitive and private, perhaps too tentative and troublesome, to disclose fully. It is a fortunate instructor who finds that he can nourish this growth ring. It is entirely conceivable that he may succeed in doing so with some students who were for him anonymous faces in a crowd of six hundred and fail completely with the single student in a private conference.

We are ready now for the next step in our argument. While we seek the goals of higher education, we can do so only by nourishing as well as possible the growing edges of students all along the educational road. A poor elementary school, we know, may strangle rather than encourage the native curiosity of children. A poor high school may bury its students under a mass of inert ideas, so that only a genius could break through to test, utilize, and vivify what he has learned. A college by cheapening its curriculum (with fudge-making and cheerleading) may effectively block young minds from ever entering the portals of higher education. And so the problem of reaching the individual and promoting his self-development runs back through the entire educational structure. At the present moment, however, we are particularly interested in how colleges may lead as many students as possible into the ranks of the creative elite.

Individual differences versus uniqueness. Since the time of Alfred Binet, if not before, psychologists have pressed for a recognition of individual differences as a guide for educational policy. Binet's purpose was to show that the art of knowing children is to separate out their real aptitudes so as to be able to give each one an education that is made to measure.[3]

Binet's own contribution to the individualizing process was, of course, the construction of a scale for the measurement of intelligence. Today there is scarcely a school child in the Western world who is not ticketed with his own private I.Q. (In the interests of historical accuracy we should note that the concept of the I.Q. was the invention of William Stern, the German psychologist, although credit for the first measuring scale goes to Binet.) Following in Binet's steps many people think that we can make education to measure if we sort children who are bright into accelerated groups and children who are dull into so-called opportunity classes. Binet himself thought that children might also be classified according to their degree of suggestibility, but this dimension proved to be abortive in subsequent psychological study.

Now the question I wish to raise is whether by classifying students as bright or dull or average we are in fact making education to measure. Children do, of course, differ in this measurable dimension. But they differ too in temperament, in basic security, in personal interests, in motivation. And what is most important of all—a fact that even many psychologists fail to perceive clearly—is that children, like adults, differ most of all in the complex pattern that results from the interweaving of their intelligence, temperament, security, interests, and motives. So infinite in number are the ingredients of personality that their permutations and combinations and final organization (influenced by an infinite diversity of genes and of environments) produce individuals who are unique. While grammarians tell us that there are no degrees of uniqueness, I shall risk a solecism and insist that each personality is *inevitably*, *ineffably*, and *ineluctably* unique. I shall repeat what I have said elsewhere, that all of the species of all of the animals of the world are psychologically less distinct from one another than one man is from another.[4]

To hear talk of this sort makes the psychologist, as well as the educator, acutely uncomfortable. What can we do, they ask, about ineluctable uniqueness? For a unique personality can you do more than send flowers to it? Fiction and drama and biography may be able to handle uniqueness, but not education nor the science of psychology. Perhaps not; but if so, what a pity! It means that psychology rejects its most compelling datum: the individual organization of complex neuropsychic processes. It means that the educator stops short of doing his job—for how can self-development be encouraged unless the self in its true complexity is brought into view? While both educators and psychologists understand individual differences, they know very little indeed about patterned personality. I predict that history will someday point to the present recognition of individual differences as only a scientific way station to the study of the integration of these differences into whole and organized human beings. At the present time we are so busy trying to understand the separate dimensions of personality, and how individuals vary on these dimensions, that we spend little time studying the intersection of these dimensions in the single person.

I suspect that the educator is far ahead of the scientist in his actual skill in sensing the pattern of a student's mental life and in identifying the unique growing edge. I doubt that he can tell us *how* he does so—which is, of course, the question that the psychologist asks. But the educator's handicap is that he works within a frame of rules and regulations, of curriculums and requirements, of lectures and mass methods, so that he cannot go the full distance in individualizing his instruction. For the most part he can only regard his students as types and handle them in groups.

Such is the scientific and pedagogical reality of the situation. We can deal with the individual in only an approximate fashion. Our educational practices can be adjusted, within limits, to types of students, but hardly ever to self-development in the strict sense of the word. So let us now ask, What are some of the more easily recognized types?

The unmotivated student. First, there is the unmotivated student who responds to no form of knowledge with warmth. One investigation suggests that about 20 per cent of the students in a major university lack motivation either for education or for higher education.[5] While they may keep their heads above academic water, they have no systems of interest that can resonate to college offerings. They elect no classes meeting at ten in the morning, certainly none at nine or at eight. Assuming that they have latent mental capacity—as most of them have—the spectacle of waste for them, for their teachers, and for the nation is distressing.

For this type of student we can only prescribe individual guidance and, if that fails, withdrawal from the academic community. Yet I am of two minds about guidance. Even though my own profession in recent years has spread the fashion of counseling and guidance widely, I sometimes doubt that any person is wise enough to guide or counsel any other. But for the time being I shall conform to my profession and encourage the drones to undertake sessions of treatment, whether these be psychiatric, psychoanalytic, nondirective, tutorial, pastoral, or decanal in character.

One type of motivational defect is seen in the lad who was "sent" to college and did not himself choose to go. The situation is often aggravated if he is sent to his father's college and if standards of performance are set for him by his well-meaning but self-centered sire. Such a situation dooms the youth to four additional years of filial subservience. He is not living his own life but is fulfilling his father's. In such cases apathy, inertness, and resistance are to be expected. I see no solution other than counseling or withdrawal from college or—in extreme cases—patricide.

With mild cases of apathy a skillful teacher may have success. A student who first enters a subject inertly may soon, to his own surprise, find his mind in ferment. The teacher, probably through skillfully juxtaposing everyday examples with generalization, has aroused a romantic emotion. Within a few months, or a year, the student may be ready to pass from the romantic state to the stage of precision, wherein he acquires sound skills.[6] If in the stage of precision he retains some of the romantic emotion, he will then enter the portals of creative higher education. But even the adroit teacher cannot start this desirable sequence unless the student has some latent capacity for response. No teacher is so good that he alone can transform inert ideas into thunderbolts.

The gifted student. Let us turn to a very different type: the so-called gifted student. Giftedness in the present context will mean the possession of both high ability and high motivation. If the unmotivated student is the principal drag and waste in a college, the gifted student is the principal challenge. A very few Shakespeares, Lincolns, or Gandhis could put the world immeasurably ahead in its search for wisdom and for peace. Even if higher education—as seems probable—cannot produce genius of the first order, our colleges can at least give encouragement to genius of the second, third, or fourth order. The world needs them all.

The basic formula for dealing with the gifted student is freedom: freedom to browse and to delve, freedom to succeed and to err, freedom to master relevant tools, and, above all, freedom to create. But freedom is not sufficient. There must be facilities; there must be high standards; and there must be encouragement. By facilities I mean libraries, laboratories, and sufficient economic security to make fruitful study possible. The requirement of standards is a delicate matter on which to speak. Yet it is my own conviction that most of our institutions of higher learning offer intellectual fare distressingly below the digestive capacity of the gifted student. I am not thinking merely of colleges that offer the frivolous course in fudge-making, but of our "best" institutions, where courses are often repetitive, routine, and devoid of challenge. Perhaps from the point of view of the average student they are adequate, but they stretch no nerve in the gifted student. Average students, it turns out, are so numerous and so time-demanding that the gifted student shifts for himself. Usually such a student does well, and the teacher rejoices, but in many cases the teacher should feel less joy than guilt, for he has, unintentionally, beckoned the gifted student downward toward mediocrity rather than upward toward maximum self-development.

A few of our colleges, to be sure, have given special thought to the optimum growth of the gifted student. Let us glance at the policies of two that have done so. The first example comes from Cambridge. In 1954 Harvard College and Radcliffe College inaugurated a program known as "Advanced Standing." In three separate ways it tries to provide freedom and incentive for the specially gifted. One channel is the admission of pupils directly from the eleventh grade into the freshman class at college, provided they have outstanding records of accomplishment and have a good coverage of secondary school subjects. No high school diploma is required. This type of acceleration in the academic ladder, it is hoped, will lead to an earlier entry into the world of individual creativeness and leadership. A second channel is similar. High school graduates who show on placement tests that in three subjects they have already mastered freshman collegiate standards are admitted directly into the sophomore class and may graduate in three years' time. Finally, students with special ability and high accomplishment in some single subject are allowed to enroll in their freshman year in advanced courses in this subject and thus progress to the stage of individual research or graduate study even before obtaining the B.A. degree. The program as a whole "reflects the Faculty's determination to seek out and to encourage students whose ability and preparation enable them to move rapidly into advanced work."

Perhaps the plan for the gifted student best known in this country is the Honors Program at Swarthmore College. It would be presumptuous of me to describe it. I may, however, be permitted to say that for many years we have admired its products as we have encountered them in our graduate program in psychology at Harvard. Speaking as an outsider and subject to correction, I would hazard the guess that the success of the Swarthmore Honors Program rests in large part upon the following features. The small size of the seminars is certainly a factor, as is the excellence of the teaching. Important too is the elimination of grading from seminar papers and from the seminar course as a whole. This device, I am convinced, is a sharp weapon against the accumulation of inert ideas. The student himself can to a degree determine his own cycle of romance and precision; he can, in a sense, linger or lunge, and explore both byways and highways. Perhaps I am exaggerating the degree of freedom he enjoys, but the fact remains that he need not at stated intervals disgorge a set number of inert facts stored reluctantly in his brain. As employed at Swarthmore I believe that the method of final external examination likewise makes for a certain maturity of mind, freeing the individual from total dependence upon the local intellectual situation. While preparing for the arrival of the external examiner, the student and teacher are on the same side of the fence. A teacher who is a collaborator has an advantage over the teacher who is an inquisitor.

The authoritarian student. We now shuttle back to another pedagogically difficult group. I have been asked: "What can be done with the authoritarian student?" Specifically, the stimulating monograph written by Professor Philip E. Jacob focuses upon this problem as a central educational challenge of our time.[7]

First, let us locate the problem. A decade ago a thick volume of research appeared in print. It was called *The Authoritarian Personality* and was written by an able group of investigators at the University of California.[8] The study had its origin in a historical concern for the devastation of humane and democratic values wrought by the German Nazis. Shockingly enough the authors find that a similar authoritarian mentality is not uncommon in our own free land. But the book goes much further. With the aid of numerous researches it depicts the cognitive and emotional style that comprises authoritarianism. It likewise presents an instrument to measure the intensity of this syndrome in the individual life. The now famous F-scale is intended as a measure of "fascist" mentality—the label clearly betraying the origin of the research. Scientifically the most important finding is that the items employed in the scale do intercorrelate. Thus if a person agrees with the proposition that "people can be divided into two distinct classes: the weak and the strong," he is likely to agree that "what youth needs most is strict discipline."

Now logically these two propositions would seem to have little to do with one another: the first indicates a tendency to bifurcate values sharply—to see things as white or black; the second item simply advocates a stricter discipline for young people. But it turns out that not only are these items related but that they also cluster together with a demand that perceptual and cognitive fields be well structured and not uncertain or ambiguous, with a conventional moralism of judgment, with an outspoken obedience to, but latent resentment of, one's parents. Perhaps most striking of all is the agreement of the F-scale with ethnic and racial prejudice. By and large the authoritarian cannot tolerate Jews, Negroes, or foreigners. He is suspicious of liberals and phobic toward Communists. He would drop atom bombs if necessary to stop propaganda coming from Russian ships at sea and designed to win Americans to the Soviet side.[9] And apart from his prejudices he shows a certain rigidity in the face of intellectual problems that interferes with his college work or at least renders him an obedient rather than creative scholar.

Now psychologists are a critical lot. When a theory of such magnitude and portent is launched they try their best to find a flaw somewhere, and they usually succeed. In the present case the flaw seems to be an overstressing of the deeper character-conditioned aspects of this syndrome. Subsequent research has shown that many people dubbed "authoritarian" are merely an acquiescent lot. Often they say "yes" to an item on the F-scale but also say "yes" to items that reverse the meaning of the F-scale items. They are yea-sayers, acquiescers, or in technical terms are marked by little more than a response set.[10]

While this criticism does not invalidate the original work, nor the many subsequent confirmatory studies, it does make us more cautious in our interpretations. Some writers today prefer to speak not of authoritarians but of personalities that are "rigid," "dogmatic," or "stereopathic." The solution, I suspect, may eventually lie in the discovery of subtypes. For example, we shall probably find a pliable conformist type who easily takes on the coloration of his environment, so that if he attends a genuinely liberal college he too will follow the path.[11] In other instances, we shall encounter classic cases of character-conditioned bigotry that perhaps no educational atmosphere can change. But whether they are skin-deep conformists or marrow-deep fascists, Jacob does show that different colleges differ considerably in the ratio of authoritarians on their campuses.[12]

The bearing of this analysis on collegiate practice is not yet fully known. One investigator finds marked differences among students as to their preference for a drill-recitation method of instruction or a permissive-discussion method.[13] Most students, it seems, prefer the highly structured drill-recitation method. Needless to say, these students may not all be authoritarian. They are living in an environment of examinations, and their attitude is "you tell us" and "we'll write it down." Yet the fact that fully a quarter of the students, bucking the system, definitely wish for a more permissive atmosphere in the classroom shows that deep personality differences are at stake.

Whether we should actually section our classes according to this preference is still an open question. One investigator reports an experiment which, unknown to the students, created separate sections for high authoritarian or stereopathic cases.[14] Judging from this one experiment, the adapting of teaching methods to students of this particular type seems to have a beneficial effect. The report says that it takes more time to break down the attitude of excessive obedience and conformity of these students, but with patience and persistence it can be done in a manner that flexes their approach not only to their studies but to social issues in general. I would hesitate to recommend that this procedure be followed forthwith in all colleges but would certainly favor continued research to gain more light on the possibilities that lie in this direction.

It is only fair to add that for deep, dyed-in-the-wool

character-conditioned authoritarians college probably can do very little. From what we know, the problem seems to lie back in the bosom of the family and in early child training. In a sense, the true authoritarian is a case of arrested development. Like an eight-year-old, he believes that to be good is to be obedient. The only "unfair" acts that he can conceive are acts that go against the command of adults in authority. This tribalistic stage of moral development lasts normally until the ages of eleven or twelve. It would be strange indeed if college did not inherit a number of cases of arrested development. In some cases, where the problem is merely one of delayed maturation, the shift from the home to the collegiate atmosphere may do the trick, but if the student has been hopelessly crippled in his early years no college can expect to repair the ravage.

Matching students and institutions. Each college has a style of its own. No institution can, or should, try to be all things to all applicants. Professor Jacob shows that students' values differ according to whether they attend public or private colleges, denominational or nondenominational, Northern or Southern. Among students in public institutions the chief educational goal sought is vocational training, skills directly useful in earning a living; whereas at private institutions the preferred goal, as most students see it, is to acquire a basic general education and appreciation of ideas. The student who attends one type of institution when he prefers the objectives of another lets himself in for needless distress.

But besides representing a type, each institution—no less than each student—is unique. There is only one Swarthmore, one Harvard, one Macalester or Reed, one Sarah Lawrence or Texas. The task of finding the most congenial environment for growth is baffling—way beyond any skills in guidance that we have today. Yet Professor Jacob is surely right in speaking of the "extreme importance of match-ing student personality and the institutional climate of values." [15] At the present time I can think of no better solu-tion to the problem than to provide the youth with informa-tion and to leave the choice to him, except as financial or academic barriers may prevent. The time of selecting a college is an excellent moment for the father and mother to bow out permanently from their offspring's decisions.

Final Word. My own conviction is that the devices we have here discussed for adapting education more closely to the needs of the individual are helpful but insufficient. The individual, let me repeat, is inexpressibly unique. We wish to win him, if we can, to the cause of higher education so that our nation and mankind may benefit from his creative contribution. But no multiplication of curricular devices or selective systems will produce genius or high compe-tence. "To educate" is a reflexive verb: one can only educate oneself. The growth ring grows from within. True, it re-quires moisture and sunlight from without. But the moisture and sunlight of higher education do not consist in its paraphernalia of plans, systems, and props, but rather in the vision of excellence it can hold before the mind of the individual student.

It is well for us as administrators, teachers, and students to step aside and survey the system in which we lead our educational lives. But it will be fatal if we mistake the scaffolding of the system for the edifice we seek to build. This edifice is personality—ever growing and creating. Educational apparatus may help here and there, but only the vision of excellence translated into precept and ex-ample will lead our students into the portals of higher education.

REFERENCES

1. H. Tristram, ed., *Newman's Idea of a Liberal Education* (London, Harrap & Co., 1952).
2. See W. A. Lloyd, *Education and Human Relations* (Johannesburg, Witwatersrand University Press, 1957), p. 2.
3. Alfred Binet, *Les Idées Modernes sur les Enfants* (Paris, Flammarion, 1910), chap. v.
4. Gordon W. Allport, *Becoming: Basic Considerations for a Psychology of Personality* (New Haven, Yale University Press, 1955), sec. v.
5. C. W. Heath, *et al., What People Are* (Cambridge, Harvard University Press, 1945).
6. Alfred North Whitehead, *The Aims of Education and Other Essays* (New York, Mentor Books, 1949), chap. ii, "The Rhythm of Education."
7. Philip E. Jacob, *Changing Values in College* (New York, Harper, 1957), see pp. 10, 44, 52, 91, 100, 122–129.
8. T. W. Adorno, Elsa Frenkel-Brunswik, D. J. Levinson, and R. N. Sanford, *The Authoritarian Personality* (New York, Harper, 1950).
9. W. J. MacKinnon and R. Centers, "Social-psychological Factors in Public Orientation Toward an Out-group," *American Journal of Sociology*, LXIII, 415–419 (1958).
10. This problem is currently receiving extensive discussion in technical journals; for example, B. M. Bass, "Authoritarianism and Acquiescence," *Journal of Abnormal and Social Psychology*, LI, 616–623 (1955); H. Beloff, "Two Forms of Social Conformity: Acquiescence and Conventionality," *ibid.*, LVI, 99–104 (1958).
11. Cf. Theodore M. Newcomb, *Personality and Social Change* (New York, Dryden Press, 1943).
12. Jacob, *Changing Values in College*, pp. 107–109.
13. L. Wispe, "Evaluating Section Teaching Methods in the Introductory Course," *Journal of Educational Research*, XLV, 161–186 (1951).
14. G. Stern and A. H. Cope, "Differences in Educability Between Stereopaths, Non-stereopaths, and Rationals," *American Psychologist*, XI, 8 (1956).
15. Jacob, *Changing Values in College*, p. 122.

VALUES: THE POLESTAR OF EDUCATION

By Brand Blanshard

In the midst of the universal clamor for more and better
technology, too little is heard about the place of values in
higher education. No one can doubt the importance of
technology. But technology is important only because it is
itself a means to values that lie beyond it. Uncontrolled by
values, it is fanaticism, and a fanatic, says Santayana, is a
man who redoubles his efforts when he has forgotten his
ends. Life without what technology has given us would
no doubt be a far more pinched and meager affair than it is,
by way of getting the perspective right, we may profitably
remember that technology as we know it was unknown to
Buddah and Socrates, to Sophocles and Aristotle, to Virgil
and Dante. Their lives were not quite bare of value, nevertheless. In the campaign for a good life, technology is the
O.S.S., the Office of Strategic Services, not the G.H.Q.,
which sets the objectives of the campaign. And it is these
objectives, these over-all ends or values, and how education
can help us gain them, that is my theme.

What do we mean by a value? To define the term is
surprisingly hard; many thinkers have thought it impossible.
But it is easy enough to give examples. As examples of
minor values, we could cite such experiences as toasting
one's toes before a pleasant fire, having tea in the midst of
a seminar, watching a world series game on television, and
taking a cool plunge on a hot day. As examples of major

values, we could cite the love of Damon for Pythias or of Darby for Joan, the hearing with full understanding of Beethoven's Fifth Symphony, the experience of Keats on first looking into Chapman's Homer, the experience of Schweitzer in ministering to his African Negroes. Is there anything that all these values have in common? Yes, three things, I think.

In the first place they are all experiences. You may say that there are many things that are valuable besides experiences, and it is true that we commonly talk that way. For economists anything has value that can be exchanged for something else one wants—for example, money or a diamond ring or a grandfather clock. But why should anyone else want these things, and why should you want things they will exchange for? The answer in both cases is the same. It is because these things are means to experiences that are wanted for their own sakes. If somebody wants your grandfather clock, it is because he can set it in his front hall and look at it and gloat over it. Things are always wanted for the sake of experiences, never experiences for the sake of things. For, strictly speaking, things have no value at all. Suppose some comet were to switch its poisonous tail across our planet and asphyxiate us tonight; would there be anything of value left on the earth tomorrow? The books would still stand in their rows on the library shelves, and the pictures would still in some sense be there on our walls. But would they have any value? None. Only if there were people to take knowledge of them or delight in them would there be any worth in them, and even then it would be the experience of knowledge and delight that had the value, not the books or pictures themselves.

Secondly, these values are not only experiences; they are pleasant experiences. I am inclined to think that every experience valued for its own sake is suffused with a flush of agreeable feeling. This does not mean, of course, that hard work, mental and physical, or even the acute suffering of a bad illness or a bad conscience is not good in a sense; only it is good in a different sense. If we call these things good, it is not because we seek them out for their own sakes, but because they are the means to later states of mind that *are* thus sought; in short, they are instrumental, not intrinsic goods. We admire people who can face suffering with Spartan firmness in the interests of a cause. But if we found a man who cultivated illness or pain for its own sweet sake, we should choose our gambit warily in approaching him; we should assume that he was a crank, and not improbably a psychopath. Indeed, I doubt whether even psychopaths attain this pitch of oddity. To be sure, we hear of masochists who find pain good in itself. I doubt whether there are such people. Those so called are probably persons who, for reasons discoverable by a psychiatrist, get satisfaction as a result of enduring pain, which is a different thing from finding the pain itself good. However that may be, can you think of any experience that would retain its value for you if you felt no satisfaction in it? Suppose you had the musical ear and experience of a Toscanini, but felt no pleasure in music; would music be any good to you? Suppose that in physics you had the flair of an Einstein but never felt the slightest glow of happiness over solving an equation or making a new discovery; would research have any value for you? I think the answer in both cases must be no. Pleasure, the feeling of satisfaction, is a component of everything that is intrinsically good.

Our conclusion so far is that all goods involve pleasant experiences. Is there anything more that is essential to them? I think there is. And perhaps the best way to see it is to take an example which perplexed John Stuart Mill, one familiar to all students of ethics. He began by saying that pleasure, and pleasure alone, was what made anything good. But he was brought up short by reflecting on the comparative value that this doctrine would assign to the lives of Socrates and a pig. Take first a month in the life of a pig, and make it no ordinary pig but a porcine gourmet whose every gustatory whim is satisfied with the most exquisite dainties of the trough. Then take a month in the life of Socrates, and make it a month in which the good man is tormented by doubt, taxes, and Xanthippe. Which life would Mill rather live? Being a singularly honest man, he voted for Socrates, thereby making untold trouble for himself. For he was by no means certain that Socrates' life was a pleasanter life, while he had no doubt at all that it was more worth living. There must, then, be something other than pleasure that makes it more worth living. What was this? I will not remind you of Mill's answer because, by pretty general agreement, it was wrong. The right answer, I suggest, is this: Socrates' life was better because, whether more pleasant or not, it involved a completer fulfillment of powers. Grant the pig as generous a gastronomic capacity as one wishes, still one must admit that its intellectual, moral, and aesthetic horizons are limited, while those of Socrates are all but unlimited. What gave Socrates' life its value was the free play of a magnificent mind, the fulfillment in thought, feeling, and practice of a great intellect and a great heart.

This gives us the clue, I think, to the third component of all values. Besides experience, and pleasant experience, there must be fulfillment of natural faculties or powers. What we take as good always fulfills some need of our nature, some urge, drive, or impulse; and if the impulse is not there, we are cut off from value in that direction. Some great men—Lamb, Macaulay, Asquith, and Dean Inge, for example—have admitted that most music was mere noise to them, that they had a congenital lack of capacity for this form of experience. If this is true, fulfillment in this sphere is for them impossible, since there is no impulse or capacity to fulfill; strictly speaking, there is no such thing as music for them, and to try to educate them musically would be cruelty, as it would be to force a blind man to study painting. "Our aims," Emerson said, "should be mathematically adjusted to our powers." Values are not adventitious to human nature. A value is a value because it speaks to our condition, answers our need, meets and completes some demand of our nature. And the more central and fundamental the demand, the greater is the value attaching to its fulfillment.

In the light of all this, we may describe a value as an experience that is at once pleasant and fulfilling. And our question now is, What is the place of values, so conceived, in education?

The answer is that they should form the polestar of education. For the aim of education is to secure a more worth-while life, in the first instance for those who receive it, in the second for others affected by these; and a more worth-while life is one that is richer in values. But while education should aim at the production of values, it has two branches that serve this purpose in very different ways. The aim of *liberal* education is to qualify us directly to realize such values; the aim of *technological* education is to qualify us for them indirectly. Since the latter is nowadays the talk of the town, let us look at that first.

Technological education is training, discipline in doing things, the acquirement of a degree of mastery over an art or craft, whether that of building bridges, pulling teeth, or setting type. There is an ancient dispute about whether this should be called education at all. Humanists have often argued that a man may be the most expert of all practitioners in pulling teeth painlessly or setting type accurately and still be ignorant, bigoted, and provincial; technical proficiency is not enlightenment. On the other hand, our most eminent philosopher of education, John Dewey, held that a technological education, rightly conducted, was every whit as good as one in the humanities. If we think otherwise, he said, it is because for twenty centuries the West has been deluded by the Greeks. Plato and Aristotle were aristocrats who thought that hewing wood and drawing water, however expertly done, were the work of slaves, and that natural business of free minds was the contemplation of unchanging truth. Dewey believed them mistaken—mistaken as to the nature of thought itself; for thought is not really contemplation, he held; it is itself an instrument for getting things done. That is why he called his theory instrumentalism. It is ironic that Dewey, a champion of technological training, should now be held responsible by many for schools that turn out too few technologists. But our question is whether he was right in holding that technical training contributes as directly or richly to values as the study of the humanities.

I do not think he was. He was a philosopher who carried his attack on philosophy, as traditionally conceived, to an untenable extreme. The attack was popular because his stress on activity, on doing things, was typically American, and a thinker who proclaimed that a hypothesis, a philosophy, or a religion must be appraised by the difference it makes in practice seemed to be saying what, for a philosopher, was surprisingly sensible. But this was hardly the sort of teaching of which we stood in most need, at least those of us who were adults. To be sure, Dewey did much to dispel the dreariness of the little red schoolhouse by insisting that life consisted chiefly in doing things, that education should be a preface to life, and that the child could learn by doing, even by playing; we are all pragmatists from five to ten. But I incline to think that a person who is still a pragmatist at forty is suffering from arrested development. A person who limits the fruits of the spirit to those that can be tested in action is not so much freeing himself from an older dogmatism as fettering himself by a new one.

In justice to Dewey, we must remember that technology has many levels and that he was talking about the higher levels, not about routine plumbing or repairing. When my car breaks down—here I speak with the authority of broad experience—I take it to a certain garage where there is a kindly staff of mechanics. I always hope that a particular one will be there, a big, cheerful, grease-stained Boanerges whose mastery in his field fills me with envy. When I last presented myself on a bitter day, complaining that my radiator was so sick that it could not hold even Prestone down, the first man who came peered about beneath the hood in helpless bewilderment. Then Boanerges sauntered round. He poked a grimy head under the hood, scoffed at the childish notion of a leak in the radiator, and announced in some thirty seconds that one of the plugs in the manifold casing must be loose. He was right, as usual. To me this was sheer wizardry. Here was a master of his craft, and because of this an obviously happy man; and here was I, a master of—well what?—who had been thinking about free will for thirty years and was confused about it yet. Still, when in my dealings with Boanerges the conversation becomes general, my envy abates. His head is always in that hood; his world seems to be bounded by it; and when he ventures outside it, the master craftsman becomes as awkward and floundering as a puppy. The hood of a car is not, after all, a stately mansion for the soul. The number of things that can go wrong with a car is limited; you can get to the end of them; and when you have got there, the next fifty years of the same looks less appealing.

Dewey would object that this is very primitive technology, that the true technologist is a man whose reflection is continuously challenged by fresh problems and whose horizons are always expanding; if an example is wanted, take Edison, or Kettering, or Langmuir, or Wernher von Braun. And we must agree that the services of these men to society have been immense. Their electric lights, motorcars, and nuclear energy are transforming the physical side of life. But that is not the point. The point is whether technological education on a high level opens the mind to values as humanistic education does. The answer is that it does not. We may gain great satisfaction, to be sure, from solving puzzles about how iron or hydrogen behaves when compressed, or frozen, or heated to a million degrees, and from harnessing the more mulish forms of matter and making them work for us. But technology, even at these exalted levels, remains a complicated game of chess, in which, though you pit yourself against nature and play for very high stakes, you are still in essence pushing physical pieces about; and pushing pieces about, even under the most complicated rules, is not a general liberation of the spirit. The objection to a complete preoccupation with matter is that matter is dead. In material things, even in the most perfect of mechanical men, there is nothing to call out our love or admiration or sympathy or emulation or even dislike. The ideal technologist is an infinitely subtle brain at work on an infinitely subtle puzzle. He needs curiosity and endurance; but any appreciation of human goodness or artistic beauty, of what is funny or tragic or sublime, any sense for music or religion or justice, would be for him, simply as a technologist, superfluous baggage. Emerson somewhere deplores our modern tendency to become specialists, so that a man, if truly seen, would appear as a great nose, or a vast mouth, or perhaps a gigantic ear. In such a world, a pure technologist would be a hypertrophied cerebrum connected to a pair of mobile hands, but without any attached heart, glands, or spleen.

Now there is a difference between a technologist and a scientist. What is this difference? Presumably, that the technologist studies nature for the sake of controlling it, while the scientist studies it for the sake of understanding it. Thus the horizon of the scientist is wider than that of the technologist; for if a certain kind of knowledge gives no promise of application, the technologist's interest fades while that of the scientist may remain as lively as ever. Indeed, Bertrand Russell says that "Faraday, Maxwell, and Hertz, so far as can be discovered, never for a moment considered the possibility of any practical application of their investigations"; and Whitehead points out that mathematics was studied for at lease two thousand years before anything important came of it "except the intrinsic interest of the study." Science, pursued in this untrammeled way, is now held to form a part of liberal education; indeed, we are being urged from all sides to make it the chief part. Let us ask, then, what return in the way of values a young man or woman may expect from this pursuit.

There is, of course, first, the satisfaction of *knowing* something of physics or chemistry or biology. How great a value is this? We may appraise such knowledge for either its illumination or its discipline. To begin with the first, what makes knowledge illuminating? Surely the light it casts upon the world at large, the extent to which it helps to make that world intelligible. Scientific study and research may be a mere grubbing among details, as one could show in a grisly way by citing some of the Ph.D. subjects in any of our graduate schools. But from time to time there appears on the scientific scene a man who shows us afresh what science can do in the way of illumination. For him the details are push buttons which

release a flood of light on nature or human nature. Isaac
Newton was one of these minds. He saw that if he could
explain the fall of an apple he could probably explain the
deflection of the moon from a straight line into its orbit
around the earth, and if he could explain that, he could
explain the movement of the earth around the sun, and if
he coud explain that, he would have the ground plan of
the universe. He believed that he had the formula for the
apple, and he tried it on the moon. It did not work, and
he laid it aside for years. Then, learning from a French
astronomer that he had been mistaken as to size of the
earth and therefore its pull, he tested his formula again
with the correct figure. Result after result seemed to come
out right. It is said that as he approached the end of his
calculations, and the great generalization came almost
within his grasp, he became so excited that he did not
trust himself and turned over the final audit to steadier
heads.

I suppose the only name in modern physics that can
stand beside Newton's is that of his challenger, Einstein.
And Einstein, so far at least as a layman can follow him,
tells us the same story as to what it is that makes science
significant. Michelson and Morley had tried what seemed
like a rather trivial experiment to check the speed of light.
They set up a platform with a beam projected from one
end and a mirror at the other end. They then measured
the time it took for the beam to go to the mirror and
back, first when the beam was traveling in the direction
the earth was moving, and then when it was traveling at
right angles to that direction. The distance it had to
travel in these two cases was different, and they assumed
that the time taken would therefore be different. But they
found that it was exactly the same. They were surprised
and baffled. Einstein was also surprised, but declined to be
baffled. Just as Newton had seen in the falling apple the

clue to a universal law, so Einstein saw that what this odd result entailed was nothing less than reconceiving of all measurement and ultimately of the relation of time and space. The little beam of Michelson and Morley he enlarged till it illuminated the physical world.

It is the same with the social sciences. While Einstein was puzzling over the experiment in Berlin, a Vienna doctor was puzzling over such unlikely details as slips of the tongue, bad dreams, and the inability to remember things. For most students, these were quite unconnected facts and not very significant ones. Sigmund Freud insisted on understanding why a slip of the tongue occurred, why one dreamed in one way rather than another, why one could recall some unimportant details and could not remember some shocking ones. He pursued his clues remorselessly until he had a theory which not merely unified the explanation of all these facts but threw more light on human nature, if one may trust McDougall's judgment, than any other man since Aristotle.

It may be said that science, studied in this spirit, is hardly distinguishable from philosophy. I agree. There is no sharp line between the two; they fade into each other. They are parts of one enterprise and are necessary to each other; if philosophy without science is empty, science without philosophy has too often proved to be blind. Philosophy, science, and what we call common sense are all stages of our endeavor to understand the world. By common sense I mean the great body of judgments that we take for granted. These judgments include much dubious metaphysics, such as that grass is green and snow is cold even when nobody is about, and much moral philosophy in the form of proverbs, often of dubious consistency, such as "Be not penny wise and pound foolish" and "Take care of the pence and the pounds will take care of themselves." Now science does not turn its back on common sense; it starts with the earth, trees, and sky that we all accept and tries to make its judgments about them more general, precise, and consistent; it is common sense extended and refined. Philosophy I take to be simply more of the same. It *is* science, concentrating now on its ultimate results and on its initial assumptions. This means, on the one hand, that philosophy goes on after science ends; it takes the main results of the various sciences and tries to put them together into a consistent picture of the world. It means, on the other hand, that philosophy begins before science does, in the sense that it subjects such ideas as space, time, and cause, and such assumptions as that nature will behave tomorrow as today, which are not commonly questioned by science, to critical analysis. Philosophy is the attempted completion of science at both ends. I should follow Plato, then, in holding that this makes it the crown of education on its intellectual side. But lest it be thought that this disparages science, I hasten to add that by philosophy I mean science become self-conscious about its beginning and its goal. As someone has said, philosophy is the study of everything else philosophically.

The notion of science has now broadened in our hands to mean the attempt to lay hold of principles in any field of study, and it will include the reflective study not only of the natural sciences but also sociology, economics, psychology, and history. The great point is that education, on its intellectual side, is the quest not of knowledge, not of facts, but of illumination or understanding. Facts, of course, are important, but their retention is not what our minds are for but what the *Britannica* is for. There is some sense in the remark that education is what remains when we have forgotten what we learned. I admire and envy a man who, like Asquith, has the sort of flypaper memory which enables him, if the subject of horse racing happens to be broached, to name all the Derby winners since the

race was instituted; but I recall also that Asquith's great
antagonist in the Commons, Balfour, had so faulty a memory that if he wanted to quote a single line, he had to take
it with him on paper. Yet Balfour, by general consent, was
one of the best-educated minds in Europe. Quickly seizing
the essential points in any issue, he would discuss it with a
philosopher's eye for principle and the logic of a master
debater.

This brings us to the second of the two values to be
found in the liberal pursuit of science, taken in the broad
sense. The first was illumination. The second is discipline.
Our education ought to supply us with a habit and a
method of attacking problems, a habit of orderliness,
clearness, persistence, and precision. How often we must
endure performances by persons, too often with degrees
after their names, which require an agonizing re-appraisal
of their being educated at all: political speeches without
form and void, radio sermons full of sound and fury, signi-
fying nothing; after-dinner oratory in which the point, if
there is one, is fathoms deep in half-relevant anecdotage!
And what a satisfaction it is, when we are hunting for light
on some complicated issue, to find an article that puts the
issue simply, offers its evidence economically, faces difficulties fairly, and draws a firm conclusion! The ability to
do that is one of the most infallible marks of the educated
mind.

How is it attained? There are plenty of prescriptions for
it on the educational drug counter. We should take more
mathematics; we should hone our wits on the tough abra-
sives of symbolic logic; we should study scientific method;
we should be exposed to philosophy; since language is the
great deceiver, we should study semantics. I do not doubt
that we could profit by any of these courses. But there are
people of excellent intellectual practice who have never
taken any of them, and plenty of muddlers who have taken

them all. The common error of such proposals is to assume
that there is only one royal road to sound intellectual practice. But the effective use of intelligence is confined to no
one field, and it may be acquired in any. How? I venture
to think that it is usually gained in two steps: first by ad-
miring it as shown in some particular person, and then by
copying it at least once.

Consider the first step. As a teacher, what seems to me
distressing is that so many students go through college
without contracting any enthusiasm for intellectual artistry
and that so long as we fail to arouse their enthusiasm, we
shall accomplish relatively little by forced feeding and
stern drills. To be sure, first-rate work does sometimes
break through to the student in spite of us if not through
us. When I was a high school student I was taught Burke's
"Conciliation with America" by a teacher who seemed to
have no conception of its quality. But that marvelous speech
had its innings in spite of all the teacher could do. I thought
it wonderful and, young prig that I was, went around
mouthing Burke. I had never met a human being who talked
like that or could think like that, but here was the thrilling
fact that one man actually had. Not that I understood
Burke; no teen-ager could; but that did not prevent my
contracting a bad case of hero worship, and I have never
quite recovered from it. In my little cabinet of master-
pieces, the speech on conciliation still stands on the same
shelf with the Fifth Symphony. Dr. Johnson once said that
you could not so much as step into the same doorway with
Edmund Burke to get out of the rain without saying as you
went away, "That was a remarkable man." I shall always be
grateful that, as a raw youngster in a Middle Western high
school, I happened to step into a doorway with Burke and
caught my unforgettable glimpse of greatness of mind.

The second step in acquiring good thinking habits is to do
for oneself in a single case what a good model does. It is far

more significant for our education to write one good essay than dozens of mediocre ones, for that one essay means that we have standards, and what we have done once we can presumably do again. No one does eighteen holes of golf in seventy-three by accident; you know that if anyone does that just once, he is a master of the game. A student who has carried through one piece of responsible research in history or biology or anthropology, so that it will stand intensive criticism for its cogency and its style, has had the ideal discipline for future work. It may be objected that discipline does not carry over from field to field. Of course there is something in this, and it makes me somewhat skeptical about precisely those subjects that have been often thought highest in disciplinary value, namely mathematics and a purely formal logic. In these subjects clarity is achieved for one rather than by one, since the concepts are perfectly definite from the beginning; one's conclusion is either completely necessary or false; and the issues are so abstract that personal feelings are not engaged. That is not the sort of thinking we do in politics or religion or even in natural science. When we are discussing liberty or democracy, half the trouble may be in the woolliness of the concepts. Rigorous demonstration will probably be out of the question; judgment will be constantly called for on degrees of importance and relevance; and impartiality may be under test at every step. I am inclined to think, therefore, that for general intellectual discipline good work in an inexact science is more valuable than in an exact science. It may be said that even this kind of discipline does not carry over. Here I can only beg to differ. Caution, clarity, precision, orderliness are the same traits in all the sciences of fact, and though eminent minds are not exempt from foolishness, I think journalists and plain men display a sound instinct when they listen with respect to anything a Toynbee or a Sherrington has to say.

We have been considering the disciplines that aim at knowledge. But what about the study of literature, music, and art? These are now a recognized part of a liberal education, and their primary aim is plainly not knowledge. Their aim is to satisfy and educate feeling. We sometimes forget that feeling is as educable as intelligence and that, so far as happiness is concerned, its cultivation is even more important. What does the education of feeling mean? Someone has given the answer in the remark that culture is the adjustment of feeling to its objects and that education is learning to like and dislike the right things. Such education is one of our most conspicuous needs. Americans are a people of strong feelings, freely expressed; they have been called the Latin branch of the Anglo-Saxon family. Many of us seem to like excitement for its own sake, and if there is insufficient outward occasion for it, we are adroit at generating it *ad hoc*. When Shriners or Legionnaires get together, or a birthday or the New Year is to be celebrated, Americans have an inexhaustible repertory of first aids to excitement: brass bands, paper hats, ticker tape, horns and whistles, snake dances, fancy costumes, and drum majorettes; and at big games there are trained cheerleaders to work up our emotions and give them organized vent. Of course exuberance and high spirits are excellent things. But this hardly implies that the value of an experience depends on how exciting it is. May I quote two or three wise sentences from the philosopher A. E. Taylor? "The mere identification of *any* fundamental activity of the human spirit with emotion, cut loose from a *specific* object, is the degradation and, in the end, the paralysis of the emotion itself. Emotions of all kinds so manifestly derive their value for human life from the character of the object on which they are directed. Emotion inappropriate or disproportionate to the objective situation by which it is evoked is the bane of life."

Now, emotion inappropriate to its object is a chief bane of American life. It shows itself in the scale of admirations felt by the American public. Let me catch a few straws from the wind. When Vice President Nixon came home from one of his trips, he was met by his small daughter, Patricia, who told him that she had started piano lessons. "And do you like to practice?" asked her father, who used to be fairly adept at the piano himself. "Yes," said Patricia, and went on to give a pointed little lecture to the Vice President: "You know, Daddy, if you had practiced a lot, you would have gone to Hollywood. And you know what would have happened? You would have become famous and everybody would remember you, and they would bury you in a nice place." I suspect that Patricia's voice echoed that of many persons of greater years. On a news counter recently I saw a well-known magazine with two figures conspicuously displayed side by side on its cover. One was Dwight D. Eisenhower; the other was a person described as having made a conquest of America, Brigitte Bardot. On my desk at home is an attractive advertisement for a new *Encyclopedia of Jazz*, which informs me that since it contains the birthdays of 1065 jazz artists it "provides an invaluable tool for . . . school jazz groups, etc." Consider this revealing sentence by a reviewer asked to write an advanced notice of a new novel for the *Retail Bookseller:* "Savage as *The Hucksters* . . . rough, tough, and violent, it looks like a best seller." To be sure, the stage and television aspire at times to higher things. Last year the producer Mort Abrahams ventured to put on his television program, *Showcase*, a novel version of an old thriller called *Romeo and Juliet*. It didn't do badly, and Mort happily commented: "This boy Shakespeare is a real comer: I'm going to use a lot of him."

These things are comic, but there are numberless people who do not find them so, and that makes them also tragic.

In the sphere of science we can protect ourselves fairly readily from quacks and frauds; there are consumers' unions, pure food and drug acts, and often simple tests of one's own that will serve to eliminate the worst in the way of soaps and cold remedies. But there is no kind of litmus paper that will show vulgarity as what it is except the inward kind called education. And by education I do not mean, of course, a college degree; I mean living in the presence of the best till one understands and likes it, till the ways of feeling of fine minds become one's own, till one catches their health by contagion as one catches other people's disease and develops a general immunity to the viruses of cheapness. "Moral education is impossible," says Whitehead, "without the habitual vision of greatness." "The way to acquire a good taste in anything," says Sir Richard Livingstone, "from pictures to architecture, from literature to character, from wine to cigars, is always the same—be familiar with the best specimens of each." An English friend of mine once sat on an educational committee with George Saintsbury, and told me that when the problem arose of how to interest the young in good literature and the group turned in some puzzlement to the great scholar for advice, all he had to say was "Leave books around." No doubt the books that Saintsbury would casually leave around would be pretty cunningly chosen. But one of the blessings of our time and country is that this kind of education is open to any determined boy or girl. There are plenty of good guides to reading, and plenty of libraries and cheap editions available to anyone with a real desire for the best. It is salutary for us academics to recall occasionally that Chaucer and Shakespeare, Keats and Browning, Jane Austen and Dickens, Mill and Shaw never went to a university. "The true university," said Carlyle, "is a collection of books."

The strange thing is that the very democracy that was supposed to diffuse acquaintance with the best is serving

in unexpected ways to prevent this. Our literate public is
the world's greatest market. Publishers depend on sales and
Hollywood on the box office; both therefore are tempted
to appeal to the lowest common denominator, the level on
which we can all meet, which is not that of ideas but of
crude emotions: fear, anger, sex, and self-glorification.
The standard formula is to mix these up into one potent
brew, varying slightly the proportions of the ingredients,
and to serve it up over and over. That is what we shall
get as long as we go on patiently accepting it. Many have
come to think of tolerance as a virtue that extends equally
to values and beliefs; I cannot agree. Not that we should
suppress vulgarity any more than we should suppress mistaken ideas, but that the very notion of values involves
good and bad and that democracy among values is a contradiction in terms.

If we really love what is good, we shall despise what
is bad and say so. There are courageous critics who are
showing us the way in this, for example Orville Prescott
and J. Donald Adams of *The New York Times*. I was delighted some time ago to find Adams telling the house of
Scribner to its austere old face that in publishing James
Jones's *Some Came Running* it was issuing a book on
"the intellectual level of a retarded adolescent" and that it
ought to be ashamed of itself. Dean Robert E. Fitch of
the Pacific School of Religion has recently spoken out
against what he calls the *mystique de la merde* in our fiction, a phrase variously translated as "the deification of
dirt," "the apotheosis of ordure," and "plain mud mysti-
cism." He says that writers like Jones and Norman Mailer
and Tennessee Williams and, at his worst, Hemingway
would have us believe that what sadistic sergeants and
moronic prostitutes blurt out in their cups is somehow
truth and reality, while thoughtful and kindly people are too
dull to be worth listening to. I will not try to appraise

this; I am not well-read enough. But of some of the things I have read it rings true.

It may be said that in these matters no grounded preference is possible; and we are sure soon to hear that *de gustibus non est disputandum*. But matters of taste are precisely what people argue about most vigorously, and if there is any force in what we have said about the nature of value, there are objective betters and worses and it is simply silly in Bentham's fashion to put pushpin beside poetry. The Greeks saw that in great tragedy one somehow fulfills oneself and becomes a new and larger man, with a new sense for the central and the trivial. What troubles me as a college teacher is that so many students leave college with apparently no sense at all of what is central and what trivial. College courses have exposed them to greatness, but it has somehow left them cold.

This is partly our fault as teachers. It is all very well to say, "We needs must love the highest when we see it"; the trouble is that without help, the highest may be as hard to see as Mount Everest is from Darjeeling. When I visited Venice long ago, I happened by chance to stay in the house where Ruskin had lived, and on the shelves was a battered copy of his *Stones of Venice*. With its aid I found how blind I was and what a revelation was open to anyone who could look at that fairy city through such eyes and with such a heart. The teacher of literature must make his students see the subject with his eyes and, if he can, feel for it some of his love. Overworked jade that he probably is, he must manage to remain on fire with his subject, for only so can he light fires under anyone else. Fortunately, to do that he does not need to be a great writer or critic himself. William Lyon Phelps was neither, but he was one of Yale's most valuable assets nevertheless, for he had the happy faculty of turning out lovers of literature in droves. How did he do it? Chiefly by a joint enthusiasm for literature and for youth. "When I wake up in the morning," he said, "I lie in bed and think with delight of my first class." Is it any wonder that the class repaid him in kind?

We have considered values of the intellect and values of appreciation, but have said nothing about the values of conduct or practice. Is not life largely action, and should not college prepare us to act as well as to think and feel? Now if action means mere behavior, the play of arm and leg, there are no values of action, for values are in the mind. Still, we all know that the man of action—the Napolean of the army or industry or public life—is a distinct type from the thinker or the artist, and a vastly important type who if often lost in the shuffle when education is under review. Can a college turn out such men, or even do much to help them? This is my last question.

Of course there are schools of business administration and welfare work and diplomacy, but no college can reproduce the conditions in which the man of affairs is going to work. So when liberal arts colleges are criticized because their graduates on entering business have to learn it from the ground up, the charge is both true and negligible. No curriculum ever devised will guarantee a Churchill or a Henry Ford. But that a college can do something even here is suggested by the fact that little Merton College, Oxford, with less than a hundred and fifty students, produced, if I remember rightly, seven archbishops of Canterbury in one century, and that Balliol under Jowett poured out administrators to every part of the empire.

The chief points about the office of the college in training men of action seem to me to be these. First, a training of intelligence *is* a training of will. As William James pointed out, a firm will is largely a matter of controlled attention, of fixing our thought firmly on what must be done, and hence a discipline of thought is itself a preparation for action. Secondly, college life on the practical side is not wholly divorced from the rest of life. It exacts hard tasks, it sets deadlines, it requires the ordering of one's time and the budgeting of one's energies. Teachers are sometimes slack and indulgent about these things, as doting parents are, but the student ought not to be so toward himself. He is enjoying a great privilege which he ought to take most seriously, and if he keeps himself to the mark, that alone will equip him to meet the deadlines of the world. Thirdly, American colleges, rightly I think, value athletics; and the participation in competitive games, if wisely conducted, gives an admirable discipline in taking success modestly, in taking defeat and hard knocks uncomplainingly, and in developing respect for justice, since sportsmanship is justice in play. If York-town was lost, as has been alleged, on the playing fields of Eton, at least Waterloo was something. Fourthly, as in the realms of intelligence and appreciation, so too in the realm of action college can marshal models across the stage for whom we feel a self-revealing repulsion or affinity. Here history is the chief resource, not so much social or constitutional history as the old-fashioned kind that makes it largely the biography of great men. We all find it intelligible that General Eisenhower, traversing Napoleon's field of action, should have remarked, "I should have liked to tangle with that fellow," or that he and Montgomery should have gone over Gettysburg together and come up with a reappraisal of Lee. What is more significant is that such people as Goethe, Hegel, and Emerson should also be fascinated by Napoleon; that Mommsen, Froude, and Thornton Wilder should have been fascinated by Caesar; and that Carlyle should have worshiped at the shrines of Cromwell and Frederick. These men of action had deep moral flaws, but they were, after all, among the "quarto and folio editions of mankind," and to read in them is to expand one's ideas of what a mere human being can do. Finally, education not only can inspire action, it can give it perspective and goals. How different the world would be if Napoleon and Hitler had been cultivated minds instead of being the one an outsized Corsican brigand and the other a guttersnipe of genius!

We have reached the end of our argument, and it proves to be as simple as it has been long. Values, we have argued, are experiences that are at once satisfying and fufilling. The purpose of education is to make us creators and centers of value. Technological education does that indirectly by supplying us tools for the exploiting of nature. Liberal education on its intellectual side provides the values of understanding, which makes us at home in our world. Liberal education on its appreciative side makes us responsive to the best that has been said and painted and built and sung. Liberal education on its practical side puts the wind of emulation in our sails and gives direction to our voyage. Values are the stars by which education may and should steer its course.

DEVELOPING COMMUNITY
RESPONSIBILITY

By Arthur E. Morgan

It is thirty-seven years since I began definitely to wrestle
with the matter of student participation in college affairs
with the aim of encouraging students to develop habits of
responsible social participation. As the years have passed,
I have come to see this question not as a distinct problem
but just as one phase of a much larger issue.

First I should like to speak of what I think students are
capable of doing, and wherein both college and students
may benefit by participation in the determination and
execution of college program and policy. The student's
life in his community will largely continue the principles
and attitudes he lived by in college, so nothing is more pertinent to our subject than his college pattern.

I shall base these preliminary remarks on experience at
Antioch College, for that is the only institution of higher
education with which I have had much first-hand familiarity. When we began the present Antioch program thirty-
seven years ago, one of my first interests was to encourage
the initiation of what was called student government. I
believed that experience in responsible self-direction could
contribute to personal development in ways that classroom
and laboratory probably could not. Its functions were relatively few but were very real. Through the first six or
seven years there was gradual extension of functions and

development of some understanding of possibilities and limitations.

Then, almost entirely as a matter of student initiative, there was a move to transform student government into "Community Government," to include both students and faculty. That has proved to be a very significant change. Through thirty years this type of organization has had a continuous, though not uniform, development. Today Antioch students have a range of functions in the administration of the college which is exceeded by few if any colleges in America.

Almost every Antioch college committee has student representatives. There are student members of the administrative council regularly elected by the community. This council, under the trustees, is the chief governing body of the college. Student members are included on committees to choose the college president, to select faculty members, on the admissions committee to select students, on the curriculum committee, the budget committee, the committee on buildings and grounds, and so on.

In their living quarters the students are divided into halls of about twenty-four persons each, with hall presidents and hall advisers. Both hall presidents and hall advisers are students. The hall advisers are upperclassmen or women, and as a rule exercise their functions in a responsible manner, commonly with a considerable degree of personal commitment.

Then there are functions which are exercised almost entirely by students. These include administration and operation of the college bookstore, the college newspaper, the college radio station, inspection of automobiles, fire protection, and especially all the varied social programs. For these purposes the Community Government has a special budget of about $45,000 a year.

On some committees there are two or three faculty

members to each student member, while on others there are two or three or more students to one of the faculty, the proportion depending on what seems most appropriate to the subject involved. Students frequently request more faculty participation, and faculty committees sometimes wish for more student help. Student community activities are by no means limited to these somewhat formally structured relationships. Faculty and students work together in drama, local government, political activities, religious programs, local social service such as boy and girl scouts, research projects, and in other ways.

Courses in history, sociology, and economics call for field studies which bring students into contact with the outside world over a wide range. For instance, in a course in business management the class makes practical studies of industries and commercial firms. One head of an industry commented to me that students were especially useful because, having no reputations at stake, they did not hesitate to make unconventional suggestions. In this case, as a result of such a study by the class as a whole, the cost of keeping the accounts of four thousand customers over the country was cut in two.

The vitality of these greatly varied relationships depends in considerable degree on the fact that in the student body there are many individuals or small groups with specific interests, and in working at these, students may have a strong sense of validity.

What about the results of this over-all program of actual and very extensive student participation? For the most part it has, I believe, justified itself. I think that few persons associated with Antioch would be inclined to reduce the general degree or range of student participation, except that students sometimes feel that too much of their time is taken. With an exacting academic program, student life at Antioch is rather rugged.

What I have said should not lead to the conclusion that student participation has a history of smooth running. Student generations are short, and at Antioch there is the added mobility of work-period turnover. With young men and women in a most active time of life, and with a sense of newly achieved maturity, there sometimes is a feeling that "now that *we* have arrived, life will begin"; the first thing is to wipe the slate clean of the past and to start afresh. A year or two ago the Community Government—substantially the student body—decided after much argument that committees and other functions had become so elaborated and complex as to cumber the operation of the whole Community Government system; that the entire system should be dissolved and a new start made. No committees would be reappointed unless they should be actually necessary. This seemingly desperate course was taken. It soon appeared that there were some committees and other functions so obviously desirable that they were quickly reconstituted. Gradually it was realized that the system was not as antiquated or perfunctory as it had seemed, but that the complexities were due in part to the very diversity of activity; and before long the new structure proved to be substantially similar to the old, with some deadwood eliminated.

Students are not children. Most qualified psychologists in the field of mental measurements are of the opinion that the college years find students at the very peak of their inherent intellectual powers. It is then that they are least inhibited in formulating theoretical concepts. Competence in applying pragmatic factors, without which the theoretical formula may not be usable, comes only with years and experience. But as the world moves, especially in a work and study program such as that at Antioch, students of from seventeen to twenty-four are not totally without experience, and in the Community Government they have members of the administrative and teaching staffs as associates and counselors, though not as paternal guardians.

Thought disciplines action and gives it direction, while action corrects thinking and holds it to reality. Alternation of thought and action is not just a clever educational device, it is a fundamental of the educational process. Students commonly come to college with an incongruous medley of conditioning by parents, playmates, teachers, the community, newspaper, radio, television, books, magazines; the pronouncements of church, state, capital, labor; and their own experiences with nature. College should be an appraising, selecting, unifying influence. This can best be exercised with a continuous alternation of study and reflection on the one hand and firsthand experience on the other.

Action without thought is no better than thought without action. Most men are men of action rather than of thought, and most of them live in narrow worlds. The scholar immersed in his study may be no more isolated than the accountant at his books or the manufacturer who lives in a narrow cell of production schedules and filling orders. Experience, unless enlightened by imagination and philosophy, may teach little.

Because habits usually are made early, unless the habit of alternating thought and action is established before the student leaves college he may step from a world of thinking into a world of action, feeling that he has come to the end of one type of experience and has begun another. Many a college and university graduate, having failed to establish this habit of alternating reflective thought and practical action, ceases to grow in personal stature through the succeeding years.

A very idealistic student who has lived in a world of ideas, as he comes abruptly to practical life, often finds himself nearly helpless in a world which seems to care little for his ideals. He may become disillusioned and frus-

trated. Either he will retreat to some shelter or he will
put his ideals into one compartment of his mind while he
lives his practical life in another. To make one's standards
work in a practical setting calls for design, forethought,
self-control and self-denial, and the gradual development
of a difficult but possible art. After college is rather late
to initiate that process.

I shall not discuss specific organizations to promote
development of community responsibility and leadership.
Hundreds of American colleges and universities have
adopted some elements of student sharing in the formulation and administration of college policy. I would, however, suggest some general considerations.

A program of student participation will not succeed
best if it is merely patched onto an otherwise full program
as something meritorious but incidental. Also, a student
who participates actively in college policy and program
does not have extra hours added to his day for that purpose.
If participation requiring substantial time, thought, and
energy is to be encouraged, it should be given place in
the curriculum and should have college credit. There are
many activities which, if well handled, will require greater
outlay than a stiff academic course. It may strain our
academic minds a bit to think of nonacademic work as
an integral part of an educational program. In academic
studies we recognize that the help of teachers is desirable.
This is no less true in the case of administrative or other
work.

There should be design and discipline to prevent over-
crowding the student's total calendar. Absence of these is
a chief weakness of some college programs. The problem
of optimum distribution of time becomes increasingly
important as new elements are added to the total pattern
of college education.

Thirty-seven years of a program of alternating work

and study for college students at Antioch have, I believe, demonstrated its value. Experience there and elsewhere has demonstrated that success does not inevitably follow the adoption of such an arrangement. More than in fields where there is abundant precedent, quality must be won by sustained, intelligent, imaginative commitment.

Now I should like to comment on some major factors which have entered into American higher education and which have had marked bearing on the attitudes students take with them from college or university to community life.

Except for the land-grant college movement initiated by the United States government, most American colleges up to the beginning of this century were established by religious bodies, and each one had the aim of helping young people to become educated men and women in general according to the prevailing pattern. But in doing so, the colleges would undertake to preserve and to advance the peculiar truth, outlook, and excellencies of the religious bodies concerned. These church colleges were interested in the intellectual development of the student, but also in his entire life and destiny.

In accord with the spirit of organized religion which had prevailed in Europe and America up to that time, the development of over-all attitudes toward life and destiny did not call primarily for inquiry, but for acceptance. The various religious organizations knew that they had the truth, and their concern was that it should not be lost in transmission. A glimpse of the widely approved educational process in church-administered colleges of the last century may be had from a biographical sketch of an exceptionally able teacher of English and literature at Union College in New York state in the eighteen sixties and seventies. It was written of him: "Three characteristics, as a teacher, stood out prominently in him. First, his earnestness and truth. Out of this came a second characteristic, a conservative caution. Clearly and sharply drawn, in his own thinking, was the line between revealed and speculative thought. In regard to the latter he was exceedingly careful. Where a sure word of scripture was not behind him, he was cautiously reticent. Two reasons seem to have shut out the Socratic method from his class room. He wished to avoid useless discussion and to place before his students a system of truth in its entirety. He was convinced of the ultimate fruitlessness of all merely impulsive discussion. The third point was his progressive and charitable spirit."

While this attitude prevailed in large degree in American church colleges, quite another movement was under way in Europe. Through many centuries, with here and there an exception, religious conformity had dominated European universities. However, at least as early as the middle of the eighteenth century a very contrasting spirit was emerging. The French Revolution accentuated this, not only in France but in Germany. The new University of Berlin "repudiated all attachment to any particular creed or school of thought." With an exceptionally outstanding faculty, it became the largest German university and perhaps the foremost in Europe. It was a center of free critical study, committed to rigorous, objective thinking by reasonably mature men, with no concern for moral or religious guardianship. There was little if any attention given to the total life pattern of the students, but only to their competence and achievement in specific fields.

Late in the nineteenth century this institution became the ideal of the American university. Anybody who was anybody in America wanted to finish his formal education there and to bring its methods back with him. During the eighteen nineties, when there were probably not 5 per cent as many American graduate students as there are now, more than thirteen hundred of them at a time were overseas at the University of Berlin. They came home to set the ideal of the American university.

No doubt something new had been needed in American higher education. When Agassiz came to Harvard in the eighteen forties he described that institution as "a second-rate high school, giving the dregs of an education." But the striking values of the Continental university so dazzled Americans that they swallowed them whole without realizing that their own native product had a great value— that of seeing education as concerned with the whole man. The pattern of the Continental university, and especially of the University of Berlin, gained steadily in American favor, and soon the liberal college attitude was on the defensive.

To accord with general educational opinion, and to meet the specific requirements of the various college-accrediting agencies, a college must load its faculty with men having doctorate degrees. In a large proportion of cases that means securing teachers who have been heavily indoctrinated with the Continental university pattern. The teacher commonly wants to teach his subject or to do research and not be "nursemaid to students."

But the old American liberal college picture has not died easily. Either through survival or through rebirth, concern for the total life of the student steadily grows. General education, student counseling, psychiatric service, required physical education, encouragement of student participation in the formation and execution of college policy, and the growth of programs of alternating work and study, all witness to this fact.

Yet the situation from that standpoint is still far from satisfactory. One of the most general of human frailties is our propensity for seeing our choices as either-or rather than for doing creative thinking which might result in a new synthesis. Would it not be desirable to seek consciously and deliberately for a pattern which would avoid both the paternal indoctrination of the old-time liberal college and the disinterest in the student's life as a whole which characterized the typical Continental university?

One of the chief functions of education is the stimulating and focusing of attention and interest. The physics teacher draws attention to key concepts which have emerged and to their significance, and insists that they be understood. But there is no sheltering the student from competent criticism of those concepts. If a young Einstein effectively criticizes the finality of Isaac Newton's ideas, he is honored for his achievement. But he must understand those ideas if he is to criticize them effectively. It seems to me to be sound education to interest students in their whole life patterns and purposes and to ask them to do substantial critical thinking on that subject. It does not follow that their minds and attitudes should be guided paternally to any predetermined conclusions.

As a rule our colleges and universities do not maintain successors to Carlyle's character, Diogenes Teufelsdroch, "Professor of Things in General." That function commonly is distributed through the faculty. If the teachers have the attitude of the Continental university and feel that they do not have or want any responsibility to students beyond teaching their own courses and serving on administrative committees, the synthesis I have suggested as desirable may not be achieved.

Even if we assume that the educational pattern of an institution takes account of the whole of the student's practical life and is giving him experience which will develop community responsibility and leadership, we are not yet fully out of the woods. A fellowship like the Society of Friends and a college like Swarthmore want more than to perpetuate the prevailing culture. They aspire to raise it to new levels.

As we are aware, the Society of Friends originated in England at a time when generally prevailing habits and attitudes were mediocre and undistinguished. The Friends sought to achieve a more discriminating and more excellent pattern of life, which they tried to exemplify individually and as a society. When in the course of time they founded schools and colleges, they had two major aims. One was to enable their own young people to have the knowledge and outlooks of educated men and women. The other was to have this educational process take place under conditions which would favor the passing on of a quality of life which they as Friends had sought so hard to achieve. They wanted a high quality of scholarship, yet the field of choice was narrowed if they were to avoid the typical products of the Continental university, persons concerned with scholarship in their fields but with little interest in the design of living as a whole. In speaking of the Friends' way of life I do not refer chiefly to peculiar Quaker formalities, as of dress or speech, but to more fundamental attitudes, such as simplicity of living, honesty, regard for cleanness and soundness of body and mind, and respect for human dignity regardless of rank or other status.

Friends' colleges were approved by the public to an extent that today among students in most of them Friends are in a minority. Yet the process of selection continues. Parents of more than average cultural and ethical discrimination seek other than mediocre educational environment for their children, and for that reason many of them choose Friends' colleges, or, what is more in accord with the time, they influence their sons and daughters to make that choice. In the minds of many such parents, the college is to be in fact as well as in theory *in loco parentis* to their children. If the college fails to take that position, is it not betraying the confidence of the parents? Yet in the present mental state of young America, the term *in loco parentis* brings about the same response as the word "colonialism" would at an Arab conference at Cairo. Students insist that what they want is not benevolent paternalism but recognition as responsible men and women. And thereby hangs a dilemma.

In order to get something of a perspective, and to see where the drift of the democratic temper may take us, let us look for a moment at the situation of the state universities and other land-grant colleges. These were a product of democratic America—of the people, for the people, by the people. Three great traditions met in these institutions: the American church college, the secular Continental university, and the practical know-how education of the American factory and farm. There was commonly a jumble and confusion of educational philosophies rather than any clear design, but this very disorder allowed each element to find somewhat free expression. Like many hybrids, the American state university, with its nearby kin such as agricultural and mechanical colleges and municipal state universities, shows so much greater vigor than its antecedent types that it threatens to swallow them up.

Democracy in America is a principle of such inherent vitality that it constantly emerges into new fields of action. The state universities began in considerable degree as a continuation of artistocratic and authoritarian administration. Yet constantly democracy has leaked through the barriers of older convention, and now it threatens to burst those gates and to enter full flood. By democracy I do not refer chiefly to patterns of administration, but to prevailing mentalities and cultural characteristics.

If we look at American democracy as we have seen it

in the past, I think we shall observe two distinct characteristics. One of these is the practical conviction, sometimes
seen graven on the front of our county courthouses, "The
voice of the people is the voice of God." What the people
think, it is right for them to think; what they want, it is
right for them to want. The second characteristic is tolerance for minorities, at least in normal times and when
they are not too troublesome.

With the voice of the people as the voice of God, there
is a tendency for the average or median culture to become
the dominant culture, for it contributes most volume to
that voice. In its philosophy the American state university
is intensely pragmatic and practical, following the philosophy of the average American. That which generally pre-
vails is justified. When Dave Beck was chosen by his
old-time neighbors, who must have known him well, as
president of the board of regents of Washington State University, was not that an announcement to the students
about how to succeed? When Kinsey found statistically
that more than half of American men are sexually promiscuous, was not sexual promiscuousness democratically
validated?

In the state university, where every tolerably literate
high school graduate must by law be admitted, and where
there are no generally accepted cultural standards but those
of the prevailing mores, what forces will long maintain
discriminating cultural standards in a democratic society?
There is such a force in the spirit of professional scholarship. Will that spirit maintain exacting standards of life as
a whole, or only in scholarship? There is the religious element in American life, which also has an influence.

The American state universities and land-grant colleges
have frequently had an ethics of short-range pragmatism.
Their presidents have sometimes been men who were
skillful at cleverly handling legislatures and who were all

things to all men. It sometimes has been possible to increase federal allotments by gently manipulating the truth. They thereby demonstrated to the students that while moralizing is good in assembly talks, practical men handle practical affairs in practical ways. At other times there has been true zeal for scholarship, and character and statesmanship of a high order have repeatedly arisen. In the broad sweep of American life there are vast resources of honesty, self-respect, and good will, and they also find democratic self-expression. It is in this mixture of elements that American young people have learned how to exercise responsibility and leadership in their home communities.

Under these conditions our far-flung system of state universities and land-grant colleges has had a reasonably honorable history. The process of democracy in education has often been marred, but it has not failed. Perhaps we should judge it not just by our ideals but also by the practical alternatives.

What are the alternatives to this democratic, secular educational system which is so frequently and so drastically decried by representatives of authoritarian religion in our country? One of the British dominions took a strikingly different course. Newfoundland escaped secular education. Tax money collected by the government was distributed to the churches in proportion to their population; about 40 per cent each to the Church of England and to the Roman Catholic Church, and the rest mostly to the Methodists. These church authorities were left to provide the educational system from bottom to top. Nowhere in all the English-speaking world was there such sorry failure in education or in citizenship as in this dominion, populated almost exclusively by hardy English-speaking people from the British Isles. Finally, after a century of inefficiency, graft, wide-scale smuggling, mismanagement, financial favoritism, and lack of educational advance, the whole dominion went bankrupt and surrendered its status —the only such failure, as I recall, of an English-speaking population in the British Empire.

What have these remarks to do with adapting the college program to develop community responsibility? It is important that there be specific ways of giving the student experience in responsibility and leadership. Yet a far more important question is, What kind of person will the student be when he leaves college? For in his community he will tend to express and to reproduce his own pattern of life and thought. What his college has done to him in making him the kind of person he is, that will he do to his community. What kind of college will make him the kind of person, as a person, which his community ought to be, as a community?

While the old-time church college in America was concerned with the student's whole life and destiny, it was spiritually authoritarian. As to over-all life and purpose the college had the answer, which it would give to the student. Fundamental questions were not encouraged. The Continental university spirit of critical scholarship, while it tended to free men's minds from authoritarian dogmas, had little concern for ethical or spiritual values. The American democratic, secular university responds to the controlling interests and drives of the people as a whole. It has no clear concept and pattern of its aim, but responds to all pressures, gives hostages in many directions, and moves along the lines of the resultant forces. Because the over-all American character has much of soundness, normalness, and vigor, this institution has had a very impressive history, though more impressive in quantity than in exceptional quality. Its product has a wide variety of impact on community life. There are variations of these educational patterns, such as that of the Jesuits, with its intensive indoctrination in a fixed pattern combined with high quality of scholarship wholly within that prescribed framework.

Where among these types of institutions can we find or create an educational design which will have the greatest promise of equipping young men and women for lives of responsibility and leadership in their communities? Especially, how can fellowships best survive and advance which are committed to spiritual pioneering and which desire to achieve and to perpetuate a way of life distinctly in advance of that of average America?

The major controls of life are not intellectual, but emotional. Intelligence implements emotion, but does not take its place. A scientist never will be a great scientist unless he cares greatly, and caring is an emotional state. A teacher never will be a great teacher unless he cares about life and destiny, and also unless he cares for students and associates as brother does for brother. Caring is not transmitted by reasoning so much as by contagion from those who care. Reason can inform, enlighten, and direct caring, but rarely if ever create it.

A craving for meaning, motive, and significance for one's life will generally characterize significant living. If the trustees of an institution have been chosen for other reasons, and do not have that, then only by accident will they secure it in their administrators; if the administrators do not have that quality, only occasionally and by chance will it be present in the teachers; if the teachers have been chosen too much for scholarship and do not have that craving for life purpose, they cannot transmit it to the students; and if the students do not acquire it, they cannot exercise or transmit it in the communities where they will live and work after college.

Several recent studies have indicated that the motivation of college students is but little effected by their college years. That, I believe, is because they have not had intimate, sustained fellowship with teachers who care greatly about life and about students.

The first requirement toward preparing students for community relations is selection of those who will direct their educational programs: the trustees, the administrators, and the teaching staff. In selecting teachers, while scholarship is important, it may not be of the highest importance. The most brilliant teaching will not greatly change motivation as to life purpose unless the teacher infects the student with that motivation, and he seldom can infect the student with what he does not have himself.

These comments may seem banal, yet the emphasis on intellectual quality and scholarship in selection of teachers, at the expense of caring about the general quality of life, is, I believe, a chief reason why college so lightly touches the over-all life motivation of students. Here the course should not be either-or, but a right relation between intelligence and scholarship on the one hand and strong life purpose on the other.

I am inclined to think that a college teaching staff might very profitably maintain a running seminar with the aim of carrying on sincere, critical inquiry to develop unity and maturity of over-all life purpose and attitude and their applications to everyday life. Student problems, student questions, and the circumstances of living would supply an abundance of cases. Here, as elsewhere, alternation of reflective, critical thinking and application to cases would be productive. If there is full respect for free, critical inquiry such a course will not develop the character either of an inquisition or of a tiresome ritual.

If an inquiring student goes to his several faculty members for counsel, he may find among them a hodgepodge of incongruous opinions and attitudes and may conclude that as to life purpose and ethical principle there are no norms of authority and that one person's judgment is as good as another's. That is fairly common student opinion today. The reason is that in this field many college teachers are illiterate and uninterested or are bound by traditional dogma. Even this prevailing situation is better than a unity of uncritical acceptance of traditional or authoritarian dogma. But those are not the only alternatives.

In selecting students, also, there should be strong emphasis on caring and on latent capacity to care. The intellectually acute student who comes to college a confirmed, disillusioned cynic or dilettante is a far poorer prospect to work with than a less intelligent student who cares strongly about life; for it takes the quality of caring to sustain critical, independent thinking.

If these considerations concerning selection of trustees, administrators, and teachers, and to some extent of students, are observed with fair effectiveness, then I should go very far in trusting the democratic process and in dealing with the students as responsible fellow men and women, not as immature persons. I should go a long way in welcoming student sharing in all phases of the formulation and execution of policy and program. If teachers care strongly about over-all life and purpose, students will be aware of that caring. Where there is trust, confidence, respect, and fellowship between teachers and students, there will be general recognition of differences of judgment and experience, just as in any good board of directors there is respect for superior experience or judgment wherever it occurs. In such circumstances the status of human equality seldom will be abused. There is a growth in dignity, responsibility, and interest which comes with being treated not as a child or a ward but as a responsible associate, and this can be a major resource in education.

The degree of democracy existing in college will largely

influence the amount exercised by the graduate later in his community, and if anything like democracy is to survive in America it must have a school for training. Recently Ralph Besse, chairman of the Cleveland Commission on Higher Education and executive vice president of the Cleveland Electric Illuminating Company, in a ceremony installing the president of a Protestant liberal arts college, said: "Before this century is over almost all human economic activity will be institutionalized in one way or another. Much of it is now. Individualism is rooted in concepts of self-determination which conflict basically with the conformity which is essential to organization unity. Moreover, though our society in its political aspects is founded on democratic concepts, our most powerful institutions—the corporation and the military—are, *and to be effective, must be authoritarian* [italics mine]. Government control of our lives will not be avoided by any development of technology. If avoided at all, it will be avoided by the leadership of supercharged people who understand history and sociology and economics and couple their understanding with personal power to persuade masses of people of their points of view. These are liberal arts skills."

What authoritarian source will select these "supercharged" operators? Where, unless by background, practice, and experience, will we develop citizenship to surmount such indoctrination? Practice of democracy is more than a helpful device. It should be fundamental to college education.

Complete freedom of inquiry, which is closely associated with intellectual honesty, is powerfully conducive to sincerity and interest in life. Where mutual confidence and respect exist along with freedom to question, there generally will be reasonable respect for human experience and judgment, and there seldom will be insistence on unconsidered divergences from generally recognized standards. When departures are made, they will be in accord with the results of critical inquiry and not from a spirit of rebellion or from uncontrolled impulse.

These several factors interact. No one of them alone is enough. Along with them, good technical methods are surely needed. Yet I think these are primary. I shall list them again.

First is the factor of caring, of strong craving for meaning and significance and also of caring for human fellowship.

Second is the recognition of students as responsible fellow workers, not as wards, and full acceptance of the spirit and processes of democracy.

Third is complete freedom in inquiry. If along with this we find imagination, creative thinking, and an appetite for adventure in ideas and in action, we are fortunate indeed; and Ph.D. degrees, if necessary, should take second place.

These conditions may be obvious, yet sometimes their relative absence is not wholly because they were unavailable but because our attention was fixed on other requirements which for the time seemed more insistent. The residue of my personal experience and reflection on college administration, with its primary aim of helping young men and women prepare for responsibility in larger or smaller communities, is that with these principles of action those schools which are cultural and spiritual pioneers can more than hold their own, while others which are stumbling along either in mediocrity or with undisciplined and largely purposeless exuberance can achieve greater significance. As a natural result, community responsibility and leadership will improve. Because we must forever rebuild the bridge of life under constant traffic, and often in the face of hostile interference, it does not follow that we cannot introduce new elements of design and work with growing effectiveness toward a fairer and more enduring structure. Working at that job develops the art, and provides the adventure, of living.

INDEX

BLUFF CITY

BLUFF CITY

The Secret Life of
Photographer Ernest Withers

PRESTON LAUTERBACH

W. W. NORTON & COMPANY

INDEPENDENT PUBLISHERS SINCE 1923

NEW YORK • LONDON

For information about permission to reproduce selections from this book,
write to Permissions, W. W. Norton & Company, Inc.,
500 Fifth Avenue, New York, NY 10110

For information about special discounts for bulk purchases, please contact
W. W. Norton Special Sales at specialsales@wwnorton.com
or 800-233-4830

Manufacturing by Worzalla
Book design by Lisa Buckley
Production manager: Anna Oler

Library of Congress Cataloging-in-Publication Data

Names: Lauterbach, Preston, author.
Title: Bluff City : the secret life of photographer Ernest Withers /
Preston Lauterbach.
Description: First edition. | New York; London: W. W. Norton &
Company, [2019] | Includes bibliographical references and index.
Identifiers: LCCN 2018032872 | ISBN 9780393247923 (hardcover)
Subjects: LCSH: Withers, Ernest C., 1922–2007. | African American
photographers—Biography. | Photojournalists—United States—
Biography. | African American civil rights workers—Biography. |
Informers—United States—Biography.
Classification: LCC E185.97.W75 L38 2019 | DDC 323.092 [B]—dc23
LC record available at https://lccn.loc.gov/2018032872

W. W. Norton & Company, Inc., 500 Fifth Avenue, New York, N.Y. 10110
www.wwnorton.com

W. W. Norton & Company Ltd., 15 Carlisle Street, London W1D 3BS

1 2 3 4 5 6 7 8 9 0

TO MAGGIE GRACE, SAX, AND OLIVIA

CONTENTS

Don't Touch Anything

1

THIS STORY CAME TO ME LIKE A DREAM. I FOUND MYSELF
in the middle of it without meaning to.

In my early thirties, I showed up in Memphis. I had no
roots there, yet I never felt more at home anyplace else.

The city felt strangely underhyped, despite its riches.
I liked that. Memphis claims it's the birthplace of the
blues. It's definitely the home of the South's first African-
American millionaire, a freedman named Robert Church
who made Beale Street into perhaps the most famous thoroughfare in the country. Journalist Ida B. Wells began
her crusade on Beale, not long before a ruthlessly dominant political machine came to power in Memphis under
"Boss" E. H. Crump. Plus, this laid-back, funky town is
where Elvis began his career in 1954 and where Martin
Luther King, Jr., was assassinated in 1968. The sound of
soul music and the scent of barbecue smoke drift through
the city uninterrupted. Imbibing this atmosphere became
my favorite pastime. The past and present merged around
crumbling buildings, neon signage, Kodachrome sky, weeds
rising from the sidewalks, and surreal sights such as Isaac

Hayes pushing his cart through the grocery store, his bald head still shining like Hot Buttered Soul, and Al Green preaching in a glorified country church before a mural of the apocalypse.

The pace of life moved at 99 percent humidity, only one percent faster than under water. The light took on a grainy quality. It might have been ragweed pollen, but there was definitely something in the air.

Memphis felt like the ancient Egyptian city of the dead, fallen with its grandeur apparent in ruin, the pharaohs and their secrets buried. How it all fit together, the King of Rock 'n' Roll to Martin Luther King, Jr., I didn't know.

Memphis people didn't answer straight. My wife, a native, told me everyone's lived in intimate oppression too long. The dynamic, she explained, is that African-American people need to survive, and whites need to not feel like complete dicks about racism. The result is a slow, roundabout way of being. Everyone has an ambling, rambling charm, a sense of automatic familiarity that's almost unnerving. The amount of conversation going on in public amazed me. Strangers chatted like friends. I grew up where you might get a hello in passing but were much more likely to get ignored. In Memphis, you couldn't buy a tube of toothpaste without hearing somebody's life story or telling your own. These people can really get you talking. I liked it, mostly. The eye contact and sense of connection struck me as perfectly genuine. Yet the longer I spent here, the stranger it felt. Because it's built on high ground overlooking the Mississippi River, people call Memphis the Bluff City. The name seemed to have more than one meaning.

Without a nine-to-five, I followed my interest in the city's culture full time, researching the nightlife of the past. My explorations guided me to the city's famed thorough-fare, Beale Street.

The street I saw in 2004 bore no resemblance to the place where Elvis found inspiration in the summer of 1954, or where Dr. King's final march met ruin in the spring of '68. Beale had been bulldozed in urban renewal and reborn as a tourist attraction *à la* Bourbon Street. To see what had been, I relied entirely on the work of Ernest Withers—he'd run a photography studio and one-man wire service on the street almost continually since the late 1940s. He left during the renewal period in the '70s and returned after its completion in the '80s.

His credo: Pictures Tell the Story.

Withers's images provided sharp detail about the van-ished world of Beale and glowed with life.

The photographer had an uncanny ability to find not just breaking news but breaking history. You know his pho-tos, even if you don't know the photographer.

In his pictures, Withers captured the emotional energy of the moment and a human essence of the people involved—the jitters outside Central High in Little Rock, Arkansas, as one of the first black students to integrate the school dropped her books on her way in, and the cool of JFK campaigning, flashing the magic grin from within a sea of sign-waving protesters, his perfect hair a helmet against a hostile background. Withers also had a gift for gaining intimate access to power—he made images of Elvis hanging out around African-American entertainers in 1956, and of Martin Luther King, Jr., sprawling across a bed wearing his white shirtsleeves in 1966. In this age of revolution, the world slowed in Withers's lens. He covered the 1960s as Mathew Brady covered the 1860s.

His work had gotten him beaten and arrested and threatened with death. His lens stared down cold-eyed killers and searched dark country back roads where outsiders like him had vanished forever. He navigated a hostile and mysterious country with audacity and sneaky wit. But in later interviews, he downplayed himself. "I was there for a purpose and the purpose was to record the events that were taking place. It wasn't that I was doing it because I was any different. It's just that I was a news photographer and the news events were occurring."[1]

He made the picture of Dr. King riding the first integrated city bus at the triumphant climax of the Montgomery Bus Boycott. When the photo ran front page across black America via the *Chicago Defender* in December 1956, an icon was born. The image still resonates, hanging in the National Portrait Gallery in Washington. Other Withers photos decorate the Smithsonian Museums of American History and African-American History, and the National Civil Rights Museum. And then we have his most enduring image, showing a group of Memphis sanitation workers gathered outside a church prior to their massive March 28, 1968, strike demonstration on Beale. They line up shoulder to shoulder, three or four deep, sidewalk to sidewalk, filling Withers's frame. They hold up picket signs, practically blocking the sky with the message I AM A MAN.

By the time I landed in Memphis, Withers had been recognized as a major photographer of the civil rights movement. His work had been shown in galleries and museums all over the country; he'd delivered numerous college lectures, received an honorary doctorate, and published four books of his photos, covering music, civil rights, and Negro League baseball.

And like Al Green and Isaac Hayes, Withers was another fabulous individual casually arrayed in the city. I'd run into him around town, and of course it was perfectly normal to say hello.

Withers dressed like a rumpled veteran journalist, in an old suit and often an American flag tie. He wore a brimless African-style hat called a kufi.

In summer 2005, after one of many stop-and-chats in the supermarket or the drugstore, I called Withers and asked if I could visit him. I'd become deeply interested in the black nightclubs and musicians from the 1940s and '50s that he'd so powerfully depicted. I wanted to get to know the people of this lost world. I didn't have a formal interview in mind. He said it'd be all right.

He kept a dark, cluttered office. His walls were decorated with framed portraits of friends and family, some choice

selections of his own work, and memorials to his deceased
sons. A large tapestry hung from the ceiling, depicting Dr.
Martin Luther King, Jr., with the all-capitalized words I
HAVE A DREAM.

Withers sat behind a metal desk, with a chair on the
other side for visitors.

I didn't sit there for long. He had another appointment
on top of mine, business, not just visiting, and so he led
me past his desk, through a curtained doorway into a hall.
There he opened a heavy wooden door to a large room of
smooth gray concrete, with a fifteen-foot-high ceiling and
shelves and tables around the walls.

"You can wait here," he said. "But don't touch anything."
He shut the heavy door behind him.

Three picture windows allowed in some hazy light. His
name and address appeared on the glass in reverse: ERNEST
C. WITHERS BUILDING, 333 BEALE.

Stacks of black-and-white photographs were scattered
and piled around every available surface in the room.

I'm in the vault, I thought. *The Withers vault.*

"But don't touch anything," I'd heard him say.

I stood with my back to the windows and leaned against
a countertop. No chairs.

I crossed my arms. Shifted my weight. Uncrossed my
arms.

Heard Withers in my head. *"Don't touch anything,"* he'd
said. *"You can wait here."*

Wait. Nothing else.

So I did.

I did the very best I could.

This meeting of his wasn't exactly flying by.

I saw the guy calling on Withers when he came in. He looked cheap, artistic, maybe foreign.

I could hear Withers in the meeting. He sounded unpersuaded. I started pacing a bit. He hadn't ruled one way or the other on pacing. I figured pacing is a time-honored part of waiting. I *could* wait here. Pacing was just waiting.

He had very clearly said not to touch anything. So while pacing, which is part of waiting, I glanced at the photographs strewn around the room. I didn't touch them. They were just lying around. Nothing dangerous or secretive. Nothing hugely valuable. Some cool, ordinary life shots. Nobody recognizable. Withers couldn't get too pissed at me for glancing at this stuff.

I leaned back at my old spot and picked up a pile of five-by-sevens from the countertop. No deep dark secrets. He'd said, *"Don't touch anything,"* but this was nothing.

I flipped through, set the stack down, and went for another. I grabbed a pile of eight-by-tens and moved the one on top to the bottom—when the big wooden door opened fast and loud, and there stood Ernest Withers.

He yelled, "I told you not to touch anything!"

I said, "I'm sorry, I didn't think these were a big deal," setting down the stack.

"What did I tell you?" he asked. He answered his own

question at high volume, pronouncing the words separately: "Don't. Touch. Anything."

Withers said he'd lost a lot of money to thieves over the years, taking his images and stealing his copyrights.

He led me back through the empty office. His other appointment had left.

I apologized, told him what I'd touched, and promised I hadn't stolen from him, it was nothing like that, I'd just gotten bored. I was smitten by the history that lay in pieces all around us.

The photographer led me straight out the front door onto Beale and locked up behind me.

When he saw that my ride wasn't waiting for me, he took pity and offered to drop me off at home. "I got one stop to make," he said.

We hopped into his car, a big gold sedan, an Oldsmobile or Buick, I think. The interior of the car, with worn velvety upholstery, looked about like the vault.

Only then did things get truly relaxed. I promised not to touch anything. He looked me dead in the eye and gave a quick growl of laughter.

That look put me in the Kodachrome zone. Every sense took on a hypnotic vividness. The world slowed down. Colors popped. Afternoon sunlight sparkled in Withers's eyes. He blasted the AC, and it tingled like after-shave. He opened a Styrofoam takeout container and grabbed a half-eaten barbecue sandwich for a bite. I glimpsed a pile of cold turnip greens and some black-eyed peas gelling in the container too.

The car smelled like sweet tobacco smoke, maybe Black and Mild. The ashtray gaped, full of cigarette butts and a half-smoked cigar that Withers grabbed and lit up as he tucked away his snack and pulled off.

He drove—in a manner many people familiar with Memphis will recognize—slowly, drifting right. It doesn't indicate any sort of impairment on the part of the driver, it just means they're having a conversation.

He headed up Union Avenue, the hottest, smoggiest, busiest street in the city proper, but focused his intense and sincere interest on me. I felt deeply at ease. In our discussion of my research, he gave thoughtful, witty encouragement.

He stared through me and said, "You oughta look into a fellow named Hayes Riley. Beale Street hustler, into what you're into."

He broke the powerful gaze as his veer right became a turn into the Walgreens parking lot—Withers's one stop.

I figured he didn't need my assistance in picking up a prescription. He left the car and the AC on, and I sat, definitely not touching anything.

He soon returned with a bulging yellow envelope in hand. This celebrated photographer had his film developed at the drugstore.

Withers dropped me off outside the apartment building I lived in and said it'd be all right if I came back sometime.

I got a reporting job, kept it for a little while, and got to know some things about the culture of political corruption, and the scoffing indifference to same, that defined

Memphis. I got to know some things about the extreme violence that has distinguished this place, known off and on for the past century as the per capita homicide capital of the United States.

I bought toothpaste, learned to tell my life story to strangers, and wondered, *What's there to feel so damn friendly about?* The overwhelming cheerfulness of Memphis was completely at odds with its reality. I would eventually understand it in spite of my young self.

Southern charm makes great cover.

Withers died in 2007. He lay in state at the altar of a Church of God in Christ temple off Beale. He wore his gold and black kufi and a dark suit.

Thinking about how Withers had photographed Dr. King in state at a nearby funeral home, I approached the casket and snapped a picture.

He looked good.

2

IN SEPTEMBER 2010, MARC PERRUSQUIA OF THE *Memphis Commercial Appeal* reported that Ernest Withers had worked as an informant of the FBI during the 1960s.

The news shocked the city and broke wide across the nation: CNN, NPR, the *New York Times*, the *New Yorker*.

This beloved, widely revered figure had done something unfathomable—he had spied on the civil rights movement for pay.

People felt shocked, outraged, confused, and betrayed.

I won't say I never felt that way, but I come from an intelligence family, and my grandfather, who had worked for the CIA during the Cold War, taught me some things that helped me understand the Withers situation.

Good operatives—from a street informant like Withers to an officer in a foreign capital like my grandfather—hold their mud. People felt betrayed because he had kept his activity secret. It had to have been bad, right, or else he would have said more. He had touched on his federal affiliation only once, telling an interviewer about being primed for organizers' strategies during the 1968 Memphis sanitation workers' strike. "I never tried to monitor what they were doing," he said, drawing a distinction between strike organizers' private planning and public activism.

> I was always interested in their outside work, but I tried not to know too much about the inside because I always had FBI agents looking over my shoulder and wanting to question me. I never tried to learn any high-powered secrets. It would have just been trouble. . . . I was solicited to assist the FBI by Bill Lawrence. . . . He was a nice guy but what he was doing was pampering me to catch whatever leaks I dropped, so I stayed out of meeting where real decisions were being made.[1]

Intelligence work requires secrecy, but not automatically because it involves evil deeds. My grandfather, by the time I got to know him, was easily the gentlest, calmest, most sweet-natured male I'd ever been around. But one thing could reliably aggravate him: former operatives who talked. Intelligence agents inhabit a hidden realm. Their work in this realm protects the safety of the normal world, where the rest of us drop off the kids at school, go to work, watch football games, and cut the grass. (Intelligence operatives know better than any of us how flawed and failed many of their pursuits are, but they remain undeterred.) My grandfather did not talk. He did, however, hint at the complexity of his undertaking and the necessity of secrecy when he told me, "We did undemocratic things in the name of democracy."

This deliciously troubling phrase still chills the back of my neck.

How are intelligence agents supposed to explain such activities to the normal world? How would Americans' ideals and innocence survive the knowledge of every election fix, propaganda campaign, political smear, coup, and assassination undertaken to protect us?

The contradiction of doing undemocratic things for democracy defines American espionage. The normal world can't live with what espionage entails, but it also can't survive without it.

And so a good operative holds their mud.

I knew—just as clearly as I could see the twinkle in my grandfather's eyes—that Withers's intelligence work wasn't necessarily evil, and that there was a hell of a lot more to the story. Most folks didn't seem to read past the headline. Many said they simply couldn't understand why a civil rights hero would partner with the FBI.

Flashing back through Withers's photography, I wondered what secrets lay buried in the images of Elvis, the Emmett Till trial, the Montgomery Bus Boycott, Kennedy, and King. I'd visited Withers's office as a novice interested in old nightclubs, but the allure of his secret story pulled me deeper.

I looked at Withers's celebrated civil rights image—the I AM A MAN photo. So much has been written about the

1968 King assassination, people have forgotten or perhaps never learned about the riot that broke out in Memphis one week earlier, the day Withers took this famous picture.

That morning, six weeks into a work stoppage of Memphis sanitation workers, Dr. King led ten thousand marchers down Beale in support of the strike. The demonstration disintegrated into mayhem, as people on hand for the march smashed windows all down Beale, police billy-clubbed and tear-gassed marchers, King evacuated to a hotel room, and a battle ensued, resulting in one death, hundreds of injuries, and widespread looting.

King had had no plans to be in Memphis beyond March 28, but the riot left him despondent, embarrassed, and discouraged. He vowed to return and redeem himself and the city. Without the disturbance of March 28, the assassination of Martin Luther King would not have happened on April 4.

———✦———

Years later, as historians and congressional investigators examined the riot as an important precursor to King's murder, a potentially important anomaly appeared. The anomaly is clearly visible in the I AM A MAN photo. In fact, it is an indispensible aspect of the scene. Throughout the daily marches during the previous six weeks of the strike, the protesters had carried cardboard signs by hand or looped them over their shoulders with string. But on March 28, strike supporters carried signs mounted on sticks, two-by-two pine posts. In the hands of sanitation workers, those two-by-twos elegantly displayed the I AM A MAN posters. The rioters turned those two-by-twos into weapons. How the posts were introduced to the March 28 demonstration, and who had introduced them, thus became key questions in the 1978 House Select Committee on Assassinations investigation of the King killing. Confusion and uncertainty about the two-by-twos permeated the House committee's questions to FBI agents, strike leaders, and Black Power advocates en route to inconclusive findings. Joan Turner Beifuss, who carried a sign that day and authored the definitive on-the-scene history of the sanitation strike, concluded, "No one ever knew where those sticks came from."

A German sociologist visited Memphis in 1982 to examine local conditions that had led to the assassination. He interviewed Ernest Withers and asked the photographer to describe the chaos of March 28, 1968.

Withers said, "Well, to show you—I mean to show you, if anybody is as much responsible for that riot up there, as anybody, I might be responsible."

Withers explained that he and some friends had bought the lumber and sawed the sticks. "We certainly wasn't doing it by plan," Withers said, but my attention remained with the first part of the statement: *"if anybody is as much responsible for that riot up there, as anybody, I might be responsible."*

Of course, the German doing the interview in 1982

didn't know about Withers's secret FBI affiliation. Withers did not anticipate that the connection between himself, the bureau, and the riot could ever be put together. Making this connection myself, I began to wonder, Had the I AM A MAN signposts been merely a photographic prop? Or had they packed a more mischievous intent?

As I listened to the recording of Withers chatting affably with the German sociologist as he'd chatted with me, I realized I needed to know how a civil rights hero had become a civil rights spy.

That day of the riot and the man behind the camera were years in the making. Only through the times, place, and people around Withers can we understand how he ended up as perhaps the key figure at a moment that rerouted history. This story covers that journey.

Pictures Tell the Story

3

WHEN ERNEST WITHERS WAS IN THE EIGHTH GRADE, HIS sister bought her boyfriend a pocket-sized Brownie 127 camera.

"I don't want this," the boyfriend said.

"Let me have it," Ernest said.[1]

Not long after Ernest picked up that camera, Marva Louis—knockout wife of World Heavyweight Boxing Champion Joe Louis—made an appearance at his school's auditorium. Marva modeled fashion and sang with traveling big bands. Black America saw her as among the most glamorous women of the time, while her husband was the undisputed hero of the race, a one-man destroyer of white supremacy.

Withers stood at the back of the auditorium, in the aisle, holding his Brownie. Marva looked so tiny through the lens, he had to get closer. He inched forward. The kids in the hall noticed and started laughing—he looked like he'd fallen under the allure of Marva's beauty. Step by step, he crept closer, until he saw the image he wanted.

As his shutter clicked, laughter and cheering filled his ears. He looked up, as if startled awake.

Toward the end of his long career, Ernest would attribute his success and longevity as a photographer to what he had discovered that day peering at pretty Marva Louis through the viewfinder of a box cam—his ability to block peripheral distraction and physically close in on his subject.[2]

———✦———

Withers grew up in North Memphis during the 1920s and '30s. Though the heart of the neighborhood stood just a mile from bustling downtown, North Memphis was its own place, encompassing distinct villages known as New Chicago and Smoky City. With automobiles scarce and loose change for public transportation limited, many residents never ventured deep into the city.

The Withers home sat along a main thoroughfare, Manassas Street, near the neighborhood school, a grocery, a dry goods store, and a picture show. Ernest and his buddies, too young to go inside the cafés, jaunted up and down the block, listening to jukebox music spill into humid nights. During the days, Withers busied himself running errands. His stepmother took in sewing and sent him to Shine Brothers dry goods for thread. He clutched a sample of the color she wanted in his hand and had to match it to one in the swath at the store. Withers would say that matching those threads sharpened his eye. He also picked up a few coins from the neighborhood beat cop, who liked to play cards in the back room of Frank and Joseph Gaia's grocery. Ernest sat on the front seat of the patrol car and made sure that no calls for car twenty-one came over the radio. The cop dropped a hot dime in Ernest's hand for an hour's trouble.

The neighborhood's primary connection to the city around it ran right through the Withers living room. During election season, Ernest's father Arthur opened the home as a voter registration and polling place. The Memphis of Ernest's youth lived under one of the most thorough civic dictatorships in the United States. E. H. Crump won the mayoral election of 1909, and over the next half-century, he grew to control every public job in West Tennessee, from the courthouse janitors to the U.S. congressional delegation. The boss ruined, banished, beat, and intimidated opponents. Many a black Republican like Arthur Withers supported whatever candidate the white Democrat Crump put up for local office. Arthur Withers had a good job thanks to Crump, and no black candidate had a chance of winning in Memphis anyway. Ernest saw his father holster a gun to protect his cargo as a special delivery driver for the post office. Arthur taught his son not to fuss about social change but to obey the law.[3]

Ernest had grown up in a racially mixed atmosphere—

the old white ward heeler Mike Haggarty lived less than two blocks from the Withers home until his death in 1929—where the one constant was the boss. Democrat Crump, on his way up, had allied with black Republicans, and he had gained power in the city through African Americans' votes. During the late 1930s, however, he exiled one of the most important black Republicans in the United States, Robert Church, Jr., from Memphis and went hostile against virtually any meeting of black citizens. This measure represented a significant step backward for black rights in a city where, as long ago as 1915, Church's Lincoln League had assembled tens of thousands of African-American voters for protest meetings and registration efforts.

During the 1940 presidential election, Crump crushed the remnants of Church's organization, and Church's second-in-command, J. B. Martin, fled to Chicago. Martin sent Church a note saying that four men had followed him around in a car and parked outside his apartment. "I don't go anyplace at night," wrote Martin, "and a very few in the day. I think I may need some protection."[4] At the time, Martin owned a portion of the Memphis Red Sox and was president of the Negro American Baseball League. To prompt his eviction, Martin had sponsored rallies of black voters in support of Republican presidential nominee Wendell Willkie.

Ernest graduated high school in this social climate, during the nation's buildup for the Second World War. He married his high school sweetheart, enlisted in the U.S. Army, and shipped off for basic training at Camp Sutton, North Carolina, in 1943.

There he received his formal training in photo lab technology, developing film and printing enlargements for the first time. His first publication appeared in the base newsletter, the *Camp Sutton Carry All.*

Following basic, Withers island-hopped the South Pacific with the 1319 Engineering Regiment. They landed on Saipan in the Marianas, following the U.S. victory over Japan there in the summer of 1944. From a primitive base hacked out of the jungle, the engineers went about constructing an airfield for Army Air Force use.

Withers's unit had no orders to make pictures and no budget for photography equipment. The chief supply officer was a shutterbug, though, and he and Withers carried their personal cameras around the island.

When soldiers saw Withers with his four-by-five— he'd moved on from his sister's boyfriend's Brownie—they would ask for snapshots to send back home. Withers and his white partner hit upon a nice little side hustle.

The photographers had a monopoly within their reach, all the demand in the world, but no supplies— until Withers discovered an almost unlimited source. The newly built Air Force base housed a photo recon squadron that had it all.

In addition to the necessities of food and tobacco, the Army rationed soldiers six beers every week. Withers and his partner pooled their olive drab cans and traded them to the Air Force photo lab techs for film, chemicals, and paper. Ernest set up a makeshift studio / darkroom / lab in the African-American section of the base, and his partner referred all the white combat veterans his way.

Ernest chauffeured a jeep for the base commanding officer as his regular job, and he hoped the boss wouldn't notice his side arrangement. But the white soldiers streaming toward Withers's place caught the CO's attention. "I thought you might have been running a whorehouse," the officer cracked, but gave the enterprising photographers his blessing.

"I guess I might have made in a run of fifteen months, some two or three thousand dollars," Ernest recalled. He sneaked the cash—which the army considered contraband—past the camp postal inspector into his letters home. Back in North Memphis, Ernest's wife Dorothy received plump envelopes in the mail, as their second baby boy grew in her belly.

Two missions that originated from the Marianas carried the *Little Boy* and *Fat Man* atomic bombs that brought an end to Ernest Withers's military career. He'd seen no combat, fired no weapons, and shot only his fellow Americans— with the camera.

He returned home as a resourceful, technically adept picture taker, versed in the craft of photography and the art of the hustle.

4

WHEN WITHERS CAME HOME, HE TOOK HIS GI BILL FUND-
ing and opened a little photography studio in North
Memphis, near the auditorium where Marva Louis had
helped him discover his destiny.

Somehow the place no longer looked the same. Ernest
had seen in the army how power made airports out of jun-
gles and cities into smoldering rubble. Boss Crump's oppression of Memphis had become increasingly pronounced
since he exiled the city's black political leadership before
the war. Crump banned the national civil rights organizer
A. Phillip Randolph from speaking in Memphis. He refused
to allow a traveling exhibit of American artifacts called the
Freedom Train to make a whistle stop in his city, because
he objected to the idea of African Americans and whites
mixing for a look at the Declaration of Independence. The
boss preached against "social equality" every chance he got.
"I'm not going to stand for it," he told the editor of the black
Memphis World. "I've dealt with niggers my whole life, and
I know how to treat them."[1]

When Ernest returned from the war, his father told him to take the civil service exam, but Ernest felt a need for variety that made the lockstep life of a postman unthinkable. Saturdays he went to Memphis Red Sox games at Martin Stadium, the local Negro League field, still owned by Boss Crump's enemy-in-exile, J. B. Martin. As the ushers packed fans foul pole to foul pole around the field and beyond the outfield walls, Ernest, with two or three cameras slung around his neck, took pictures of everyone who wanted a keepsake of the game, and many who didn't ask. He simply walked up to them as he had done to Marva Louis and activated the charm. *My name is Ernest Withers, and I think you make a wonderful picture*, and the shutter clicked before anyone could decline.

As soon as he spent the last frame of film, Ernest hurried home. He converted the bathroom into his darkroom, developing his rolls with the lights off and washing prints in the bathtub. His boys got sick of the sour chemical smell. His wife Dorothy dried the five-by-sevens in the oven. Ernest grabbed them, headed back to the stadium, and delivered them smoking at a dollar apiece, provided he could find the people in the shots and they paid.

After the games, he'd head down to the field, where he posed his sons with Satchel Paige and took pictures of Memphis Red Sox like Casey Jones and Pepper Sharp, or manager "Goose" Curry, as well as a promising young pitcher who would go on to greater renown as a country music singer, Charley Pride. In the cinder block locker room, Withers photographed young Willie Mays celebrating a win with his Birmingham Black Barons teammates. "My team was Memphis, but my best friends in Negro League Baseball were members of the Birmingham Black Barons," Withers recalled. "I had good friendships on other teams, too. The Cleveland Buckeyes had Sam Jethro, the man Branch Rickey considered the best player in black baseball. Unfortunately, Mr. Rickey decided that Jethro might be a little too rough for the big leagues and he chose Jackie Robinson instead because he was a great ballplayer, but he was also much more polished."[2]

Withers shot funerals for hire and occasionally serviced the national black press, selling pictures of bandleader Jimmie Lunceford's last rites to the *Pittsburgh Courier*. Though Ernest scraped together a living, his father continued to press him for civil service. In 1948 a new city job opened up that suited Ernest better than the post office.

Even Boss Crump could be reasoned or shamed into the occasional shrewd concession to black voters. Following an incident in which the Memphis police killed an unarmed African-American man, Crump—perhaps in need of a goodwill gesture to balance his racial crackdown—allowed twelve African-American officers to join the Memphis Police Department. Ernest Withers graduated from the police academy and became one of the first black patrolmen in his hometown.

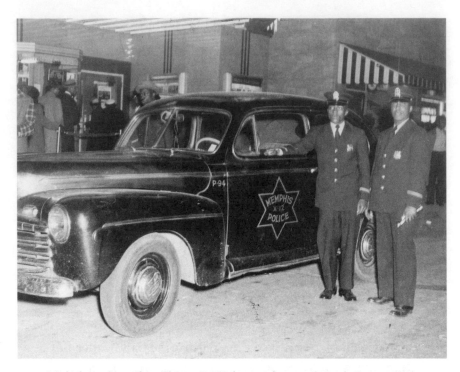

Memphis police officer Ernest C. Withers, right, patrols Beale Street, 1948.
Special Collections Department, University of Memphis Library.

These cops couldn't carry guns or arrest white people. But their beat kept them segregated on the most compelling stretch of pavement in the city, Beale Street. Though his time on the force would be brief, the new job changed Withers's life forever, moving his center of operations from sleepy North Memphis to the vaunted Main Street of Black America.

Withers relocated his photography setup to a rented room above the Palace Theater, in the thick of the midnight world, on the block of Beale between Hernando and Fourth streets packed with hot dog cafés, rib joints, theaters, liquor stores, and nightclubs. Gambling, bootlegging, prostitution, and cutthroat music flourished.

Down the street from Withers's new studio, at the corner of Beale and Hernando, Sunbeam Mitchell ran a nightclub and hotel on the second and third stories above a drugstore. Sunbeam would sell a half-pint of illegal booze in front of the chief of police, and shoot anyone who started trouble in his place, long before asking questions.

Sunbeam had one of the wealthiest white businessmen in the South behind him, Abraham Plough, owner of St. Joseph's Aspirin, with manufacturers in Lima, Santiago, Buenos Aires, Caracas, Kingston, Stockholm, and Tel Aviv.

Plough sold Black and White Triple Strength Bleaching Cream, guaranteed to bring you lighter skin in just seven days. He would soon add Coppertone suntan lotion and Maybelline cosmetics to his empire.

Less publicized was Plough's liquor wholesaler, which he'd founded just before the repeal of Prohibition, that held a virtual monopoly on popular "old" whiskeys like Old Crow, Old Charter, and Old Grand-Dad, in West Tennessee. Sunbeam emulated his sponsor, developing an interstate corporate model for his vice business, transporting whiskey, women, and song together from Memphis to Arkansas and Mississippi.

The liquor business blurred the otherwise bold lines that divided the city, black from white, right from wrong, classy from trashy. Boss Crump had made an unwritten rule forbidding black nightlife businessmen from receiving liquor licenses, keeping them in de facto Prohibition, making them bootleggers, beholden to crooked cops and political sponsors.

With Plough as his sponsor, Sunbeam didn't need to get into politics.

One block from Sunbeam's stood the fortress of another mixed-race conglomerate, made up of an Irish ex-boxer named Kid Dugan, Mr. Crump's hit man Red Lawrence, and an old-time ward heeler. "Up over Kid Dugan's was the Sportsmen Club," Withers explained, "owned by a fellow named Hayes Riley, who was somewhat of an underworld figure."[3]

Hayes, as people called him, had participated in vote fixing, in exchange for openly running craps games and bootlegging on Beale, since the 1930s. Like his predecessors in the Beale Street kingpin lineage, Hayes Riley was light-skinned. He cultivated a reassuring manner for whites, having worked in their service as a bellhop and a cabin boy—neat, dapper, and charming. But he was a mean son of a gun, and his black constituents knew well that the grin concealed a pistol. He developed such a reputation that his two pretty daughters had to move away from Memphis—every boy who took a fancy to them lost interest upon learning the girls' last name. Despite his underworld reputation, Hayes dined with the city's mayor and police chief in Beale nightspots.

Through his police work, Withers began to understand the street's inner workings. As one veteran explained the power structure of Beale Street:

If a black guy has something a white man has use
for, the white man will be interested.

He tells the black guy, if you keep your ass out of
the ground, I'll keep it out of jail.

The HNIC, the head nigger in charge, is the one
on the plantation that's over the rest of them, that
controls the others. That's where power came from.[4]

Proximity to power kept Sunbeam Mitchell and Hayes
Riley out of jail. And as Ernest recognized, proximity to
power was the revolver holstered to his daddy's hip and the
nice house in which he grew up.

Sunbeam allowed the city's African-American police—
segregated from the locker room at the station downtown—
to dress and to receive messages at his nightclub. The place
contained a whorehouse and a hot-sheet hotel with rooms for
rent by the hour, plenty of space to accommodate the black
cops, and ample reason for Sunbeam to befriend the law.

Twirling his baton on his rounds, Ernest kept a friendly
flirtation going with a cute ticket taker at the New Daisy
Theater, a big modern movie house on the same block as
Withers's photography studio and the black police headquarters at Sunbeam's.

One night she complained to him of having a headache.
He told her he had some aspirin—St. Joseph's, maybe—in
his locker and invited her up to get one.

This liaison led to the birth of Withers's first daughter.
She would always be part of his life, and while her pres-

ence in the world complicated his own, he never blamed the child. But like his move to Beale Street, Ernest's dalliance triggered consequences. Ernest's wife became determined that she wouldn't stop having children until she had a daughter of her own.

On the police force, Withers figured out that just as sure as white cops could carry guns and black ones couldn't, and white cops could arrest white criminals and black ones couldn't, white cops could sell whiskey and black ones couldn't. In August 1951 the Memphis Police Department dismissed Withers for "conduct unbecoming an officer."

His FBI file contains a summary that states, "Withers was caught . . . in the act of dividing money with a male Negro, [name redacted] said money being proceeds from the sale of whiskey by [redacted] which whiskey was provided by Withers."[5]

With charming candor, Withers argued that he'd been set up. "Beyond a reasonable doubt, I was in a guilty position, I would not say that I was not," he explained. "But I was guilty of aiding and abetting one black fellow who was set out to get me to do so, and I lost the job as the results of it."

Was he innocent, guilty, or framed? Was he simply functioning normally according to the rules of a crooked universe?

He knew now that being on the right side of the law couldn't protect him, and that living on the wrong side of the law offered no relief from racism, but he had the courage nonetheless to push limits.

He could find no delicious gray area, however, in his children's hunger. Dismissal from the police department left him only one way to make a living. But as of 1951, Ernest Withers was where he belonged, at the heart of the city's culture.

5

NOW A FULL-TIME FREELANCE PHOTOGRAPHER, ERNEST worked every available angle, shooting weddings, funerals, and family reunions for hire. He photographed society luncheons for the black papers, ladies in big hats clustered around fancy white tables. He worked advertising jobs. Beale Street entrepreneur Cliff Miller's daughter Christy recalled modeling for a Tastee Bread newspaper ad as a little girl: "We were sitting around the table, and I was ready to eat, so I stuck my hand in the bread, Mr. Withers snapped a picture, and they used that."

After his kids' bedtime, Withers toured the downtown nightclubs he'd become familiar with on the police beat. His primary trade was in table shots, making dollar mementos for patrons on a night out, much as he'd done at Negro League baseball games. He shot people sober and sold them drunk, running from the club to his Beale Street office to hurriedly develop film, make prints, and return to close sales before the night's end.

In time, he built in his mind a name-to-face directory of African-American Memphis, from upscale church to lowdown dance hall, expanding as his lens crossed boundaries normal folks avoided.

In between table shots at Sunbeam's and Currie's Club Tropicana, he made images of the entertainment to pass the time. At first he hung his pictures of famous musicians around the office to give himself some photographer-of-the-stars cachet.

In this Menlo Park of midcentury American music, Withers caught Lionel Hampton and Ruth Brown hypnotizing huge crowds at the Hippodrome, every patron with a big smile and a little bottle. He shot boyish, thin B.B. King and future legend Bobby "Blue" Bland with ill-fated Johnny Ace on piano inside the groundbreaking radio station WDIA. The R&B hit parade passed through: Roy Brown, Gatemouth Brown, Percy Mayfield, Louis Jordan, and Ray Charles all posed for Withers, and so did lesser-known local geniuses like Little Junior Parker, Bill Harvey, and Roscoe Gordon.

Smoke practically pours out of the images. This visual record of one of the most fertile times and places in American culture helped make Withers a legend in the later years of his career, and it now makes one of the cornerstones of his photographic legacy.

Just as American music evolved before his lens, the Withers style too was taking shape. He captured spontaneous emotion. The photographer reapplied his earliest lesson—he moved in on his subjects as he had Marva Louis, impervious to distraction.

Behind his camera, Withers grasped the truth that slipped away from him elsewhere in life. He learned how to communicate through composition. He adopted the credo "Pictures Tell the Story."

His photograph of white radio deejay Dewey Phillips onstage in an all-black nightclub illustrates the truth about race relations more profoundly than any thousand words. Withers positioned the white deejay at the center of the image, dividing the frame in half with two groups of the African-American audience on either side of Dewey. Phillips can see half the crowd, and virtually every face in that half of the crowd looks right into Phillips's face, beaming, laughing, joyous in the spotlight. The other half of the crowd stands in the dark behind Phillips. There are a few grins, but virtually every other face scowls, sulks, and glares.

———◆———

Despite the tension evident in Withers's photo of Phillips, racial integration had already begun to reach the wider public in the entertainment arena. White kids sat in the balcony at the colored W. C. Handy Theatre to hear black artists like Roy Brown shout "Good Rockin' Tonight" or Jackie Brenston and Ike Turner rock "Rocket 88." Black men likewise were invited to the most comfortable crow's nest in the South, at the Joy over in West Memphis, to watch Miss Tarana unwrap herself from a cellophane gown, not quite mixing with white men below but sharing their thrills.

Withers's photograph of Memphis deejay Dewey Phillips at the Hippodrome, Beale Street, 1951. Copyright Dr. Ernest C. Withers, Sr., courtesy
of the Withers Family Trust, Thewitherscollection.com.

The nation as a whole began to unwrap itself. On May
17, 1954, the U.S. Supreme Court declared racial segregation unconstitutional. A black newspaper editor in
Memphis compared 1954 to 1865, calling it a new jubilee,
and at least some African Americans welcomed the idea of
opening their part of the world to white people. A black
police officer on the street said, "I don't want to be the white
man's brother-in-law, I only want to be his brother."[1]

Though white faces didn't exactly flock to Beale Street
all at once, a new energy, a feeling some would compare to
magic, filled the air. The nation's first black-programmed

radio station, WDIA, cranked its signal up to fifty thousand watts, blasting Beale Street as far as New Orleans and St. Louis. The Supreme Court had recognized black equality, and Black Memphis had a new vitality. It felt connected.

⊢——◆——⊣

Inside an expansive nightclub tucked away on a side street off Beale, exotic murals of tropical birds and trees decorated the walls, and mirrored chrome columns bordered the dance floor. When the band started playing, a huge Puerto Rican known as Mambo grabbed a lady and started cha-cha-ing, as the dance floor bustled.

Clifford Miller set the tone in the Flamingo Room with leading-man charisma. He dressed impeccably, puffed constantly at a cigar or his pipe, and never appeared creased or ruffled. His presence ensured good behavior from the clientele, usually, and the outline of a .25 automatic in his pocket reinforced the idea, but things sometimes got wild nonetheless, and when fights broke out, Cliff simply lifted his hand and the Goon Squad, his security force, moved in fast. George Stevens, Henry Ford, and Durango were Goon Squad mainstays. They stood on the edges of the room, around entrances and exits, observing. When called on, they ejected troublemakers memorably, tossing them down the catwalk toward Beale. Anyone who ever saw that would act right in the Flamingo, because that staircase was long, narrow, and made of steel.

Cliff hired the Phineas Newborn Orchestra as his house band. They opened their show up-tempo with a tune called "Calvin's Boogie," featuring the band's twenty-year-old guitarist. Calvin Newborn played hot, but his acrobatics onstage drove the crowd to a frenzy. Dressed in pink coat and slacks, with his guitar on a long electrical chord, he worked every corner of the room, sliding on his knees across the dance floor, leaping from the stage, and playing all the way into the ladies' powder room.

Ernest Withers first photographed the Flamingo Room on the night of a Barn Dance in April 1954. The club handed out miniature western hats, and the crowd wore overalls and sack dresses, sipping corn liquor from jugs marked XXX. Men lassoed their dance partners. The Newborn band donned straw cowboy hats, blue denim jeans, and neckerchiefs. The bass player strapped on a toy six-shooter and clutched a corncob pipe between his teeth. The group sprinkled country and western tunes into its repertoire of jazz and R&B for the night. Though barn dances were popular among white fans of hillbilly music, almost as popular as mimicking African-American style and caricature, the Flamingo was the only black place to turn these tables.

This genre-bending took place right around the time an unknown, underage white musician named Elvis Presley visited the Flamingo Room.

Durango from the Goon Squad let him in the back door.

6

UNLIKE THE TYPICAL WHITE SLUMMER, ELVIS DIDN'T wildly carouse. Unlike Dewey Phillips, another of the approximately three white hipsters in the city, Elvis sought no attention. But Elvis did not move without purpose.

Ernest Withers commented, "Elvis didn't go to Beale Street to advertise himself, he went down there searching for talent."[1]

Many memories of young Elvis at the Flamingo recall him in the wings—exactly where the back door led—observing the action from beside the stage.

He witnessed a spectacle designed to give audiences something to hear and something to see.

The Phineas Newborn Orchestra revolved around a showbiz family of seasoned professionals whose résumé featured a stint on the road with Ike Turner and Jackie Brenston for the 1951 hit record "Rocket 88," recording sessions with B.B. King, and tours with Lionel Hampton. They took the gig as the Flamingo Room house band in time for the February grand opening and played there every night of early 1954.

They performed a lush variety of styles. Wanda Newborn could sing like Billie Holiday, and the old man and
bandleader could play his drums every way from low-down
blues to break-leg samba. Phineas had two brilliant boys.
His namesake became a jazz piano prodigy whose excellence
would rival Art Tatum and Oscar Peterson, but Phineas
Newborn, Jr., had already moved on from Memphis, leaving the spotlight in the family band on his guitar-playing
brother Calvin.

Calvin's looks, acrobatics, and offstage exploits made
him the most sensational performer on the illustrious
street, even with B.B. King in town.

Calvin was a sleepwalker, and as a child he'd injured
himself falling into a tub of scalding water. Lying flat on
his stomach in the hospital for weeks to let his burned back
heal, he began to dream of flying. When he got out, Calvin
leaped from buildings and moving trains, hoping to defy
physics. "I became Flying Calvin," he said.[2]

At the Flamingo, Calvin flew from the stage, soaring
into the first row. Once he landed, "I played my guitar like
I was having sex with a woman," he recalled, "thrusting my
hips into it faster until I fell to the floor."

He knew what he was doing. Calvin had witnessed the
magic of simulation during a stint on the road a couple of
years prior.

"I got it from battling Red Prysock," Calvin recalled,
referring to the heartthrob lead sax player with the Roy
Milton band, who Newborn had played with in 1952.

"Wherever he went, I followed, right into the ladies' restroom, and the ladies went wild. After the first gig we played in Atlanta, all the chicks followed him to his room. Late that night I peeped through the keyhole and couldn't see nothing but his ass and some legs in the air. I knew then what wiggling your legs and swiveling your hips would do."

Complementing Calvin, other enchanting personalities graced the Flamingo stage. The club held a drag revue showcasing the likes of Sissy Charles, a hulking queer blues singer who ran a whorehouse down the street "that was outta sight," Calvin said.

"He was the madam of the place, Sissy Charles, he'd open the door buck naked with his joint hanging out. My brother used to go there all the time, go from girl to girl until the money was gone."

Shake dancers, like local star Miss Shake Right and imported talent like Black Velvet from Detroit, billed as SEXOTIC and SEXCITING, enlivened the Flamingo night.

Females in the Flamingo audience would walk right up to the bandstand in the middle of a song to pass Calvin a number, only to feel the slide from his wife Wanda's trombone hit them in the head.

Calvin's antics peaked in competition, and on the weekend of June 5 and 6, 1954, that's what rolled up in a yellow Fleetwood Cadillac. Pee Wee Crayton, a guitarist every bit as smooth as Calvin—and maybe prettier—arrived for what Cliff Miller billed as a "Battle of the Electric Guitars."[3]

"And that's when Elvis started coming to the Flamingo Room," Calvin recalled.

One version of Elvis's arrival is that Cliff Miller's dad, a postman, delivered mail to the Presley home on Alabama Avenue in North Memphis. He got to know the family and became aware of Elvis's fondness for rhythm and blues music. The elder Miller arranged for an invitation to the club and provided a pass that Elvis would need to get through police enforcing segregation on the street.

Meanwhile the Flamingo's leading family ran the Newborn Music Store, just east of the club on Beale. They sold records and gave lessons, and Elvis reportedly enjoyed coming to the store to pick through its gospel selection. The whole family pitched in at the shop, giving lessons and selling disks, and matriarch Mama Rose Newborn fixed lunch in a little kitchenette in back. Elvis got her blessing to join the Newborns for baked ham and black-eyed peas, and an invitation to the Flamingo soon followed.[4]

Lewie Steinberg, a bass player who performed with the Newborns, said, "Calvin would play his guitar and then put it behind his head. And then get all on the dance floor and then get him a running start and hit the floor on his knees. He'd just hit that floor and slide on his knees and be playing that guitar."

He added, "Elvis would sit on the left-hand side of the bandstand over there, watching Calvin."

Emerson Able, another musician who frequented the

Flamingo, echoed this memory. "I saw him there over beside the stage, looking inconspicuous, watching Calvin."

Steinberg said, "That's where he got all his moves and stuff, from Calvin. He learned all this stuff from Calvin Newborn."[5]

A local black newspaper on June 25, 1954, ran a photo of the Newborn band sporting country rags and announced that the Barn Dance had become a weekly Monday-night feature at the Flamingo. The show featured "regular dance music as well as specialized western novelty tunes," that is, an African-American band playing a mixture of black and white styles.[6]

Elvis's historical significance is due more to his music than to his moves. If indeed Elvis *started coming* to the Flamingo on June 4 or 5, 1954, as Newborn recalled, then he may have witnessed the exact sort of fusion in the club that he would go on to become famous for.

June 1954 would be the last month of anonymity in Elvis Presley's existence, and it is a rare dark patch during a life that has otherwise been thoroughly examined. The sources that historians have relied upon for Elvis's beginnings were absent from Memphis during that month. Elvis's girlfriend Dixie Locke—who would illuminate much about those days just before he became famous—had gone on vacation, and the bandmates and entourage who would become fixtures after Elvis hit it big had not yet arrived on the scene. Elvis never commented on the Flamingo himself.

Weeks after his purported visits to the Flamingo Room,

and barely a mile away from the club, just beyond the end of Beale Street in a little storefront studio, Elvis made his first real record, a cover of the blues song "That's Alright Mama." White musicians with a twangy country western sound accompanied Elvis, who strummed his guitar and sang. Sam Phillips, who'd founded the small independent Sun Records, produced the session. The raw, original power of African-American music had enticed Phillips into the business in 1950, but the financial realities of selling black records in a segregated world had made him yearn for a white singer with the same soul as guys like B.B. King, Little Junior Parker, and Rufus Thomas, who'd all preceded Elvis in Sun's studio.

In hindsight, Presley's blend of white hillbilly style with black rhythm and blues in "That's Alright Mama" conceived a new genre, rock 'n' roll. Clearly, though, this fusion had come together in the Flamingo Room before Elvis made it famous.

If anyone in the world is entitled to beef with Elvis, it's Calvin Newborn, an important but largely ignored predecessor. Calvin had his own ambitions, though, and never wanted to be the king of rock 'n' roll. He and his brother were onstage every night at Birdland in New York—the jazz mountaintop, Calvin called it—by the time Elvis became thing one. When Calvin looked back at Elvis, he saw no rip-off but a white man who courageously thumbed his nose at a sick world by embracing black culture. "Elvis portrayed rebellion which was against a lot of different things," Newborn said. "He wore his hair differently. He wore clothes like a black person. He ate pork chops and gravy sandwiches. He was a soulful dude."

The once-hidden history of race in Elvis's musical background has since become one of the most debated aspects of the king's career. It's a story Ernest Withers would help to tell in pictures. As the photographer would recall, "seeing [Elvis] as often as I saw him . . . in and out of the clubs on Beale Street in a segregated period . . . I knew him and saw his compassion, and I listened to his conversation." Withers's sensitivity to Presley's unusual character would influence the photographer as he made some of the most meaningful images of the singer.

Fittingly, the city's dictator, Boss Crump, died in 1954, just five months after the Supreme Court issued the *Brown v. Board* decision and three months after Elvis recorded "That's Alright Mama."

7

ERNEST WITHERS TURNED THIRTY-THREE THE YEAR
after Elvis cut his first record. He'd worked as a professional photographer for nearly a decade. He'd developed a
style, a work ethic, and many of the intangibles needed to
make him more than a picture taker: he had the courage
to move in on his subject, the mental focus to block out
interruption, and the ability to capture a story in an image.
Until now, he lacked the platform to deliver his work to a
wide audience.

Withers got his break in journalism at the moment photography emerged as the most powerful new weapon in the
rebellion against racism. The news—and image—of a conspicuous act of evil roiled Beale Street in the late summer
of 1955: that August, Chicago teenager Emmett Till took a
trip to Mississippi and returned home in a coffin.

Afterward his mother demanded to have his body displayed as it had been discovered, saying, "Let the people see
what they have done to my boy."[1] A photographer from the
nationwide African-American magazine *Jet* took pictures of
the murdered boy's desecrated remains. Circulated around

the country, in *Jet* and in black newspapers—hitting Beale with the September 10 issue of the *Tri-State Defender*—the image provoked a new level of outrage. It prompted a group of black teenagers in Memphis to assault a white couple in retaliation, and calls for justice emerged from all corners of the United States

The trial of Till's killers, in a courthouse in little Sumner, Mississippi, attracted top-level media attention from across the globe. Ernest Withers was among the photographers.

A short, wide sheriff's deputy with an antler-handled revolver on his hip greeted Withers at the courtroom entrance. Withers, holding his camera in one hand and a chewed-up cigar in his mouth, raised his arms. The deputy frisked him.

Finding nothing dangerous, the deputy gestured Withers toward a card table set up at the far wall of the courtroom: the so-called black press bureau. A pair of reporters from up north sat there smoking, watching Withers make his way toward them, his scruffy jacket hastily thrown over short sleeves.

Withers stopped and pointed his lens at a group of old white farmers seated in the audience. Before he could shoot, one of the farmers rose, cursing, "Nigger, don't take my picture!"

Withers replied, "Don't worry. I'm only taking important people today."

As Withers set his camera on the black press table,

one of the reporters muttered, "Man, you'll get us lynched down here."[2]

Withers took a seat, and the county sheriff stopped by. "How you niggers doing this morning?" he asked.

The reporters silently seethed.

Withers opened his mouth. "We're in good shape," he said. "You looking out for us just fine."

The sheriff gave Withers a hearty pat on the shoulder and moved on.[3]

———•———

The African-American press functioned in a highly pressurized atmosphere. In its eyes, white media disseminated demeaning stereotypes of black people, diminished black achievements, and highlighted black debauchery and had done so as a matter of daily business for several hundred years. The founding principle of racism, that African Americans were inferior to white people, had guided every American policy and custom from slavery to segregation and to the current unequal protection of the law. Words white people printed made up a false galaxy of racial perceptions that swirled through the national psyche. Black reporters felt a duty to challenge such biased coverage, to go beyond the white version of events.

At the Till trial, one gangly reporter looked particularly uncomfortable stuffed behind the folding card table. At six foot four, L. Alex Wilson was stooped at the shoulders from a lifetime of hunching over his notebook. He wore glasses and had an inquisitive facial expression, eyebrows raised and mouth hinting at a frown. His typical uniform consisted of a snap-brim hat, a tailored suit, and high buffed shoes.

Wilson worked as editor of the *Tri-State Defender*, one of two African-American weeklies in Memphis. But he had caught the assignment to report on this trial for the flagship *Chicago Defender*, the publication with the largest daily circulation in black America. Since its founding in 1905, the *Defender* had chronicled lynchings and segregation, while imploring African Americans to migrate north.

Born in Orlando, Florida, in 1908, Wilson had studied journalism at the University of Wisconsin and served in the Marine Corps during the Second World War. He won the Wendell Willkie Award for best feature writing in African-American news for 1949. He served as *Chicago Defender* war correspondent from Korea, which primed him for duty in the American South. The company sent him to edit and manage the Memphis *Tri-State Defender* in 1952.[4]

Described by one of his understudies as "distinctly non-gregarious,"[5] Wilson was nonetheless a fearless newspaperman and brilliant motivator. He told his newspaper staff that an altercation with the Ku Klux Klan influenced his journalistic style. He'd run from the Klansmen, he said, but felt ashamed and vowed that he'd stand his ground in the future. "Any newsman worth his salt," he said, "is dedicated to the proposition that it is his responsibility to report the news factually under favorable *and* unfavorable conditions."[6]

Wilson encouraged writers to depict events clearly, letting the myriad twists and ironies of black oppression in the land of the free speak for themselves. He placed the story of the race struggle in the context of the Cold War. In its global propaganda battle against the Soviet Union, the United States portrayed (and perceived) itself as the force of good against evil, the land of liberty against oppression. But as Wilson often wondered, how could a country wave the flag of justice for all when it treated its people of color the way the United States did?

Ernest Withers considered himself blessed to find such a mentor. Over the next few years, as he developed a knack for capturing pivotal moments, L. Alex Wilson would bring him along, as he did to the Emmett Till murder trial.

⊢——◆——⊣

Black media did more than provide the world with a complete story of the Till trial. It also provided the judge and jury with information more complete than the court itself had gathered.

Supposedly no one had seen Till's murder take place. The prosecuting attorney had found a few witnesses who could testify only to the circumstances of Till's disappearance. The black press acted on a tip to bring a handful of material witnesses out of hiding.

Sharecroppers had seen Till riding in back of a pickup truck driven by one of the defendants, but they had gone into hiding out of fear for their lives.

Withers, Wilson, and others had joined with law enforcement officers and NAACP officials to form a search party. They'd spent the night searching for those witnesses. They donned overalls to blend in with local farmers and sped across unlit gravel back roads in the plantation district, following rumors to shacks throughout the Mississippi Delta.

The search had to be clandestine. In Mississippi, any information about African Americans organizing anything progressive or subversive led to deadly backlash. Two NAACP men registering black voters had been assassinated in public during 1955.

So the state NAACP operated underground, like the resistance in Nazi-occupied France during World War II. Members kept their allegiance covert and communicated secretly. Around whites, to avoid trouble, they portrayed themselves as whites wanted to see them, shucking and shuffling. They used stereotypes to their advantage. Operators of safe houses and secret meeting places hung crudely lettered, misspelled signs on their homes or businesses to signal their presence to insiders yet appear harmlessly ignorant to their oppressors.[7]

But when it came to disseminating and protecting crucial information, the underground had numerous disadvantages. Chiefly, black people could never infiltrate the Klan or the White Citizens' Councils (the more public white supremacy organization in Mississippi), yet the underground itself could easily be infiltrated by spies—"Judas niggers," as reporter Simeon Booker labeled them.[8] The underground had to operate with minefield caution, not knowing which local black folks could be trusted.

The underground believed a "Judas nigger" had directed Emmett Till's killers to the boy.

In order to do Till justice, the resistance had to find witnesses who didn't want to be found and convince them to come to court and recount what they'd seen to people who didn't want to hear them. The resistance next had to smuggle those witnesses out of the state alive.

One of Wilson's *Defender* reporters had been in the search party with the NAACP's Mississippi field secretary, Medgar Evers. At three in the morning, they'd found a pair of reluctant witnesses hiding in a shack on a remote cotton farm. Another three witnesses materialized and agreed to come forward. They all waited in their work clothes in the judge's chambers for the gavel to open the new day of the trial.

The rest of the sleep-deprived black press bureau, totaling eight African-American journalists, arrived in court and sat at the table. A hundred cigarettes burned around them. Locals seated nearby popped open beer cans and soda bottles. The reporters joked about how grateful they were to be sitting beside a window. If things got crazy, they said, they could jump out, even though they were on the second story.

They knew better than most what potentially explosive days of testimony lay ahead. Just when it felt like the smoky, humid air in the Sumner, Mississippi, courtroom couldn't get any tighter, in walked Emmett Till's mother. Mamie Till-Bradley strode past the defendants and took a seat beside the window.

The court first heard the much-anticipated statement of Moses Wright, Emmett Till's uncle. Wright said the men accused of killing Till—Roy Bryant and J. W. Milam— had come to Wright's house in the night and taken Emmett away. That had been the last time Wright saw his nephew alive.

As Wright took the stand, the judge warned the many press photographers to refrain from taking pictures during his testimony. Tall, lean, and stiff-limbed, he wore clean white long sleeves, a black tie, and yellow and brown suspenders.

"Look around, Uncle," said the prosecutor. "Do you see any of the men who came to your house that night?"

The terror that had kept so many other eyewitnesses in hiding now weighed on Moses Wright. If he testified honestly and identified the suspects, he risked jeopardizing his own health and that of his remaining family members, perhaps even triggering a courtroom race riot. So it would have surprised no one for him to claim that he hadn't seen the suspects or couldn't identify them.

But if he suffered that bout of amnesia, justice would have no chance.

Wright stood in the courtroom silence. He extended

his arm and pointed a knobby index finger at defendant J. W. Milam. "There he is," he said.[9]

The court rumbled.

Just at the moment when Wright defied an entire history of brutality and intimidation, a camera shutter clicked. Ernest Withers ignored the judge's order against taking pictures.

As *Jet's* Simeon Booker recalled, "One of the wire services bought his roll of film on the spot, and the iconic photograph was carried by newspapers around the country."[10]

The next morning brought out the first surprise witness that the journalists had helped uncover, eighteen-year-old Willie Reed. On the stand, Reed recalled that as he walked along a dirt road, a few hours after J. W. Milam abducted Emmett Till, a green and white '55 Chevy pickup drove past him carrying three African Americans in the back.[11]

The prosecutor showed Reed a picture of Emmett Till. "Is this the same boy as one of those in the truck?"

"Yes sir," Reed replied. "That is the same boy."

Reed explained that he had followed the truck down to a barn.

"Did you hear anything?" asked the prosecutor.

"I heard someone yelling. They were yelling, 'Oh!' . . . More than once. A whole lot of times."

Reed identified the same man Wright had pointed out as Emmett Till's captor. He said he saw the man exit the barn wearing a gun.[12]

After Reed's testimony, Mamie Till-Bradley, cherubic

and youthful, dressed in mourning, thanked him, reaching her hand out to hold his, as Ernest Withers snapped a picture.

That afternoon, after questioning the four other surprise witnesses, the prosecution rested its case.

As the evening sun sank, Willie Reed walked six miles across blossoming cotton patches and uncharted paths to retrieve a few belongings from his home. Next, with the help of the Mississippi NAACP, he escaped to Chicago.[13] There he changed his last name from Reed to Louis, the middle name of Emmett Till, and lived the rest of his life. The resistance relocated four other prosecution witnesses to Chicago, including Moses Wright.[14]

On September 24, the jury began its deliberations. Mamie Till-Bradley left the courtroom before the announcement of the verdict. This woman who had let the world see what Emmett's killers had done to her boy, could not bear to see them let off.

She pushed through the courthouse gossips on the steps, her eyes down. Ernest Withers stood poised with his camera to capture the moment.[15]

Inside, the jury deliberated for a few minutes more than an hour, including a soda break, and returned the verdict Emmett's mother had expected. They found Roy Bryant and J. W. Milam not guilty.

In an interview with *Look* magazine the next year, knowing they couldn't be tried twice for the same crime, Bryant and Milam confessed.

Walter Reed, Willie Reed, Mamie Till-Bradley, Dr. T.R.M. Howard, Charles Diggs, and Amanda Bradley at the trial of Emmett Till's murderers, September 1955. Special Collections Department, University of Memphis Library.

Covering civil rights in Mississippi further developed Withers's philosophy of photography.

"I mean I had fear," he recalled, "but I had a sense of self-confidence and a tactic that you would always have in life, that you know how to act anywhere you go, to keep yourself, if you can keep your head on all about you. It's the same philosophy that really makes one act and live safely, so I had no problem. I was somewhat emotionally empowered, but I did not let my emotions override my duty to shoot the necessary pictures."[16]

Despite Withers's energetic, gutsy performance during the Till murder trial and his importance to its legacy, the experience embittered him to the business side of photography. "I worked one solid week in the Emmett Till case," he recalled in a 1992 interview. "My salary for seven days, night, day, morning, and evening, was $35. You would think that that was an awful little amount of money for that much service."[17]

Back in his Beale Street studio, Withers worked to benefit from his experience. He and a printer friend published a pamphlet on the trial. He advertised it, not in the *Defender*, his freelance employer for the assignment, but in a competitor, the *Pittsburgh Courier*:

> EMMETT TILL KIDNAP-MURDER CASE PHOTOS NOW ON SALE IN PAMPHLET FORM! Only $1.00 . . . On-the-spot, authentic pictures taken before, during and after Emmett L. Till Murder Trial at Sumner, Miss. Pictorial story of how 14-year-old Chicago boy was caught up in a whirlpool of "Jungle Fury" in the "Congo" Delta of Mississippi! LIMITED SUPPLY . . . ORDER NOW!

But aside from reprinting the image of Emmett Till's face in death, which was widely circulated already, the pamphlet was far less sensational than this pulpy ad copy promised. In a preface for the pamphlet, Withers anticipated his critics: "'Crass Commercialism' one cynic might snort, or another label it as 'Outright Exploitation.'"

But in a tantalizing disclaimer he admitted, "We are not only depicting the plight of an individual Negro, but rather of life as it affects all Negroes in the United States . . . not in an attempt to stir up racial animosities or to question the verdict in the Till Murder Case, but in the hope that this booklet might serve to help our nation dedicate itself to seeing that such incidents need not occur again."[18]

Tisby, the printer, reeled off a thousand copies of the pamphlet, and the two men rented a post office box at the train station, where people could send a dollar to get one. Tisby kept the only key, though, and, Withers feared, more than his share of the incoming bucks.

At the time, Withers and his media colleagues fretted little over intellectual property issues. He happily sold rolls of film, especially to high-paying white photographers who couldn't get the access he could, and he didn't mind them publishing his work under their own names.

Perhaps in this same spirit, he took liberties with the work of others. Though the Till pamphlet is marked "Entire Contents Copyright 1955 By Ernest Withers Photographer," Withers didn't photograph the image of Emmett Till's corpse, and there's no reason to think he obtained the copyright from photographer David Jackson. Additionally, four of the other images in the booklet ran in the *Tri-State Defender* of September 17, 1955, credited to Moses J. Newson, a *Defender* reporter.

Newson recently said he hadn't known about copyrighting pictures back then and doesn't mind that Withers used his.

On his first assignment after the trial, Withers headed right back out with the local paper's society editor to photograph a housewarming fete.

8

THE IMAGE OF TILL'S CORPSE NEVER LOST ITS POWER,
despite the failure of Mississippi to bring the boy's murderers to justice. It embedded itself in the minds of millions
and activated a new intensity, a new determination among
African Americans, galvanizing a nationwide push for civil
rights.

In December 1955 the news hit Beale Street that black
citizens in Montgomery, Alabama, had boycotted city
buses. A front-page story in the *Memphis World* (the *Tri-
State Defender's* competitor) was probably the first account
anyone in Memphis had read of the minister acting as
spokesman for the group leading the embargo: "Rev. King,
a recent recipient of the Ph.D. degree . . ."

The report went on to explain, "The bus controversy
stems from the arrest several months ago of a Negro woman
who was fined for not complying with state and local segregation laws. A similar case recently triggered the boycott."[1]

This case referred to was that of Rosa Parks, a Montgomery seamstress and NAACP member who'd taken
a front seat on the bus while riding home from work and

refused to move for a white passenger. Her seemingly spontaneous act of defiance had been planned. And as she sat on the bus, Parks steeled herself by recalling the image of Emmett Till's face.

The boycott struggled on for a year, while its spokesman gained prominence.

In early June 1956, a federal circuit court ruled that racial segregation on Montgomery city buses was unconstitutional. Alabama officials immediately appealed the federal court's decision. In the newspapers, a photo of King in professorial robes, accepting a university honor, accompanied the story. "The protest will continue," King remarked. The final decision would be up to the U.S. Supreme Court.

———◆———

While King forced the issue of racial segregation toward the front of the American mind, a young white man reviled for his rebelliousness slipped through the boundary in Memphis.

On the steamy night of June 19, two weeks after the federal court ruled against Montgomery bus segregation, Elvis Presley came to the midway of the Memphis fairgrounds.

His arrival was news by itself. Elvis was fresh off NBC's *Milton Berle Show*, where he had debuted his new single, "Hound Dog," before virtually the entire TV-watching nation. The camera had shot him full body, without his guitar, gyrating his hips, showing mainstream America Elvis the Pelvis for the first time. The performance launched Elvis into previously uncharted levels of superstardom and prompted a social outrage yet unseen in the rise of rock 'n' roll. The *New York Times* TV critic panned his act as original only to the "blonde bombshells of the burlesque runway," while one citizen concerned with moral decline announced the formation of a committee to "do away with this vulgar, animalistic, nigger rock 'n' roll bop." As outrageous as Elvis may have appeared to the *Times*, his act was typical fare for the Flamingo Room.

He appeared at the Memphis fairgrounds on a Tuesday, and as everyone well knew—and as signs posted at the Memphis fairgrounds reminded them—this was Negro night. At the midway, Elvis and a girlfriend moseyed around and found the Cat Rack, a game where players tried to knock down toy cats like bowling pins with a baseball.

"Is that Elvis Presley?" someone in the crowd asked.

"From the way people have been talking about him, I expected him to look better than this," another fairgoer said.

Elvis knocked down two cats and won his girl a prize.

Another voice wondered, "Is he going to sing?"

"I want to hear 'Heartbreak Hotel.'"

"'Blue Suede Shoes' or nothing" came another request.[2]

Elvis sauntered out, causing little further commotion.

By showing up on Negro night at the Memphis fair, however, Elvis threatened polite society more than his pelvis had on TV. Yet, other than a brief mention in a local African-American weekly, it escaped notice.

The next time Elvis crossed over, Ernest Withers would be there.

In a two-week span near the end of 1956, Withers made his most important images on the integration theme, featuring two enduring symbols of race rebellion.

In early December, Memphis radio station WDIA—the first in the nation to broadcast all African-American programming—put on its annual Goodwill Revue at the Ellis Auditorium downtown, to benefit local charities in time for Christmas. The festival featured the top R&B acts on the radio and the road. Ray Charles and B.B. King would top the bill, with WDIA deejay Rufus Thomas as emcee.

Nine thousand people showed up. Both halls of the downtown civic auditorium had to be opened to accommodate the crowd, so that the stage sat amid thousands of fans on each side.[3]

Elvis and George Klein, a high school classmate and part of Presley's "Memphis Mafia," sneaked into the wings and mingled with Ray and B.B.

As Withers snapped pictures, he overheard Elvis tell King that the price of everything had doubled since he'd hit it big. "Thanks man, for the early lessons you gave me," he added.[4]

B.B. would recall, "He'd tell people I was one of his influences. I doubt whether that's true, but I liked hearing Elvis give Memphis credit for his musical upbringing."[5]

Onstage, emcee Rufus Thomas introduced himself as Rocking Horse, the man who'd brought rock 'n' roll to the tribe.[6]

After bringing out an act, Rufus slipped into the wings. The show's director wanted to send out Presley, but Rufus refused: "Don't do that. You do, the show's over."

Nearby, Elvis joked with WDIA's Teen Town Singers, a glee club, who were wearing Native American costumes for the show. Withers framed Elvis's face, laughing, between headband feathers worn by African-American kids with painted faces.

The backup band on the show that night, also wrapped in Native raiment, was none other than the Phineas Newborn Orchestra, of Flamingo Room fame, albeit without Elvis's inspiration Calvin Newborn. Calvin had already gone to New York, where he recorded the album *Phineas' Rainbow* with his brother for RCA, the same company that released Elvis's "Hound Dog."

Finally announcer Nat D. Williams told the packed house, "Folks, we have a special treat for you tonight: here's Elvis Presley."[7]

Elvis parted the curtain and walked onstage with the Teen Town Singers war-dancing behind him.

Withers followed the Teen Towners, rushing for the footlights. Elvis bowed, applauded Rocking Horse, and shook his leg as Withers snapped a picture. Thousands of girls rushed the stage, "like scalded cats," according to one observer.[8]

Elvis had planned his escape route in advance. He grabbed his buddy George Klein, and they headed out the stage exit for a waiting Cadillac.

Withers's photograph of Elvis Presley, with Carla Thomas visible in front of Elvis, December 1956. Copyright Dr. Ernest C. Withers, Sr., courtesy of the Withers Family Trust, Thewitherscollection.com.

The story, and the picture, depicted Presley's support for the most heated American social issue. As B.B. King explained, "Remember, this was the fifties, so for a young white boy to show up at an all-black function took guts. I believe he was showing his roots. And he seemed proud of those roots."[9]

Elvis was already being scrutinized for his "lewd" stage act. Now, by posing in a familiar, respectful stance with African-American artists, he knowingly risked his mainstream reputation even further. He and B.B. subtly conveyed messages of equality and integration. Elvis had nothing to gain for taking such a public stance.

Withers's photos of Elvis help us see something we still wonder about and discuss today—the importance of black artists to Presley. In a photo of Elvis laughing with B.B. King, he captured part of this story—and the king's acknowledgment of it.

That image reveals just as much about the photographer. Withers was becoming more than a picture taker. He digested the backstory of Elvis Presley and concentrated it into an image that ultimately sent an ideological message. He had become a crafty communicator through his medium.

In those final weeks of December 1956, Withers had no time to wait for the reaction to his latest photo. Before his picture of the two kings hit newsstands, he was already driving out of town with L. Alex Wilson, to cover more breaking history.

9

HANDSOME, YOUTHFUL MARTIN LUTHER KING, JR., understood the pressure toward perfection. He had come to fame without personal liabilities, with no hints of radicalism, Communism, or homosexuality.

His oratory drew on the charismatic Baptist style, classic except that it was imbued with the philosophy of Indian leader Mahatma Gandhi, who King called "the guiding light of our technique of nonviolent social change." Gandhi had used passive civil disobedience tactics to challenge the British Empire in India. In Montgomery, King and his followers had emulated that nonviolent approach, advocating a widespread boycott and enduring mass arrests. As L. Alex Wilson wrote, "Through the astute, capable leadership of Rev. King, the unity of the Supreme Court, and the cooperation of understanding whites to bring democracy to a citadel of segregation, integration was born here."[1]

On Thursday, December 20, 1956, U.S. marshals delivered official written notice to W. A. Gayle, the mayor of Montgomery, that bus segregation violated the U.S. Constitution. The case, known as *Browder v. Gayle*, had bounced through the federal courts for much of that year. Now the Montgomery mayor, named plaintiff in the case, could do nothing more to maintain racial segregation. That evening at a mass meeting, King ended the successful boycott, announcing, "Negro citizens of Montgomery are urged to return to the buses tomorrow," as applause overtook his speech.[2]

"Our aim has never been to put the bus company out of business, but rather to put justice in business," King told the celebrating crowd. Such deft verbal turnabouts caught the ear of reporter Alex Wilson, who recognized them as a signature of King's oratorical style.

After the speech, Wilson and Withers discussed the philosophy of image making. The weight of American imagery was racist—how were they to shift that weight with their coverage? How was Withers to photograph King and their people's struggle in general? *How do I know what picture to take?* Withers wondered. *How do editors know what image to run?*

Wilson answered Withers by suggesting that as he took a photo, he ask himself: *Is it true? Does it hurt? What good does it do?*

The next morning Wilson shook Withers awake at four. "Come on, boy," he said.[3] Already impeccably dressed, Wilson was determined to catch the first bus out of the station.

At five, under the sparkly morning stars, the two men could feel nervous excitement heating the winter air. A prayer from the previous night's rally ran through Wilson's mind: *"You have kept us in your hands, O Lord, now keep your arms of protection around us, we need you, right now."*

The story of the Montgomery Bus Boycott was about to become the biggest integration news of the decade. By now, the weakness of the 1954 *Brown v. Board* Supreme Court order to desegregate public schools was apparent: it had prompted more backlash than change. By contrast, the Montgomery story had a simplicity that *Brown* lacked. It was about a group of cooks, maids, seamstresses, and maintenance men who banded together to break segregation— *and they had done it.* The legal decision that the boycott achieved wasn't a ruling left to a million scattered entities to implement with "all deliberate speed" like the *Brown* case—this was right now.

At half-past six, L. Alex Wilson and Ernest Withers became the first black men to ride the front of a Montgomery city bus. (There were already two African-American women seated directly behind the driver.)[4] The bus reached the corner of Dexter and Lawrence streets, in sight of the Alabama state capitol and the church King pastored. Here the cradle of the Confederacy met the insurgent civil rights movement.

Wilson and Withers transferred to another bus, riding several lines over the next hour, observing a mostly courteous transition. Wilson interviewed an African-American passenger who'd woken up early to make sure he could get on board. "I had had some curiosity about the front seat of a bus," the man remarked. "They had been guarded so religiously that I felt they were made of air cushions and that probably there was a lever which would automatically release gold coins into one's pocket when he sat down."[5]

At seven-thirty, Wilson and Withers got out at Court Square downtown. As Withers snapped pictures, Wilson, notebook and pencil poised, approached Dr. King and asked for the latest.

"Our nonviolence program is proving its worth," King said. "From what I have personally observed and the reports I have received . . . everything is going along favorably. It should be remembered that we have to go through a period of adjustment."[6]

Wilson scribbled by the glow of a bus headlight, towering over King as they strolled together, off from the crowd.

"We feel certain that the shock phase will soon pass away," King said, "that the white reactionaries will discover as they are discovering, that they are fighting a losing battle. . . . The future looks bright."

Withers followed King onto a packed bus. King took a window seat up front, next to his top adviser in the boycott, Rev. Ralph Abernathy. As King gazed out the window, Withers framed his shot.

He positioned King and Abernathy next to the profile of a scowling old white man ahead of them—giving the appearance that these young black men had integrated the bus right under the old white man's nose. Behind them, a white man stands at the very back of the bus. All passengers sitting in rows between the two black men in front and the white man in back are visible, mostly female, all white.

Like the daring snapshot of Moses Wright pointing at Emmett Till's killer, Withers's image of King is excellent photojournalism, deriving drama from its effective staging. The scowling white man at the front is actually a minister and a boycott supporter, despite what his age and color imply. Nevertheless, the picture tells the story.[7]

Published nationwide, Wilson's words and Withers's photographs helped portray Martin Luther King, Jr., as a new hero to black America. Their coverage ran on the front page of the *Chicago Defender*.

The boycott's strategy, its organization, and the boycotters' tenacity to continue for a year all made Montgomery the most meaningful story since Emmett Till. Nothing like it had ever happened. In 1956 King's good looks, charisma, and vitality, the opposite of the Till image, conveyed a psychological basis for hope and for the future.

Withers provided the country its first widespread exposure to King's magnetism and electricity. Today the picture Withers snapped on the bus that gray December morning hangs in the National Portrait Gallery.

Yet Withers came away rankled. "I remember ninety-nine hours in Montgomery and a paycheck of ninety-nine dollars," he would reflect. "And when you really figure ninety-nine hours in Montgomery, the amount of time that it took to get there, was a whole lot of time and whole lot of life's danger spent."

Nonetheless the other side recognized the power of Withers's image and moved to suppress it. When the *Tri-State Defender* published the Montgomery story on December 29, the papers sold briskly, much to editor Wilson's delight. But black customers complained they couldn't find any copies. A group of white citizens, Wilson found out, had launched a campaign to empty the streets of the *Tri-State Defender*. They had bought bundles of the issue, collected them together, transported them to a bridge, and dumped them into the Mississippi River.[8]

10

FOUR MONTHS LATER, ON A FRIDAY NIGHT AT METRO-
politan Baptist Church in Memphis, Ernest Withers and
L. Alex Wilson sat among a few hundred early followers of
Dr. King.

Behind the pulpit, inside the two-story Palladian
church, King faced a young crowd. Three fraternities from
the two small local African-American colleges, LeMoyne
and Owen, had pooled resources to sponsor the program.

Since chairing the Montgomery Bus Boycott, King had
grown from a local preacher in Alabama to an "internation-
ally known leader," who'd visited Africa. He now came to
Memphis for the first time to "bring an inspiring message
on non-violence in the Negro's struggle for first class citizenship."[1] It was Easter weekend.

King's message foreshadowed one of the twentieth century's oratorical triumphs—his "I Have a Dream" speech,
which he would deliver to a significantly larger crowd in
Washington six years later. After warning that the U.S.
oppression of African Americans could drive them to Communism, King concluded,

Freedom must ring from every mountainside. Let it
ring from the snow capped Rockies of Colorado, let
it ring from the prodigious hilltops of New Hamp-
shire, let it ring from the mighty Alleghenies of
Pennsylvania, let it ring from the curvaceous slopes
of California. . . .

When that happens we will be able to sing in our
generation a new song with our fathers of old:

Free at last, free at last, great God almighty, I'm
free at last.[2]

King highlighted the federal government's deafening quiet on segregation, other than in judicial rulings.
President Eisenhower had remained mum on the issue,
in deference to Southern white voters. "Oh, we look up to
Washington and what do we see?" King asked. "My friends,
the executive branch of the federal government is all too
silent and apathetic. The legislative branch is all too eva-
sive and hypocritical. We have got to say to the officials in
Washington, from the president on down, that we expect
you to have some concern for these problems."

Washington would not remain on the sidelines much
longer.

⊢——◆——⊣

After King's speech, Ernest Withers came home to a preg-
nant wife. Ever since he'd fathered a girl outside the mar-

riage back during his time on the police force, his wife Dorothy had been determined to have a daughter of her own. They'd kept trying and now had seven children, all boys—Ernest Jr., Perry, Clarence, Wendell, Dedrick, Dyral, and Andrew.

All would work with their father as photography apprentices, tagging along on jobs, and some would take up the craft. Ernest Jr. and Dedrick, known as "Teddy," would go on to successful ventures in politics. Four of the boys would precede their parents in death. Andrew, known as "Rome," has been a most vigilant supporter of his father's legacy, helping to make the family home—three bedrooms and two thousand square feet, where they all grew up—into a museum and appearing at local events with a camera around his neck and a kufi atop his head.

On September 19, 1957, Rosalind Withers was born. She delivered the joy that a healthy child brings, and the relief to her daddy that his family was now complete. Roz would be the last Withers child.

As Ernest tallied nine kids in Memphis, nine more in Little Rock were making news. They were to be the first African-American students admitted to Central High School in the capital city of Arkansas, if only they could get inside. As L. Alex Wilson explained, "In Little Rock, Ark., USA, Gov. Faubus ordered out the National Guard . . . to prevent nine students from entering Central High."[3]

After a federal circuit court ruled in favor of integrating the high school, the governor had no legal means left to block the students from entering the building on September 23.

That September Monday the ever-dapper Alex Wilson parked his car two blocks from the school in downtown Little Rock, but Ernest Withers remained back in Memphis with his wife and baby girl. Around the perimeter of Central High, police barricades had been set up to keep protesters off school grounds.

Wilson walked with reporter Moses Newson, a former Memphis resident who was now with the Baltimore *Afro-American*, and reporter Jimmy Hicks, like Newson a veteran of the Till trial. The fourth black journalist in their group was Little Rock–based photographer Earl Davy, whom Wilson had recruited to replace Withers for the day.

Wilson noticed a surly but silent pair of white men on the sidewalk close behind. He turned to Davy and said he would not run from them. Wilson and Newson walked on ahead, with Davy and Hicks behind. They moved to the center of the street.

At 8:45 the school bell rang. A group of whites standing around the police barricade saw the four African-American journalists heading toward campus. Up went a shout— "Look, here come the niggers."[4]

Two men at the front of the mob moved to face Wilson and the journalists and spread out their arms to block the way. One of the whites wore a shiny metal helmet. He said, "You'll not pass."

Wilson said, "We are newspapermen."

Hicks said, "We only want to do our job."

"You'll not pass," said the man in the helmet.

A city police officer came forward to ask what business Wilson and the others had. Wilson handed over his press credential.

The cop told Wilson, "You better leave."

Wilson headed across the street, away from the mob. He could feel it on his back. He turned and saw the policeman standing still as the crowd flooded toward him.[5]

Meanwhile the man in the metal helmet chased photographer Davy up the street, kicking him from behind. As the photographer collapsed on the sidewalk, the metal helmet man took Davy's camera and smashed it to pieces.

An Associated Press reporter jumped into a phone booth and dialed the newsroom to dictate his account of the action.

Wilson, in his silvery suit and snap-brim fedora, stood against the mob. He thought about Elizabeth Eckford, one of the nine students who'd quietly endured insults from this bunch.

The first kick came from his left side. He blocked it and did not strike back. Another man flew into Wilson's view, swinging a right hook, grazing his jaw.

Wilson suddenly felt the full weight of a man land on his back. The impact knocked off his fedora, but he caught it.

The man wrapped his arm around Wilson's neck and

squeezed. *Snap* went a lens shutter. Local news photographer Will Counts captured the assault on film.

Someone in the crowd yelled, "Look, they're going into the school."[6]

The mob paused its attack to watch the nine African-American students cross the lawn, behind Little Rock NAACP executive Daisy Bates, and disappear into Central High for the first time. The AP man in the phone booth assumed that the four reporters under attack had deliberately created a diversion in order to allow the students to slip inside.

As the door closed behind the Little Rock Nine, Wilson bent to one knee and flipped an attacker off his back. The man picked up half a brick. With fifty people behind him, he wielded the brick, yelling, "Run, damn you, run."

Wilson looked at the man. He creased his fedora, put it on, and walked away.

Pain crashed into the back of Wilson's head. He reeled but pulled himself up and found himself looking into the tear-filled eyes of a white woman.

Wilson felt her sorrow but knew she couldn't help.

As Will Counts backpedaled to keep photographing the action in front of him, Wilson heard "Don't kill him" from the crowd behind him and felt surprised to find himself free.

"We'll teach you Yankee niggers about coming down here," he heard.[7]

Down the block, another of the mob yelled, "The niggers are in the school." That pulled the attackers away from the black reporters and toward Central High, stampeding over the remains of Davy's camera on their way.[8]

The mob hit a police barricade and went no further.

Inside the school, the Little Rock Nine took cover in the principal's office.[9] They were soon evacuated for their safety.

With Little Rock on the brink of a riot, President Eisenhower called on the street mobs to cease and desist. When they did not, he announced that he would use federal force to disperse them and to enforce the federal court order that permitted the nine African-American students to attend Central High.

Ike mobilizing the 101st Airborne Division to Little Rock and removing the Arkansas National Guard from the segregationist governor's hands represented the strongest federal commitment yet in support of racial integration.

The morning after the mob attacks, one thousand paratroopers converged on Little Rock. Eisenhower ordered U.S. soldiers to escort the Little Rock Nine safely into the school. He spoke carefully to avoid offending his Southern white constituents, justifying his use of force not as a gesture of support for integration but as a necessary response to the defiance of lawless mobs.

One fact nevertheless became clear to supporters of integration: between local, state, and national forces, only the feds could be trusted to protect the rights and the bodies of African-American citizens in the South.

Two days after the mob attack, Withers was photographed out on the sidewalk where the mob had assaulted Wilson. He is chomping a big cigar, his camera slung around his neck and his suit jacket askew in the sunny morning.

He watched a U.S. Army station wagon park in front of Central High against the backdrop of a mass of white students. A uniformed soldier popped out of the car and opened the door like a chauffeur for the young African-American women in the backseats. Three students got out and started toward the school. One of them, Minnie Jean Brown, dropped a piece of paper and, with her arms full of books, bent down to pick it up off the asphalt street. Withers snapped a picture, capturing the jitters.

Soldiers, with rifles at arms, escorted the young women through the white mob.

———————◆———————

The soldiers weren't the only federal presence around Central High after the melee. FBI special agent William H. Lawrence of the bureau's Memphis office had come to Little Rock to join the local agents piecing together reports on the racial violence.

The FBI's appearance in Little Rock was notable. After Emmett Till's murderers were acquitted, Mississippi African-American leader Dr. T.R.M. Howard had publicly called on J. Edgar Hoover to investigate why Southern FBI agents could never find the killers of black citizens.[10] Federal interest in the Till murder had been nonexistent. Federal interest in

Montgomery had been cynical, as J. Edgar Hoover saw the bus boycott as a potential invitation to Communists.

But in Little Rock, agents at least indicated an interest in identifying the perpetrators of mob violence.

Agent Lawrence was a Northerner, from Ohio, and so probably was a good choice to work on racial intelligence in a Southern city. He played good cop, and his sincerity was apparent in his grammar—he capitalized the word *Negro* in his written reports, unlike the Little Rock agents documenting the event and unlike many newspapers reporting on Central High.

In his investigation of the attack on the black newspapermen, Agent Lawrence caught up with one of them, Moses Newson, at Little Rock's black hotel, the Charmaine. Newson gave Lawrence little to work with and no reason to follow up with him, as Lawrence documented in his report of their interview.

> Newsom [*sic*] stated that due to the speed of
> the . . . action and the ensuing confusion, that he
> could not furnish any descriptions of any of his or
> his associates' assailants and could not recognize
> any of them if he were to see them again. . . . He
> stated he has developed no information and pos-
> sesses no information concerning the identities of
> any agitators or inciters to violence who may have
> attempted to prevent racial integration of Little
> Rock Central High School."[11]

Newson's stonewalling was a strategy for dealing with the bureau, as African Americans had seemingly little trust for Hoover men. Nevertheless, the fact that the government was putting boots and wingtips on the ground in Little Rock was a more emphatic federal intervention than at previous civil rights showdowns. The FBI men diligently interviewed witnesses, followed up on a possible racist conspiracy, and even tracked down Sonny Whitehead, who admitted he had put Alex Wilson in a headlock. Yet white Little Rock agitators seemingly suffered no punishment. Whitehead claimed that Wilson had knocked him down on the street while he was running from the mob, a dubious characterization of Wilson if ever there was one, and that Wilson had pulled a knife. "I cannot describe this knife and only saw the blade on it, which appeared to me to be about six inches long," said Whitehead.[12] No one else at the scene reported seeing Wilson's knife, and no blade appeared in Will Counts's photographs of the attack on Wilson.

While the bureau searched Little Rock for clues, Eisenhower sounded the theme to millions of Americans that Withers and Wilson had heard Dr. King deliver in Memphis just a few months before. "Our enemies are gloating over this incident and using it everywhere to misrepresent our nation," the president said. "It would be difficult to exaggerate the harm that is being done to the prestige and influence, and, indeed, to the safety of our nation and the world."[13]

Americans were sifting through the disturbing Little
Rock episode just as truly majestic international news
broke—the Soviets had successfully launched a satel-
lite, *Sputnik*, into space. The headlines blurred: while the
United States was blocking children from going to school,
the Soviet Union was taking the first big leap toward con-
quering the galaxy.

In December 1957, a photograph of Little Rock resident
Sonny Whitehead choking L. Alex Wilson outside Central High School appeared in the official Soviet newspaper *Pravda*. Soviet interest in the African-American plight
only intensified U.S. government scrutiny of Communism
in the civil rights movement. After Little Rock, Mississippi
senator James O. Eastland convened a federal hearing on
Communist activity among African Americans in the mid-
South that put everyone vested in the fight for equal rights
on high alert.

"It's getting harder to discern true friends among liberal
whites," wrote Nat D. Williams, a Beale Street lifer, mentor to Ernest Withers, and author of a nationally syndicated column in the *Pittsburgh Courier*. "And the climate in
the South today is definitely in the direction of suspecting
that any white man who befriends the Negro's cause, as of
now, may pretty surely be safely charged with Communist
connections and feelings."[14]

The federal investigation and paranoid atmosphere surrounding Communism placed the highest premium on
American loyalty and patriotism in the civil rights move-

ment. Any person or organization involved had to be clean of Red, or they risked harming the crusade as a whole. Of course Communism, as an alternative to the system that oppressed African Americans, appealed to plenty of civil rights activists and organizers, but it also gave the FBI its justification for spying on them.

During these days of intrigue, in January 1958, the FBI's Memphis office requested Ernest Withers's records from the bureau's central identification division in Washington, which included a list of his criminal offenses and his fingerprints. The document identified Withers as a potential informant on criminal cases.

11

MEMPHIS WAS HOME TO THE WORLD'S LARGEST African-American Pentecostal denomination, known as the Church of God in Christ. By 1958, COGIC had been sponsoring activism for nearly fifty years and boasted a membership of millions spanning the globe. Members called themselves "saints," while outsiders called them a cult. The church's founding elder and presiding bishop was its extraordinary leader, Charles Harrison Mason.

Diminutive and spry at nearly one hundred years old, Mason had led an almost unbelievable life. Born into slavery in 1864, he practiced as a minister in the Baptist faith early in his career, but the church excommunicated him in 1895 for the zeal of his preaching. He thereafter wandered, spreading the word as he felt it needed to be expressed.

At the turn of the century, Mason came to Memphis, where he conducted spontaneous, open-air revivals in the Beale district. He told the people that he was sanctified, that they too could become sanctified, and that those who truly felt the Holy Ghost shouted and trembled in its possession. Sanctified, moral black people would transcend racism, he told them, and white people couldn't help but respect them for living right.

In 1906 Mason traveled to Los Angeles to attend services at the Apostolic Faith Mission on Azusa Street, where a new faith, Pentecostalism, was just emerging. Believers defined their faith according to the experiences of Christ's original disciples on the day of the Pentecost: as described in the New Testament, the Holy Ghost descended and baptized them in fire.

Pentecostal worship transformed Mason. He witnessed black men and white women laying hands on one another in rapturous prayer. "I saw and heard some things that did not seem scriptural to me," he wrote, "but at this I did not stumble. I began to thank God in my heart for all things, for when I heard some speak in tongues, I knew it was right, though I did not understand it. Nevertheless, it was sweet to me."[1]

At the Azusa Street mission, with hundreds of people speaking in tongues all around him, he experienced spiritual rebirth:

The sound of a mighty wind was in me, and my soul cried *Jesus! Only one like you!* My soul cried and I soon began to die. It seemed that I heard the groaning of Christ on the cross dying for me. All of the world in me cried until I died out of the old man [I had been]. The sound stopped for a little while. My soul cried *Oh God, finish your work!* Then the

sound broke out again in me. I felt something raising me out of my seat without any effort of my own.
I said, *it may be my imagination.* Then I looked down
to see if it was really so. I saw that I was rising.
Then I gave up, for the Lord to have his way with
me. . . . When he had gotten me straight on my feet,
there came a light which enveloped my entire being
above the brightness of the sun. When I opened my
mouth to say *glory*, a flame touched my tongue.[2]

Mason returned home and introduced Pentecostalism to Memphis. He baptized the faithful, both black and
white, in the Mississippi River. He shared an inflammatory
message:

Have we not all one father?
Have not one God created all of us?
God created all of us!
There is no such thing as a white God or a black God!

Mason preached from Mark 16:17, "speak with new
tongues." He could speak, pray, and sing in tongues. He
interpreted messages from God, sent to him via misshapen
tree roots and vegetables. He conducted all-night revivals,
scheduled to allow members of other churches to come and
vent and commune with the spirit in a way that more conservative denominations forbade. With Mason, they could
dance and shout their praise, testify to their faith as they

felt it. Bands of tambourines, organs, pianos, and guitars played throughout his services.

Mason called his deformed vegetables, roots, and tree branches "freaks of nature" and loved them just as he loved the ostracized people of his flock, people poor or black who'd been told they weren't equal. He preached that they were no less children of God than the prosperous whites—a downright subversive gospel in turn-of-the-century Memphis.

During World War I, the Bureau of Investigation (the agency's name before it added "Federal") took an interest in Mason's pacifist teaching, suspicious that he sympathized with America's enemies. During World War II, the FBI monitored Mason's home and his sermons, and it interviewed him about pacifism and his patriotism. In a letter to President Franklin Roosevelt, Mason explained, "We declare our loyalty . . . [but] believe the shedding of human blood or taking human lives to be contrary to the teachings of Jesus Christ."[3]

All the while, the Church of God in Christ gained membership. COGIC's annual holy convocation, a three-week revival, drew more than ten thousand saints from across the country to Memphis.

Mason remained iconoclastic. In 1940 faith healer Vera Boykin danced and healed the sick at COGIC revivals around St. Louis. Known as the dancer with a miracle touch, she cured, twisted, and gyrated before the crowds that flocked to her. But she also outraged church officials when she danced in a revealing costume on a table before the pulpit at Kennerly Temple in St. Louis. The temple elders pleaded with Bishop Mason to come stop her indecent behavior. He traveled to St. Louis at their behest. Seeing Vera Boykin perform, he got up on the table and danced with her.

Nor did Mason have any trouble challenging white authority in Memphis. When his church burned in 1936, he petitioned political boss E. H. Crump for a donation to help rebuild. Boss Crump didn't like it, but Mason threatened to relocate the church's headquarters, taking with him thousands of votes and tax dollars, plus the lucrative convocation. He secured a ten-thousand-dollar pledge from the city. Mason built the largest church auditorium in Memphis. Mason Temple, opened in 1945, would be the site of numerous history-making gatherings and speeches, including the "Mountaintop Speech" that Martin Luther King, Jr., delivered on the eve of his death.

The bishop had a son and namesake, Charles Harrison Mason, Jr., born in 1913. Known as "Bob" Mason, he followed a fraught path, partially in his father's steps but anxious to distinguish himself. He lettered in two sports at LeMoyne College in Memphis and began a career as a musician. His calling to join the ministry came late in life, in mid-1954, when he assumed from his father the pastorate at the Home Temple of the Church of God in Christ.

While the faithful believed his father to be a man of holy blessings, some saw Bob as eccentric. Of course, eccentricity had been a central tenet of COGIC from its beginning, with its tolerance of difference and its forgiveness in the born-again sense. Rumors of young Mason's alcoholism circulated, however—a violation of COGIC morals.

As public housing projects and restrictive covenants kept black residences segregated from those of whites nationwide, Memphis's unique spiritual phenomenon, COGIC, led the push for housing integration.

Back during the Montgomery Bus Boycott, Bob Mason purchased a home on Glenview Avenue in South Memphis, a few blocks of mostly single-story houses with small yards. The first African American to do so, he moved in during the summer of 1957, just prior to the militarized integration of Central High School in Little Rock.

In response to Mason moving in, white residents formed the Glenview Plan, reportedly two hundred strong. They pooled $15,000 to purchase Mason's house from him. He refused to sell but said nice things about his neighbors in the press. Neighborhood tensions grew when two more African Americans, including another minister, bought on Glenview.

In early February 1958, Bob Mason began conducting a three-day-long fast and prayer service at his church. While he was away from his house, he left his ten-month-old child with a babysitter. At one-thirty on the morning of February 7, the sitter looked out the front window and saw a wooden cross flaming in the front yard.

Police later explained to Mason that the cross-burning was a prank. He publicly accepted that explanation, but he moved his wife and baby into a relative's home. During the coming days, through the dark hours, he stayed awake alone on Glenview to keep watch over his property.

A few weeks earlier Lewis Thompson, who lived about a mile away on Cannon Street, had been murdered in his own driveway. Thompson ran a store and had the night's proceeds on him, but he wasn't robbed. The case was a mystery.

One night as Mason was sitting up, a stone crashed through a windowpane of his house. Another night whiskey bottles landed in the yard. Mason cleaned up the messes and kept to his routine.

On February 13, he attended choir practice at his church. Home Temple, on the corner of Georgia Avenue and Lauderdale Street, was a sacred place to COGIC saints. The grand three-story building, with eighteen-inch-thick brick walls, stood for the church's prosperity and solidity. After rehearsal, at around nine-thirty, Mason drove home in his sharp new Olds 98.

The next morning, at one minute before five, an alarm summoned firemen to Mason's church from a station four blocks away. When they arrived at COGIC's Home Temple, the exterior was intact, but the inside was full of fire. More alarms were sounded to bring men and equipment, but within twelve minutes, one of the thick walls caved in.[4] The fire spread toward the mortuary next door, where the funeral director wheeled out three cadavers and loaded them into hearses, stunning some of the firemen battling the blaze.

Rev. Charles Harrison Mason, Jr., left, as firefighters extinguish ruins of the Church of God in Christ Home Temple, February 1958. Special Collections Department, University of Memphis Library.

At sunrise, Bob Mason arrived at his church. In his overcoat and hat, he stood and watched as firemen carrying hoses raced around all sides of the building, desperately fighting the flames for two hours. Water from their hoses froze into icicles on power lines. Fire reduced the pews inside to ash, consumed the old Bible on Mason's pulpit, and shattered the stained-glass windows. Another high brick wall collapsed and crumbled. Ash and dust swirled, and plump snowflakes began to fall.

Parishioners arrived, church ladies with hats and handbags, and elders, stoic and dapper with trimmed mustaches. Newsmen reached the scene.

Ernest Withers snapped a photograph of Mason posed grimly in front of the rubble.

When asked about how the blaze might have begun, Mason said, "I don't believe that the cross-burning was a prank now. Nor was this fire started accidentally. Both show deliberate and concrete planning."[5]

A fire marshal echoed Mason's concern: the inside-out pattern of the blaze indicated arson.

Fire was the central COGIC symbol, linking the modern-day saints with the disciples of Jesus in their searing connection to the Holy Spirit, as in Acts 2:1–3:

> When the day of the Pentecost arrived, they were all in one place. And suddenly there came from heaven a sound like a mighty rushing wind, and it filled the entire house where they were sitting. And divided tongues as of fire appeared and rested on each one of them.

Fire also connected much of the neighborhood's recent tortured history. Five years before, almost to the day, Boss Crump had permitted the home of his old rival, the South's first black millionaire, Robert Church, to be burned. The mansion had stood not a block down Lauderdale from COGIC's Home Temple.

Over on Glenview, the white neighborhood association kept the pressure on Mason. The Glenview Plan attorney said, "The people of this area are law-abiding citizens and therefore have not harassed him." But did that mean they had accepted Mason as a neighbor? "Nothing could be farther from the truth," said the lawyer.[6]

The attitude that had prospered under Boss Crump lived on in the words of Henry Loeb, a newly elected city commissioner who stood with Glenview's white residents: "We ought to go out to the Penal Farm . . . to find more suitable locations for Negro homes."[7]

Loeb stoked the cool rage of L. Alex Wilson, who wrote, "If [Loeb] is interested in being a valuable asset to this changing community, he should . . . embrace the struggle to change his inner self."[8]

—————◆—————

On Sunday, March 2, a realtor arrived on Glenview Avenue with her clients. Evelyn Taylor was the first African-American woman in Memphis to become a licensed and bonded real estate broker. At first, she had sold houses on the side while working private nursing jobs: she used the phones in her patients' homes for realty calls and borrowed a family's chauffeur to help put out yard signs. She initially listed one-bedroom shotgun dwellings on twenty-foot lots with a john in the back and no running water.

When her generous patient with the chauffeur died, Taylor was ready to sell houses full time. The white president of the local real estate board recommended that she market Glenview, and she took out an ad in the *Commercial Appeal* saying, THOSE WHO WANT THE BEST WILL FIND IT HERE.

When she and her clients arrived on March 2, white residents unfurled a large sign to greet her: CROSS BURNING ROW—LUXURY HOMES.[9] One owner on Glenview told her, "Now Evelyn, you can show my house, but don't bring no niggers in my front door." She reminded the man, "If the nigger *buy* the house, he'll own the front door."

Taylor received harassing phone calls, and all manner of emergency vehicles clogged the street during her later showings. None of it really bothered her. She pitied racists and knew that she was serving her customers with a nice roof over their heads and a twist of social revolution. She had fun doing her part. Still, her clients faced near certain peril.

The night after Taylor's March 2 showing, three calls to the fire department reported a blaze at Mason's house. No one was at home. Firefighters arrived to see flames licking out the attic, charring a gable over the entrance. They smashed through the front door and put out the fire before it inflicted serious damage. Investigators found wiring in the attic that had been stripped and cardboard that Mason said he hadn't put there.[10]

Nevertheless two more African-American families soon moved to Glenview.

Two days after the attic fire, Bob Mason appeared at the FBI's Memphis office, carrying a letter he'd received in that morning's mail. He handed it over to an agent. The cursive writing read:

> Do you remember what happened on Cannon street several weeks ago, to your brethren in color?
> It <u>can</u> happen to <u>you</u>.
> <u>Remember</u> <u>Cannon</u> <u>street</u>, this man wanted bus intergration. [*sic*]
> Heed this warning
>
> XX

"Cannon street" referred to the murder of Lewis Thompson, shot dead in his driveway back in January. The case remained unsolved. "Intergration" or any racial dispute had not been publicly announced as a possible motive for the murder.

At the FBI office, an agent asked Bob if he had any criminal record. Mason replied that while living in Detroit and Montclair, New Jersey, he'd been arrested sixteen times on charges of drunk driving, public drunkenness, and disorderly conduct. He'd given up that life when he took the pulpit in his father's church. He had founded an African-American chapter of Alcoholics Anonymous, and though he remained a restless soul and spent many a sleepless night in local taverns, he did so as a recruiter for both COGIC and AA.

Whoever Mason talked to at the bureau told him they couldn't offer him any protection. Later that day the local FBI conferred with police about the preacher. A police detective investigating the fires had developed a theory: Mason set the blazes himself.

The author of the threatening letter remained anonymous but was not finished. Realtor Evelyn Taylor received the next handwritten message:

> Do you remember what happened on Cannon Street not many moons ago, to one of your brothren [*sic*] in color?
> He was very interested in bus integration, he asked for what he got.
> Stay off Glenview St. or else.
> Matches are 8 cents per box.
> Shells cost more but worth the price.
> The <u>preacher</u> lost his Chuch. [*sic*]
> The <u>off</u> – <u>brand</u> preacher had a fire at home – all set, by himself to reflect on the white people. Remember to watch your stepp, You are a kinky headed Negro, stay in your place
>
> XX

Taylor brought the note to the Memphis Police Department but was told there'd be no investigation, even though the police claimed to have four detectives on the Thompson slaying, and Taylor held a possible clue. The FBI eventually developed a suspect in the harassment of Mason and Taylor, based on handwriting analysis conducted at the national crime lab on the two pieces of hate mail, but no arrests were made. The murder of Lewis Thompson remains unsolved.

⊢———◆———⊣

A young lady named Edna Smith showed up at Mason's home on Glenview, saying she'd been an acquaintance of the reverend's wife, heard about the troubles, and wanted to help. She went grocery shopping with Mason and his brother-in-law. She watched Mason pay by check, then returned to the store with three checks from Mason's account, saying the reverend wanted her to get them cashed for him. The scam got her locked up on a forgery charge. In police custody, Edna claimed she had been working as a prostitute at Mason's house.

The afternoon following Edna's arrest, two detectives showed up at the most notorious house on Glenview Avenue and arrested Mason for aiding and abetting prostitution, charging in effect that a minister was a pimp.[11] The flimsy criminal charges evaporated, but the intense persecution finally forced him out of Glenview. In 1959 Bob sold his house and moved into the Mason family home.

His father, the founding bishop of COGIC, died in 1961. Though Bob preached for a time, he slid back into his old ways. On February 3, 1966, he got into a fight in a small tavern near the Mason family house and suffered a head injury. That night fire gutted the back end of the sprawling house. Reportedly, Mason was not home when it burned, but a relative found him there unconscious a few days later. He never recovered. A friend took him to the hospital, where he died at 2:45 in the morning of February 7, 1966, eight years to the day—almost to the hour—after the cross burning in his yard on Glenview Avenue.

But thanks to Mason's resolve in '58, and Evelyn Taylor's gumption, Glenview turned out to be a triumph in the city's African-American revolution. As more houses on Glenview sold to black residents, Taylor persuaded white owners that selling to African Americans made the city a better place, that they were taking part in a positive change. A man who bought a house on Glenview in the early stages of the change recalled that back in his apartment in the Beale Street area, the tenants' only water service had come from a fire hydrant out back. He had heard rapes taking place in his old neighborhood, and it was not completely out of the ordinary to see a dead body in the alley.[12]

As the Glenview story cooled off, Ernest Withers lost his journalistic mentor. In February 1959, L. Alex Wilson left Memphis to become editor of the African-American daily *Chicago Defender*. The job rewarded Wilson's intrepid fact-finding and comprehensive front-page reporting from the three biggest stories of the era: the Emmett Till trial, the Montgomery Bus Boycott, and the desegregation of Central High in Little Rock.

The wounds Alex Wilson had incurred on the beat were also catching up to him. After being attacked outside Central, he felt a tremor in his hand. He worked through the discomfort, keeping the problem secret even from his wife. But the tremor spread through Wilson's arms and became uncontrollable. He sought medical treatment in Chicago and in the early fall of 1960 underwent surgery. He never returned home from the hospital. His young wife, his three-year-old daughter, and his mother all survived him.

After watching her son go beneath the ground, Wilson's mother said, "Alex always wanted to be a newspaperman. He would come home in the afternoons . . . when he was very young, and go up to his room and write and write and write."[13]

For Ernest Withers, no one would ever replace the man who'd guided him as philosophical conscience and career booster. But he soon began a new partnership. For Withers, Wilson's departure, and the Glenview saga, marked the end of his phase as solely a civil rights photojournalist. From this point on, he would cover the important race news—the Freedom Rides, Black Power, riots, and the death of Martin Luther King, Jr.—as both a photographer and a spy.

Holding On to Jerusalem Slim

12

AFTER GLENVIEW, ERNEST WITHERS AND FBI AGENTS showed up in the same places: Clinton, Tennessee, where a bomb destroyed a recently integrated public school; downtown Memphis, where NAACP-coordinated sit-ins and pickets protested segregation of public facilities and private businesses; and rural West Tennessee, where the feds and African-American journalists cracked a conspiracy that had deprived black citizens of the franchise for the better portion of a century.

In early 1961, FBI special agent William Lawrence was considering using Withers as a confidential informant. He contacted Memphis police chief James MacDonald seeking background information on Withers.

MacDonald had been an assistant chief ten years earlier, when Withers was dismissed from the force. Now he checked the photographer's personnel file and told Lawrence that Withers had been busted for selling whiskey and removed from the department. Withers had picked up a couple of suspensions while on the force as well, for failing to appear in court as a prosecuting witness and for fighting with an auto salesman.

Lawrence asked the chief for his character assessment of Withers. Definitely opportunistic, MacDonald said. Intelligent but troublesome. Withers had required an excessive amount of supervision on the force. The chief didn't trust Withers. He didn't like him. But he didn't question Withers's loyalty to the country, and he thought Withers would cooperate with any government agency—as long as he could see the advantage.

Lawrence concluded that Withers fell short of the bureau's standard of reliability, "wherein his activities can be directed or controlled." But he wanted to give Withers a chance nonetheless, "because of his many contacts in the racial field, plus his willingness to cooperate with this Bureau, as attested by his recent furnishing of information."[1]

Six weeks before Lawrence asked MacDonald about Withers, the photographer had given the FBI agent a picture of a voting rights activist in a cotton-farming, sharecropping area outside Memphis.

Beginning in 1958, African-American residents of Fayette and Haywood counties filed complaints against white county election officials for refusing to allow black citizens to register to vote. Those who had tried to register were kicked off the land they farmed. They were also economically blacklisted, denied the farm loans and store credit they'd traditionally used to make their living. A document containing their names circulated through key businesses in the region. A local bank president said: "The men on that list, I won't even talk to, unless they already owe us money and are coming to pay it off."[2]

The evicted farmers built a compound of canvas army tents in a muddy bottom on an African-American property owner's acreage. It came to be known as Tent City.

Over the objections of West Tennessee's U.S. attorney and FBI director J. Edgar Hoover, the civil rights division at the Department of Justice authorized agents from the FBI's Memphis office to investigate. The agents conducted scores of interviews, while the black press exposed the blacklist and applauded the federal participation.

In late January 1961 a federal judge issued a restraining order against the white Haywood County residents who'd prevented potential voters from registering or punished those who successfully registered and voted. "The F.B.I. had thrown its full weight into the case," noted the African-American *Pittsburgh Courier*. "In other words, the U.S. Department of Justice was not 'playing.' It meant business. This was no show for political purposes, or to allay complaints from Negroes. This was 'it,' the real McCoy . . . truly protecting the rights of Negro citizens."[3]

In previous civil rights cases, African Americans had typically greeted FBI and other investigators with suspicion and silence: for one, Memphis journalist Moses

Newson had stonewalled Agent Lawrence in Little Rock. African Americans in the Tent City case responded differently. They were accustomed to violent local law enforcement. In 1941 the current sheriff of Fayette County had led a lynch mob that murdered an NAACP member for registering black voters. But the fact that the feds now cared enough to respond reassured them. In 1958, when African Americans filed the first voting discrimination complaint in the counties, two agents showed up from Memphis to investigate—and several African-American community members came out to meet them. The very presence of someone official attempting to help gave the community a morale boost.[4]

During this time, Ernest Withers furnished Agent Lawrence with a photograph of a Haywood County activist. His exact intention remains unknown, but his cooperation came during this period of alliance between FBI agents and African-American journalists to investigate Tent City and the white conspiracy trying to rob black citizens of the franchise. At least at this point, Withers cooperated with the bureau in the context of an effort that black America viewed positively.

Meanwhile the new U.S. president reinforced such grassroots optimism that the federal government might start to support full black citizenship. At John F. Kennedy's first live TV news conference, *Chicago Defender* reporter Ethel Payne asked him, "Does your administration plan to take any steps to solve the problem at Fayette County,

Tennessee, where tenant farmers have been evicted from their homes because they voted last November, and must now live in tents?" Kennedy answered:

> We are. The Congress, of course, enacted legislation which placed very clear responsibility on the executive branch to protect the right of voting. I supported that legislation. I am extremely interested in making sure that every American is given the right to cast his vote without prejudice to his rights as a citizen. And therefore I can state that this administration will pursue the problem of providing that protection with all vigor.[5]

Withers soon became involved with another case that had a national impact.

———— ◆ ————

On a July afternoon, six months after he screened Withers with the police chief, Agent Lawrence contacted the photographer to ask about the Freedom Riders, who were scheduled to come through Memphis. Groups of racially diverse volunteers from colleges, seminaries, churches, and synagogues were riding buses together to challenge local segregation in interstate travel accommodations. Withers told Lawrence he didn't know anything about them but could find out.

He contacted his local NAACP branch, located around the corner from his office, and learned that a group of

Freedom Riders would arrive on a Greyhound and spend the night at Owen College. He got back in touch with Lawrence and shared the news.

That evening Lawrence stood at the Memphis Greyhound depot and watched a bus arrive. Five men stepped off and entered the Post House, a café in the station. Three were white—two rabbis and a college student—and two were African Americans, a sociologist and a student.

The Post House had been an all-white establishment up to that moment. As Lawrence watched, the five men sat down side by side at the counter. They were served without incident. A few reporters and policemen were the only other witnesses to one of the less eventful racial demonstrations of the year.

After their meal, the five men caught a taxi. Two white policemen, two black policemen, and two FBI men, including Lawrence, followed the cab to a dormitory at Owen College, confirming Withers's tip.

The police, saying they wouldn't hang around for an all-night stakeout, left the two FBI agents outside the dorm. A short while later one of the Freedom Riders walked out of the building. Lawrence approached him and questioned him. The man told Lawrence the group would take the next day's 12:40 p.m. bus to Little Rock.

Lawrence returned to the Greyhound station the following midday and saw the five men eating lunch in the newly desegregated Post House. They got on the bus just prior to its departure time. "The two Negroes were observed sitting in the front of the bus," wrote Lawrence.

At a quarter till one, the Greyhound chugged toward Little Rock. The rabbis, the sociologist, and the students had encountered no opposition or harassment of any kind.[6]

Lawrence paid Withers fifteen dollars for the information.[7] Not six months before, Lawrence had doubted Withers's potential, writing, "It is not believed that Withers can meet the Bureau's reliability requirements as a PCI (RAC)," that is, an informant with specialized expertise in racial matters, "wherein his activities can be directed or controlled." The photographer had begun to overcome the agent's doubts.[8]

———————◆———————

To brand anyone who talks to the government as a snitch is hasty. Withers's relationship with Lawrence must be understood in context. All the top NAACP officials in the city during this time talked to the FBI: Jesse Turner, Vasco Smith, Maxine Smith, Hosea Lockard, A. W. Willis— even Benjamin Hooks, who would go on to become national NAACP chairman and a commissioner for the Federal Communications Commission. They communicated, usually with Agent Lawrence, about the organization's various plans for integration in the community. These local leaders were simply following national leaders like Roy Wilkins and Thurgood Marshall, who maintained open lines with the Department of Justice. Furthermore, the FBI initiated a Liaisons with Groups Sponsoring Integration program that enlisted such grassroots civil rights warriors as Mississippi's Aaron Henry and Amzie Moore as "informants."

The FBI classified, for its own purposes, each of these knowledgeable individuals as a "Confidential Source of Information, Racial." We don't know what any of them knew about how the government viewed them and treated them in its paperwork. They communicated their perspectives about tense, complex local racial circumstances in hopes that the bureau would help the Justice Department protect American citizens' rights, continuing the positive momentum of Little Rock and Tent City. Of course, the NAACP had its own need for power and control. FBI cooperation helped reinforce it as the civil rights establishment, the movement's leading source of vision and direction. Perhaps a bit like Hoover's bureau, the NAACP believed in the rightness of its cause and saw certain other organizations as harmful. NAACP leaders were happy to help the bureau locate troublemakers that threatened the stability of the cause and the country. That said, the racial intelligence program that these sources participated in, under a variety of bureaucratic pseudonyms over the years, was almost entirely political both in nature and in execution.

The FBI was best at solving major crimes, like kidnappings, bank robberies, and serial murders. But through Hoover's boundless sense of responsibility, the bureau had taken upon itself the more slippery, subjective goal of maintaining a stable American society. Racial integration had the potential to create social disorder. And anything that could destabilize America would be attractive to Communists. And so investigating racial matters was an important function of Hoover's bureau.

Espionage requires secrecy from the general public, but a civil rights spy in the Cold War didn't need a separate psychological compartment. To properly appreciate the strange situation of a civil rights hero like Withers becoming a civil rights spy, we must absolutely understand one thing: the movement, if it were to succeed, needed total independence from Communism, because of the way its enemies attacked it. Hoover had been monitoring every NAACP chapter for Communism and effectively marginalizing successful black leaders as socialists since the days of Marcus Garvey.

Both the FBI and the civil rights movement had a strong interest in accurately identifying Communist leaners among the movement's leaders, albeit for drastically different purposes. The bureau used this information to justify investigating and disrupting the movement as a national security threat, while the movement needed the information to weed out radical individuals whose presence, even well-meaning, could cause turmoil. Since anyone could be smeared as a Red, the movement needed someone smart, objective, and friendly at the nitty-gritty street level to conduct research, obtain information, and pass the truth on to what was potentially the movement's most dangerous enemy but damn sure was the Communists' most dangerous enemy.

Withers also saw danger to the movement coming from individuals with the potential for violence. He positioned himself as a volatility gauge, describing to Lawrence any activists who appeared to be "emotionally unstable," egotistical, vain, or likely to organize dramatic protests for public attention that could lead to anger and physical confrontation.

Agent Lawrence worked from the idea that Director Hoover had articulated in an early 1956 report on racial tension and civil rights: that where reason gave way to emotion, violence could result. The concept dovetailed with the teachings of Withers's journalistic mentor. L. Alex Wilson had cautioned Withers against emotional excitability and taught him to spot publicity-hungry people who glommed onto civil rights to boost their egos and profiles rather than participating out of devotion.

Lawrence even resembled Wilson a bit: he too was tall and thin, wore glasses, a bit stiff in gait and stooped at the shoulders. Memphis attorney J. Michael Cody remembered the agent as "nice, pleasant. Nothing ever aggressive. Not like you were under any kind of suspicion from the FBI. He always had his dopp kit [travel bag] with him, and I thought he must constantly travel. It didn't occur to me until later that he was recording me."

Agent and informant shared an affinity for sincere, responsible leadership and a mistrust of attention seekers and agitators. Still, Withers had to talk his way out of trouble with his handler when, early in their relationship, some of his photos appeared in the country's leading Communist weekly, the *Worker.*

Withers swore it happened accidentally. He'd received a request for photos of Tent City—site of the voting rights case that had brought Withers and Lawrence together—from an organization called the Southern Conference Educational Fund. He had sent the photos and received a check for thirty dollars from the SCEF. Nobody said anything to him about publishing the photos in the *Worker.*[9]

Lawrence and Withers discussed the mishap and turned to a person there who fit their definition of interesting.

Jim Forman, at thirty-three, was an activist at large, showing up wherever racial tension simmered. Withers had met him twice. At Little Rock in 1958, Forman had carried a *Chicago Defender* press credential (which Withers thought might be fraudulent) and traveled with a suspected Red, Louis Burnham of the *National Guardian.* And at Tent City in the fall of 1960, Forman had delivered food and clothing on behalf of the Chicago Emergency Relief Committee for Fayette County.

Withers, as his reporting to Lawrence attests, mistrusted outsiders who intervened in local civil rights issues. He saw a distinction between his own activity as a photojournalist, observing and recording events, and Forman's efforts to influence events. A local movement could transform the country, as it had in Montgomery and Tent City.

But outsiders might come into a situation for publicity, without knowing the local dynamics, and create trouble that locals would ultimately have to deal with.

Forman appeared in Memphis in the late summer of 1961. Withers chatted with him, figured out where he was staying locally, and paid attention to him. Forman didn't strike Withers as Communist material.

But Forman, he learned, had recently associated with a dangerous person in Monroe, North Carolina. Monroe's NAACP leader, Robert Williams, had allegedly visited Fidel Castro in Cuba and advocated violence to desegregate the South. What would Williams's next move be? Withers pressed Forman, who replied that he planned to head right back to North Carolina to take part in a protest with Williams. Withers asked about details, but Forman evaded—Withers asked too many questions. Withers let it go and passed along what he had to Lawrence.[10]

Lawrence asked Withers to get pictures of Forman. He soon delivered seven prints of a photo he'd taken of Forman the previous year in Tent City. Lawrence paid him a dollar apiece for the images and sent them to other bureau offices, "since it appears Foreman [sic] is a racial agitator who has a propensity for appearing on the scene of many racial controversies."[11]

While Withers secretly provided investigative information, he also offered important perspectives that an FBI agent otherwise lacked. In late 1961 he told Lawrence about a positive shift in African-American public opinion regarding the Memphis police commissioner, Claude Armour. The integration of public schools in October "elated" the community, he reported. Citizens appreciated the impartial, businesslike manner in which officers had handled the assignment.[12] He channeled this sort of information to positively reinforce civil rights gains and help clear a path toward future advances.

Withers took it upon himself to deepen his background knowledge of civil rights tactics and leaders. He studied law journal articles about sit-ins and scoured out-of-town newspapers for impactful race developments. He offered Lawrence not only raw data on individuals of interest but also broader context based on his own research. He became a high-functioning intelligence gatherer who took his informant work seriously. More than a desire for money seemed to motivate him, though he definitely kept the information—and the resulting cash—flowing. The records show no evidence that he used his access to the bureau to grind any personal ax or get anyone in trouble.

Far more than his study of law journals, however, Withers's position on the street kept him in the right place to catch new developments on their way up. Criminal activity swirled around him.

13

ACROSS BEALE STREET FROM ERNEST WITHERS PHO-
tography stood Bernice's Beauty Shop.

Owner Bernice Nichols employed her daughter, while
three other ladies rented chairs in the salon. To support
her staff of hairdressers, Nichols hired her young nephew
Nathaniel Lewis, who went by the name Pedro.

"I went down there as an errand person," Pedro recalled,
"going to Vogue Beauty Supply at Second and Beale every
day to get tint, shampoo, peroxide, anything that the shop
needed. I would go down to Banner Laundry across from
Church's Park and pick up the uniforms for the women
who worked in the shop—my auntie, her daughter, and the
ladies who rented booths. Drop off the uniforms from yesterday and pick up the fresh uniforms for today. I was eighteen at the time."[1]

Pedro, born in 1943, had grown up in one of the many
insular sections of South Memphis. He and his clique sang
doo-wop under the streetlights and brawled with rival
neighborhood sets. He felt the urge to go farther.

His aunt assured him he'd find something else on Beale

Street. "From police to prisoners, everything stops at the beauty shop," Bernice said.

Bernice's Beauty Shop opened new worlds to Pedro. After finishing his morning chores, he headed back out. "I would go over by the poolroom and begin to move around the district," he recalled. "I went down Third Street, over to Vance, but Beale Street had so much to offer, you didn't stray far. I coasted along, meeting hustlers, learning the layout, where the wino corner was, and seeing the guys dressed a little better on the opposite corner. Over at the poolroom were the guys in alpaca sweaters and tailor-made pants. You had to start off on the wino corner, because you weren't allowed in the pimps' and hustlers' setting."

The guys in alpaca sweaters soon recognized Pedro as their kind. "I started this thing on Beale, selling 'blossom,'" he said. "I made a concoction out of Asthmador cigarettes. They smell close kin to weed." Asthmador was an herbal cigarette made of dried green leaves, marketed to treat asthma, and readily available at the pharmacy by Bernice's.

"When I used to clean my weed, I would save the seeds and mix it with the Asthmador," he said. He packed this "blossom" into a small manila envelope, the kind popular among Beale Street pot dealers. "We called that a nigger nickel, because white folks would never use a bag that small. So it was better shopping with them, in that regard." He told customers, "It's five for one bag, but I've only got two left, so just give me eight for both."

From there, Pedro recalled, "a lot of people that came

in and out of the beauty shop took me under their wing. I knew how to align myself with those who knew their way. Where they were accepted, I was accepted. It's like a hustlers' club, somebody have to invite you in."

This hustlers' club was no mere metaphor or state of mind. The institution that honed Pedro's skills on Beale Street in the early 1960s had ancestry in Elizabethan England, as documented by the Recorder of the City of London in 1585.

> There was a school set up to learn young boys to cut purses. There were hung up two devices, the one was a pocket, the other was a purse. The pocket had in it certain counters and was hung about with hawks' bells, and over the top did hang a little sacring bell; and he that could take out a counter without any noise was allowed to be a Public Foister; and he that could take a piece of silver out of the purse without the noise of any of the bells, he was adjudged a Judicial Nipper.[2]

In a second-floor room above a Beale Street storefront—visible through the cloudy window of Ernest Withers's photography studio—a new generation of light-fingered magicians modernized these ancient techniques.

"You up in there where they got dummies tied up," Pedro said, "hanging off the ceiling with little bells on the dummy, where you learn to get the wallet out the dummy's pocket and keep the bell from ringing. It's like a school up there."

In another corner, scholars practiced till-tapping. "You go into a store like you getting ready to pay for something, spill your change all over, and the girl is helping pick it up," Pedro explained.

> Of course, you don't spill until she's done hit the cash register and the drawer come open. Then you spill. You always get paid if you can see her ass and elbows. That means she's bent over and you're going over in the twenty tray. Now, you don't snatch 'em up because then you going to hear that 'plunka' from that little lever that holds the money down in there. You got to know how to pull the money out. That's another thing that you practice up in the school."

Expert craps shooters demonstrated how to cup a crooked pair of dice on the inside part of the knuckles. For their turn, they picked up the fair dice being used in the game but rolled the crooked ones out of their fingers. The real skill came in snatching the rigged dice after their roll and delivering the clean dice for the next player's turn.

"It's magic!" Pedro marveled. "Look at the grace!" The level of control—from fingertips to heartbeat—had him spellbound. "That's why I use the term Beale Street University," he said. "Beale Street was like a campus, and you walk the campus with different professors. The professors were very talented in their lines of learning."

Boosters made up a critical sector of the Beale Street economy, stealing luxury goods and selling off the hot stuff to a police-protected fence, namely Hayes Riley, who resold the items, sometimes to the legitimate elites. A booster could freelance, but Hayes would make things difficult for an independent. Might as well just go along with the system.

Hayes's political ties had remained strong even after the end of the Crump machine. Back in 1954, after all the old bosses were gone, he had a dinner date with the mayor, a city commissioner, and judge made that national black news.[3]

With a professor guiding him, Pedro visited the lair known as the Sportsmen Club that Hayes Riley ran, right across Beale from the beauty shop. Here he gained acceptance into the street's players' club. Hayes not only fenced there but also hosted many of the academy graduates, pickpockets, craps shooters, and pimps.

This crew was not welcome in many of the street's other clubs. At the Flamingo Room, Cliff Miller's goon squad would chuck them out, and everybody knew Sunbeam Mitchell at Club Handy wouldn't hesitate to shoot first. A locked steel door separated the Sportsmen Club from the rest of the world. The place was exclusive. If you wanted in, you banged on the door, and someone slid open an eye slot to make sure you were a member.

Inside, a cold bottle of beer and a shot of Robitussin—*serp*, they called it—cost a dollar. Guys would sit right in the big open windows, smoking, or gather around and watch their colleagues work the street below. Pedro mocked a nodding serp head—"look at him over there suckin' his own dick."

Pedro had come to Bernice's Beauty Shop searching for alternatives to singing lamppost doo-wop and brawling under the viaducts of South Memphis. He found some. But while the underworld thrilled Pedro, he felt as marginalized there as he did in the real world. Light-skinned African Americans such as Hayes Riley had go-between power, moving freely from police and politicians on Main to the black underworld of Beale. Hayes benefited from segregation. Likewise, Pedro felt that legitimate NAACP leaders also enjoyed their power. He suspected that they lacked his incentive to truly revolutionize the city.

He wrestled with his fate and his available choices. "Why am I black?" he wondered. "Why am I going through these things?" He hated the white world's insistence that he and his family live with less. He loved his parents but pitied them for accepting the rules.

"I guess all black people, they mama worked for white folks," he said.

> They send clothes home, and Mama want you to wear them clothes Miss gave her. Miss want us to pray for her mother in the hospital. I said, "If she gets back up again, all she's going to do is treat you like a nigger. And you want to bring her back? Why don't you let God do what he's going to do? Save that prayer for yourself. We need those prayers."

Then she had to babysit them bad little white children. They call her nigger and spit in her face. They say, "I'm not doing what you say, you're just a nigger." You got to take all that insult of being less than human. Yet you want me to pattern after that?

I'd heard so much repetition—"black folks ain't nothing, you'll never be nothing, you got bad hair, you're bad people"—you never hear nothing good. Anything good was all about white folks.

Pedro pointed to the picture of Jesus hanging on the wall and asked his mother, "How can you stop suffering if a white man is your comfort?"

———•———

All the hustling outside his door didn't bother Withers. He got interested in Pedro's world as the young man's journey along Beale Street took a philosophical, political turn. In between shifts at the beauty shop and lessons at the second-floor underworld academy, Pedro encountered the Nation of Islam.

Mohammad Mosque had opened three doors down from the beauty shop in late 1960. Pedro saw the brothers selling the official Nation of Islam newspaper *Muhammad Speaks* in the middle of Beale. "Some of them, if you seemed interested and asked questions, they might start giving you a paper and some information that you did not know," he recalled.

The brothers on Beale had traveled the underworld and knew where it led. They could save Pedro the trouble of going all the way to the penitentiary to meet salvation.

"Their character was sharp," Pedro said. "I noticed a difference in the person. It gave me the desire to see myself in a different light, to see black folks actually being something." He found the brothers' message every bit as refreshing as their image. "Don't call your black sister a bitch," he heard the Islamic men say. Christianity hadn't told him that.

The brothers' insight reduced the complex problems of race to a core issue. They said:

> You inherited a religion that was designed to keep
> you in slavery, suffering, and death.
> Slave master don't live by that book.
> He expect you to live by it.
> Why should you live by it?

Pedro had navigated barrenness in the real world and the underworld. Islam showed him something else. "From this desert, I saw flowers growing," he explained. "I said, 'It must be something to this. The white man didn't do this.'"

The Nation of Islam introduced a radical idea. The black church had born, bred, fostered, and sustained the push for equal rights to this point, but black people could never fully triumph over racism through it. "Because," as Pedro said, "you were still holding on to Jerusalem Slim's hand."

Jesus, Pedro's "Jerusalem Slim," represented the most powerful psychological hook that whites had embedded into black consciousness. NOI wisdom held that the white man gave the black man religion the same way he gave Indians blankets: you had to be careful of what was in there. "Fear is nursed in your mother's milk," Pedro said. "All the fear white men instilled in black people is in the psyche." Islam provided the necessary alternative: "In Christianity, it was 'Love thy enemy.' In Islam they say 'Do unto the enemy as he do unto you.' Do like America. And what does America do? To the people that believe the Book, nonviolent people, they sic dogs on 'em, they beat the hell out of 'em, they shoot water on 'em, they cattle-prod 'em, do the worst damn things they can. America disregard 'Thou shalt not kill,'" Pedro said. "But it's a little different if you gonna fight back."

Pedro Lewis became interested in the Nation of Islam at the same time Ernest Withers began observing the group for the FBI.

⊢———✦———⊣

In a 1956 presidential cabinet briefing titled "Racial Tension and Civil Rights," FBI director J. Edgar Hoover had identified the "Muslim Cult of Islam" as one of the organizations destabilizing the social order through racial agitation. He described NOI members as "religious fanatics who claim allegiance only to Allah and whose leader is Elijah Mohammed. . . . This cult is anti–United States and violently antiwhite."

The director warned that Elijah Muhammad had dispatched members to "spread the teachings of the cult through the South."[4] And so the Nation of Islam and its chapters became the subject of an FBI security investigation.

But the NOI meant very different things to Pedro Lewis and to J. Edgar Hoover: one saw a flower in the desert, another saw a violent cult. Through his reporting on the Memphis mosque, Withers mediated between the street and the power structure.

Agents William Lawrence and Joseph Kearney had grilled Withers about the Muslims back in early 1961, when the bureau was considering enlisting him as an informant. Withers had initially evaded their questions. He called Lawrence later, though, to pass along that the NOI had a new meeting place. Withers said he couldn't talk long but would get back in touch soon. In the years to come, Withers would provide a steady flow of information about NOI to the FBI. His observations countered Director Hoover's harsh view of the group.

Withers told Agent Lawrence about an NOI member who made a positive transformation, from a "Beale Street character," with a long rap sheet, to a neatly dressed, devout member, selling papers outside the photo studio. He described an NOI brother visiting Memphis from Little Rock as "very dedicated and clean-cut."[5] Withers could easily have accused the visitor of fomenting hatred and advocating violent uprising—nobody would have known—and thereby caused the young Muslim trouble.

Yet another temple member was a janitor who spent his free time in the public library researching the Muslim faith, Mecca, and Egyptian history, becoming quite well versed in these subjects.

Withers described a local NOI minister as ingratiating, friendly, and dedicated, a man who worked construction, gave his boss a good day's work, didn't preach NOI on the job, and got along well. The minister told Withers he didn't even truly hate white people or advocate fighting them but needed to keep the rhetoric in his sermons flying to ensure the interest and enthusiasm of the flock.[6] He asked Withers to join, but the photographer replied that such an affiliation would be bad for business. The minister said he understood.

Withers promised he'd do nothing to hurt the NOI and would help when he could.[7] He allowed some of the brothers to store their inventory of their newspaper, *Muhammad Speaks*, in his studio. The storefront also hosted many lengthy discussions about Islam, risking Withers's reputation in the community but ingratiating himself to a group that was of federal interest.

He noted how Muslim women walked up the street in the afternoon, past his office toward the mosque, backs straight, heads high, dressed in full-length gowns and turban-like head scarves. In early 1964 he turned over to the FBI an NOI tract that stated, "True Muslims are soft spoken and impeccably dressed, well groomed, serious faced, do not advocate violence, do not smoke or drink. We are taught to love our woman and not to get drunk or beat her; moreover, to respect and protect her because the Negro woman is the most beautiful woman there is on earth."[8]

The Nation of Islam addressed a sense of crisis within the crisis. Pedro felt scorned and rebuked within American society but lacked connections either to church or to professional-class civil rights groups. Not only did he have needs that neither Jesus nor the NAACP met, he doubted that these entities could alleviate the poverty and violence that shook his world. With Ernest Withers and the FBI paying close attention, the militant NOI message of black independence from the white world would reverberate throughout the 1960s, helping to push the race discussion from desegregation to Black Power.

14

ON THE MORNING OF OCTOBER 1, 1962, ERNEST WITH-
ers met up with James Meredith at the Memphis home of
Meredith's attorney, A. W. Willis. It was the first day of
fall classes at the University of Mississippi, where Meredith
had enrolled as the school's first black student.

A riot had broken out at Ole Miss the night before, as a
thousand students and outsiders violently protested Meredith's enrollment and arrival on campus. Two people per-
ished, including journalist Paul Guihard of the Agence
France-Presse.

Meredith and Willis rode out of Memphis toward Ole
Miss, seventy-five miles southwest in the town of Oxford.
Withers and journalist Larry Steele followed one car behind.
As the caravan crossed the state line into Mississippi, a
highway patrol vehicle jumped on Willis's tail. "I prayed,"
Withers recalled. "I never prayed so much in all my life."[1]

FBI agents and National Guard stood at the entrance to
the university. Withers took some pictures, and his reporter
colleague took some notes. Withers, explaining that he had
achieved the goal of seeing Meredith set foot on campus,

didn't stick around: "We came in to prove that he was here and got the 'h' out."

In the aftermath of the Ole Miss riot, Withers reunited with another protégé of L. Alex Wilson. Dorothy Gilliam had worked at the *Tri-State Defender* around the time of the Little Rock Nine and later become the first African-American female reporter at the *Washington Post*. "All hell was breaking out in Mississippi," Gilliam recalled. "The *Post* sent me down to see what the mood was in the black community." She drafted Withers for help. "I knew [he] knew how to negotiate," she said.[2] She also liked that Withers had Tennessee license plates on his car, believing that Northern tags brought unwanted attention.

Withers and Gilliam visited Medgar Evers, the state's NAACP field secretary and a veteran of many Mississippi battles. Withers had met Evers nearly eight years before, when Evers led the search for witnesses to the slaying of Emmett Till. Evers had also spearheaded the mission to relocate witnesses to Chicago who'd risked their safety by testifying against the suspects.

Now, despite the Ole Miss riot, Evers promised that African Americans would apply to the state's other segregated universities. "We don't intend to let this thing fizzle with Meredith," he told Gilliam.[3]

But the violence in Mississippi didn't fizzle either. Eight months later Evers was dead.

As one news organization attested in an obituary, Evers had survived the Allied landing at Normandy, only to fall mortally wounded in front of his home, while carrying a batch of JIM CROW MUST GO T-shirts.

———◆———

On June 15, 1963, three days after Evers's death, Withers traveled from Memphis to Jackson, Mississippi, to cover the leader's last rites. He brought his son Perry and his editor, Thaddeus Stokes, of the *Tri-State Defender*. At the funeral, Withers captured a sorrowful moment as Evers's widow Myrlie braced their son with an arm around his shoulders and absorbed the little boy's tears into her handkerchief.

At the conclusion of the funeral, an announcement came that the City of Jackson had issued a permit for mourners to march from the Masonic temple, where the service took place, to the funeral home that would prepare Evers's casket for shipment to Arlington National Cemetery. Withers, along with his son and his editor, followed the cortege. Thousands marched two miles in one-hundred-degree heat behind the hearse, past silent police dressed like soldiers on the sidewalks.

After the casket reached the funeral home, a few hundred marchers turned around and headed back the way they'd come. People sang freedom songs and danced.

Three blocks south of the funeral home, at an intersection the marchers had just passed without trouble going the other way, they encountered a barricade of policemen standing side by side in shiny hard hats, with shotguns shouldered.

The permit had legally allowed the march to proceed only from the Evers funeral to the funeral home, and after that, the march became illegal. The police might have let it go. Instead, they initiated a standoff with the marchers.

The show of force outraged many of the mourners. They'd just bade farewell to a vital, young leader cut down by gunfire. The main column of marchers stood still, staring ahead at the police line. A few moved ahead tentatively. "I could hear the dogs barking," Withers recalled.[4]

Two large army transport vehicles backed up behind the police barricade. Withers wondered if soldiers were arriving.

A few young women danced toward the officers, jeered, and taunted, "You gonna shoot me?" "Go on and shoot me!"

The mourners began chanting, "Shoot—shoot—shoot!"

Bricks and bottles flew at the police barricade. "Then the officers started grabbing the demonstrators who were out in the street and began beating and kicking them and pushing them toward the trucks," Withers recalled.

A crowd of onlookers had gathered on the sidewalk. A white man lunged through the police barricade toward the marchers, wielding a long-bladed knife. Withers took pictures—"All of the time I was standing on the sidewalk, photographing one horrible scene after the other amidst the screams."

A burly white man from the crowd entered the fray. He threw Withers off the sidewalk, into the street, knocking off a piece of his Mamiyaflex camera, which consisted of a boxy rectangular body with two short lenses. As he reached down to recover his equipment, he felt the thump of a nightstick. He tried to step away, but each step led from one nightstick blow led to another. His ribs ached, and a knot swelled on his forehead.

From the sidewalk, Withers's son Perry watched in horror as his father flashed into view, absorbed a nightstick blow, and disappeared again into the melee. Perry climbed a telephone pole for a better view.

Two policemen grabbed Withers under his arms and hoisted him into the back of one of the big green transport trucks.

Withers climbed in, pressed his handkerchief to his forehead, and felt it stick to the skin. He pulled off the cloth and saw it stained with blood. "As a news photographer," he would write, "I have covered numerous racial incidents in the South, which began with the Emmett Till trial. . . . But it was only following the Medgar Evers funeral in Jackson, Miss., that I shed my first drops of blood in the line of duty."[5]

Out in the street, the crowd moved back from the police, while attorney John Doar explained to those who could hear that he had come from the Department of Justice to observe the march. "And anybody around here knows that I stand for what's right," Doar reportedly said. "You can't win with bricks and bottles." He asked the mourners to peacefully disperse, and they did.[6]

The police continued to throw men, women, shoes, and

handbags into the green transport truck. It sped away, with Withers and fifteen or so other people inside. The driver made abrupt stops and sudden starts, shaking up the passengers.

Next to Withers stood a college professor, John Salter, a veteran of Jackson demonstrations. Withers asked him if he had a smoke. Salter took out a fresh pack of Pall Malls and handed several to a grateful Withers.[7]

A woman near Withers said she suspected the police had arrested him for photographing their application of the nightstick and would confiscate his film. The police wouldn't search a female, she said, and suggested he give his film to a woman for safekeeping. He handed his rolls to a young lady in a white dress.

The rough transport arrived at the city fairgrounds, and the police hustled the prisoners into a stockade. One of the cops yelled, "All right, we want this nigger photographer to come on out."[8]

Withers stepped forward and was asked, "What did you do with the film?"

He said he'd lost it in the street scuffle, but the cop replied, "We know you gave it to one of them nigger women."

Withers said he didn't know anyone on the truck.

The cop announced, "We'll search all of these nigger women till we find it." With the prisoners crowded into a pen for booking, the police called over an African-American woman in a blue uniform to pat down the females, while one of the officers thoroughly searched Withers in front of everyone.

The policewoman discovered Withers's film hidden on the woman in white. The police charged him with disturbing the peace and transported everyone downtown to jail.

At suppertime, the prisoners were fed, "and I observed that the food was better seasoned than it had been in Memphis jails," Withers said.[9] Meanwhile his editor Thaddeus Stokes called a Jackson police official, vouching that the photographer was a credentialed newsman and not a street protester. He sprung Withers, who escaped the incident without charges.

On the way out, Withers retrieved his film. It had been exposed, destroying the pictures of the police and their riot batons. Withers had been on the assignment for black papers in Cleveland, Baltimore, and New York, in addition to the *Defender* publications. The loss of the two film rolls deprived major segments of the black population of objective coverage of an important moment.

When he got home, Withers cleaned his forehead wound with witch hazel. He didn't plan on filing charges or taking any action beyond telling his story to the local *Defender*.

Six days after Withers's arrest, President Kennedy convened a White House meeting to stimulate discussion of creative solutions to civil rights issues. One of the participants was Memphis attorney Russell Sugarmon, who had helped to organize a Memphis branch of the Kennedy Club, the grassroots organization that helped convert

African-American voters, including Ernest Withers, to the Democratic Party, as the Republicans shed their ideological connections to the Party of Lincoln.

Three days after Sugarmon met with Kennedy, Withers showed up at the Memphis FBI office to register a complaint. He explained to Agent Lawrence that he wouldn't be complaining except that his attorney, Sugarmon, advised him to do so after returning from the Kennedy meeting.

In his statement to Lawrence, Withers described the ambush-style arrest of Jackson demonstrators: "The police shoved and pushed the arrestees, and I saw several instances where the police . . . hit the arrestees with billy clubs as they herded them onto the trucks. I took pictures of these arrests."[10]

He had not willingly joined the fracas, he explained, but had needed to retrieve a piece of his camera that had broken off and landed in the street.

Lawrence immediately sent a memo to Director Hoover's office, detailing Withers's story and emphasizing the seizure and destruction of the film.

By this time, Withers showed little physical evidence of the beating, other than a swollen spot behind his left ear. Lawrence took color pictures of Withers straight on and of the small bump on his head and sent the negatives to the director's office, with a request that the DOJ's civil rights division receive copies of developed pictures. The next day Perry Withers and Thaddeus Stokes gave Lawrence statements that corroborated Withers's account of events.

The Withers case offered a new and different legal challenge: the exposure of his film looked like a potential violation of his First Amendment rights, a federal crime. The case also exposed the challenge of finding justice in a department divided between the civil rights division and Hoover's FBI. Attorney General Robert F. Kennedy, head of the DOJ, loathed and feared yet enabled his subordinate, Hoover. Withers's case attracted the attention of high-powered Civil Rights Division attorney Burke Marshall, a colleague of John Doar, who'd helped disperse the Jackson standoff. Like Doar, Marshall was understood to be a civil rights sympathizer.

Hoover's office carefully instructed the FBI New Orleans special agent in charge to investigate Withers's First Amendment case. The office made it clear that Marshall—not Hoover—wanted to know whether the arrest of Ernest Withers occurred "because he was taking photographs or . . . he was believed to be a demonstrator."

Two New Orleans special agents met with the Jackson assistant chief of police who'd released Withers. He claimed to have no knowledge of film or photographs belonging to Withers and said he never ordered officers to expose seized film.

The Jackson police officials interviewed during the investigation contradicted the accounts of Withers, his son, and his editor almost entirely.

John Salter, the activist who gave Withers cigarettes in the paddy wagon, recalled that contrary to the law enforcement version, "standard police practice [for] anyone, other than police agents, photographing anything in a demonstration context was to either seize and break the camera or to seize it and take the film."[11]

Another Jackson police official said he had seen the arrest personally and that the officers didn't beat or mistreat Withers in any way. The mass arrests had taken place upon the refusal of street protesters to disperse.

The U.S. attorney at Jackson thought the case had no prosecutive merit and the investigation should cease. As for Withers's exposed film—proof of a First Amendment suppression—Agent Lawrence seems not to have logged it, thus disregarding potential evidence. In a photo of Withers accompanying the *Defender* story of his arrest, he holds two unwound rolls of film in his hand, identified in the caption as "deliberately exposed."

———•———

Nothing about the Jackson episode hindered Withers's intelligence gathering.

That fall Marjory Collins, a freelance photographer and writer, came through Memphis and got in touch with Withers to see his photographs of Tent City. She said she'd been in Fayette and Haywood counties doing research, on assignment for the *Southern Patriot*, a monthly publication of the suspected Communist front SCEF.

Withers reported on her visit to Lawrence. She had a

press card for the *National Guardian*, Withers said, another publication long associated with Communism that had just as long attracted the interest of the FBI. And while in Memphis, she contacted SCEF by phone.

She carried a letter containing suggestions about who in Memphis might help her. (From the pertinent FBI report, it is not clear how Withers learned about the letter or how Lawrence obtained a verbatim copy.) Also in Collins's possession was a pamphlet about the projected expansion of a program called Operation Freedom from Tennessee into Mississippi. It mentioned various Mississippi Delta racial leaders, whose personality characteristics, educational backgrounds, and financial resources and relationships Withers described to Lawrence. He also let Lawrence know that Collins stored her personal belongings in a locker at the Memphis bus depot.

When Collins parted, Withers asked her to keep in touch, and she obliged, sending word from New Orleans, which Withers passed along to Lawrence.[12]

At Lawrence's urging, Withers obtained a press card identifying himself as a contributor to the *Southern Patriot*, the SCEF monthly. He wrote to SCEF for the latest issue of *Patriot* and other printed material it published. SCEF sent Withers its annual plan and financial information for the coming year of 1964, including the names of field staff, which ended up with the FBI. One of them happened to be the man who had given Withers the Pall Malls in the paddy wagon in Jackson.[13]

15

THOUGH HE WAS NOT YET THIRTY-FIVE YEARS OLD, REV.
James Lawson came to Memphis in 1962 as a distinguished character in the nation's civil rights struggle. He moved to the city to pastor the Centenary Methodist Church.

Born in Uniontown, Pennsylvania, in 1928, Lawson grew up in Ohio, son and grandson of Methodist ministers. During the Korean War, he could have filed a clergy deferment to spare himself from the draft, but he refused and served a penitentiary sentence for violating the Selective Service Act. Following his parole in 1952, he spent the next three years in India doing missionary work, where he learned of Gandhi's peaceful civil disobedience tactics. He came to believe, as had Gandhi, in confrontations with injustice through strikes, boycotts, marches, fasts, mass civil disobedience, and imprisonment.

Lawson returned to America and came south to study divinity at Vanderbilt University. In Nashville, he led workshops on nonviolent resistance. His pupils organized early sit-ins. The university learned of this activity and expelled him. A 1960 *New Republic* profile highlighted Lawson's "considerable hardheaded calculation."[1]

Dr. Martin Luther King, Jr., referred to Lawson as the country's leading nonviolence theoretician and gave Lawson a planning role in the Southern Christian Leadership Conference. Lawson also helped form the Student Nonviolent Coordinating Committee, thereby having prominent positions in two of the major 1960s civil rights organizations.

Upon his arrival in Memphis, Lawson immediately drew Withers's attention. Withers had previously clipped articles about the 1960 Nashville sit-in movement for his background research. To Agent Lawrence, Withers described Lawson as "a self-admitted advocate of non-violence in the campaign for full Negro equality [who] has studied this special type discipline in India."[2]

Lawson struck Withers as a bad fit for Memphis. Where the typical Southern preacher was charismatic, Lawson was intellectual. Where the typical Southerner spoke in broad allegorical terms, Lawson could be clipped, direct, and even cold. He was the ultimate outsider—scholarly and Northern, aggressively pacifist.

Lawson's new congregation, in Withers's view, was a conservative bunch. His personality might suit their Methodist sense of calm professionalism, but his activism had the potential to run afoul of his flock and the city. He cared nothing for the nonconfrontational Memphis civil rights tactics. "Lawson is in favor of as many mass racial protests as possible," Agent Lawrence summarized, "despite the fact that the local NAACP leadership is more conservative and is generally averse to demonstrations."[3]

The Memphis NAACP had built itself into the largest branch in the South. After sponsoring a few sit-ins and marches in 1960, the leadership had shifted away from pressure tactics toward negotiation. These consistent, reliable professionals organized the city's African-American voters, opened up downtown stores to black customers, desegregated some of the public schools, and maintained a clean, Communist-free machine. They felt suspicious about protests. Memphis had developed a style of negotiated, gradual desegregation that credited both the white and the black establishments. The director of police could remark, with unintentional clairvoyance, "We don't have a division between races here like in many other southern cities. We have been able to solve our problems without blood flowing in the street. Not one drop of blood has been shed here. Someday it will go down in history how Memphis solved its racial problems."[4]

A year into Lawson's time in Memphis, Withers called him a possible "thorn in the side" of the local civil rights establishment. The NAACP had made him a board member, but he spoke his own mind. He criticized one leader for stifling a protest of the white Cotton Carnival celebration of Southern heritage, and when the police dogs and fire hoses broke loose in Birmingham, he pushed the NAACP to organize sympathy demonstrations. His impatience resonated with African Americans who felt left out of decision making, both in their movement and society at large.

On top of Lawson's tactical and strategic differences with the local NAACP, the minister had a possible ideological problem. When photojournalist Marjory Collins visited Withers's studio, she had carried a letter from *Southern Patriot* publishers Carl and Anne Braden, who were suspected Communists. Their letter listed several people who might help Collins on her research assignment, including that of Rev. James Lawson—"one of the most articulate spokesmen in the South on non-violence."

In March 1964 Withers arranged a meeting between visiting journalists and local civil rights leaders. He introduced the journalists to local NAACP president Jesse Turner and to Lawson. At this meeting Withers, and hence the local FBI, learned about Lawson's weekly classes on nonviolent demonstration tactics.[5] Lawson was doing in Memphis what he had done in Nashville—preparing the people for conflict.

———◆———

Around this time the West Tennessee Voters' Project—or in FBI parlance, "the Communist-infiltrated WTVP"— a new organization of outsiders, traveled to Tent City for civil rights activity. Its members were undergraduates, graduate students, and professors from Northern universities, especially Wisconsin and Cornell. They came through Memphis and conferred with local NAACP activists.

They met Withers too and felt connected to him, as he appeared to be sympathetic. He affected a casual appearance. His hair could get shaggy, his glasses were horn-rims, and he dressed not exactly to impress. He never had the newest car and sometimes went without, bumming rides downtown to work. As a photographer, he could pass for a starving artist, and his résumé meant no one could question his importance to the movement. He didn't have to say anything—his pictures told the story. He blended in with them, and they blended with him.

He allowed them to stay in his studio, which he decorated in sympathy with their causes. WTVP members asked him about potential financial donors, while he picked up information about their plans.

They invited Withers to photograph their events, hoping he could place the photos in *Jet* magazine. They even offered to pay for his film.[6] His photos of them appeared in the local *Tri-State Defender*, but many more ended up with the local FBI.

Agent Lawrence even sent three of Withers's shots to the personal attention of William C. Sullivan, FBI assistant director and head of racial intelligence, at the bureau in Washington. His memo specifically credited "Ernest C. Withers, Confidential Source . . . who has gained the confidence of the WTVP workers." The three photos showed "a virtual illiterate Negro tenant farmer . . . who the white project workers established as the 'Chief Administrator' of the WTVP," a white leader of the WTVP "holding on his lap a young . . . Negro girl," and a white attorney from the civil rights division of the Department of Justice. "I thought these photographs would be of personal interest to you," Lawrence wrote to Sullivan.[7]

At a celebration in Memphis following a freedom march in Brownsville, Withers observed several white students and professors from the North having fun with the young African Americans from the rural Tent City area. It looked like unsustainable social chaos to him. He didn't think the outsiders understood how naïve and dangerously impressionable the young people they were trying to help were. He also knew that young rural African Americans shouldn't expect life with white people to be full of college girls ready to party.

The episode inflamed his sense of responsibility for gradual social change. He told Agent Lawrence that the outsiders played on "local teen-age Negroes who get a thrill out of marches, demonstrations, and picketing, and further get a sexual thrill out of being able to freely intermix with these white college students."

Lawrence, for his part, reported that Withers "fears that many of these young Negroes will get a distorted view of society and are engaging in and experiencing a socialistic-oriented 'beatnik' type experience for which they are educationally, emotionally, and culturally ill-equipped to deal."[8]

The bureau tailed WTVP outsiders to the home art gallery of Mary Chilton (where Big Star lead singer Alex Chilton grew up), which law enforcement circles knew as "a 'hang out' for both male and female homosexuals and Lesbians." Lawrence further warned, "There have been some inter-racial parties at this address in the past."[9]

Withers secretly compiled private information on WTVP members. One volunteer took some pictures and sent the film for Withers to develop, not knowing that Withers would, in Lawrence's words, "confidentially make copies for the FBI."[10]

A WTVP activist from Madison, Wisconsin, wrote to Withers,

> Dear Ernie,
> I'm looking at your card now and it says, "Pictures Tell The Story," and I remember that spread you had in your office of that guy who was killed in Viet Nam. . . . But, I did not write to talk about that . . . I wrote to ask if you could send me two or three copies of the picture you took of me sitting on the steps of the Freedom House in Somerville. Do you remember . . . the one you had hung up on your wall?

Withers handed over this letter—signed "Yours in Freedom"—and the photo of its writer to Agent Lawrence. He sent the photo to the activist as well, asking for news about the voters project.[11]

Withers developed lewd information on WTVP activists. He told Agent Lawrence about one young local African-American man who "exposed his privates in front of a group of white women" during a march. The young man told Withers that "he did not know why he had done this, that he had an uncontrollable impulse to do this."[12] Withers subsequently turned over a photo showing a young white female with her arm around this young man.[13]

He reported to Lawrence that he had heard an organizer lament that "some of the white female volunteers had as their predominant motivation that of seeking sex." One female student, he wrote, had been "openly promiscuous with several young Negro and white . . . workers in Fayette County," while "others too had to go home prematurely for this same reason."

A leader of the WTVP, whom Withers had primed, confirmed that many Northern college students "were more interested in seeking out inter-racial sexual experiences than in doing legitimate volunteer work. He said these people were indiscreet and their actions hurt the WTVP."[14]

———◆———

Soon after Withers's "beatnik-type experience" at the WTVP party, days of nationwide protest were held against U.S. policy in Vietnam.

Agent Lawrence thought that "if any one person in Memphis might participate it would be Rev. James Morris Lawson, Jr., since he is an avowed pacifist and made a trip to Vietnam in June, 1965." Lawson's trip had been sponsored by the Fellowship of Reconciliation. He had written a report and told Withers he'd mail a copy to him. Withers, Lawrence noted, "in turn will make it available to this office."

On the morning of the first day of the protest, Withers called Lawson to find out about plans to demonstrate against the war in Memphis. Lawson said he knew of none.

Agent Lawrence noted, "Withers said many leading Negroes fear Lawson, feeling that he is too outspoken and too prone to criticize the U.S., but can do nothing to get him to leave Memphis."[16]

16

MEMPHIS'S FIRST MARCH AGAINST U.S. POLICY IN VIET-
nam was to take place on Saturday, April 23, 1966. It would
commence at noon with a five-mile walk across the city to
the main post office, where participants would mail antiwar
letters to elected officials.

Agent Lawrence asked Withers to cover it. The photographer agreed, saying he could mix in like a newsman on
the job. He'd photograph every participant in the march, he
said, with good facial views for solid identification.[1]

Lawrence himself showed up to observe, probably in a
car at some distance. He saw Withers arrive over a half-
hour before start time. As the five-mile walk began, Withers
moved through the crowd taking pictures. Lawrence marveled at his skill. Withers even convinced a couple of kids
from a college newspaper to lug his equipment along the
route.

Rev. James Lawson got out of a car and joined the march,
distributing flyers detailing reasons to oppose the war. He
seemed to feel comfortable with the ubiquitous photographer, confiding to Withers, as they walked downtown, that

the march had been his doing, though numerous organizations sponsored the event and shared credit.

All the while, Withers memorized the names of the people he photographed. He even noted the make and license plate number on a car of supporters who cheered the marchers at one corner. His productive afternoon continued as the publishers of a subversive underground newsletter invited him to their secret headquarters.

Sometime after one-thirty, the demonstrators arrived at the downtown post office and mailed their letters. Even with the march over, Withers and Lawrence stayed to observe discussions taking place around the demonstration, and to see how marchers interacted with bystanders.

Afterward Withers contacted Maxine Smith, executive secretary of the NAACP in Memphis, to gauge the branch's outlook on the antiwar movement. Smith said the local NAACP had opposed it and forbade its young members to participate. The organization as a whole purposefully refused to get involved with the war in one way or another.

Withers asked Smith about the branch's most controversial member. She said she couldn't influence James Lawson and that his statements didn't reflect NAACP thought.

A few days later Withers delivered to Agent Lawrence eighty eight-by-ten photos that he had taken during the march, with thirty-three participants identified.

The informant expressed outrage at the marchers' anti-American statements, their arrogance and mannerisms.

Furthermore, those beatniks were lucky the cops were there—they would have gotten beat up without police protection.

The U.S. Army had taught Ernest Withers his trade, and he had become an independent businessman thanks to the GI Bill. He was a veteran of World War II. His father was a veteran of World War I. His great-grandfather had worn blue in the Civil War. Soon his three eldest sons would all be in the U.S. Army. Whatever combination of cash and anti-Communism had motivated Withers's espionage up until now, the antiwar movement made it personal.

Withers's views of the counterculture are echoed in a J. Edgar Hoover column published in the FBI's monthly bulletin the next February. Dangers awaited young men at institutes of higher learning, Hoover warned, among them "a turbulence built on unrestrained individualism, repulsive dress and speech, outright obscenity, disdain for moral and spiritual values, and disrespect for law and order."[2] The whole counterculture had been spawned by a Communist Party conspiracy, according to the director.

———•———

In early June 1966, an ideological shift in the national civil rights movement began when Stokely Carmichael became the new chairman of the Student Nonviolent Coordinating Committee (SNCC, pronounced *snick*).

Born in Trinidad, raised from the age of eleven in

Harlem, and educated at Howard University, Carmichael knew Mississippi well, from sharecropper hovels in the Delta to the inside walls of the state penitentiary. Arrested as a Freedom Rider in 1961, he had spent his twentieth birthday in the state's notorious Parchman prison farm. Three years later, during the drive known as Freedom Summer, he had returned to the Delta to register voters. In May 1966, he'd been elected to chair SNCC over the popular incumbent, twenty-four-year-old John Lewis.

He took over an organization in transition. Late the next year, Lewis would speak in Memphis, where Withers heard him explain that he had resigned from SNCC because key organization people were chanting for violence.[3]

SNCC had grown out of the sit-in movement of the early 1960s and developed an extensive grassroots network of civil rights activists throughout the South. SNCC leadership had operated Quaker style, allowing consensus to arise through deliberation. In strategy, the group had distinguished itself from other organizations by focusing on empowering African-American individuals rather than pushing for integration or top-down social change.

Carmichael began to question nonviolence while being beaten in prison. When President Johnson refused to seat the grassroots Mississippi Freedom delegation at the 1964 Democratic National Convention, he and other SNCC organizers lost faith in the federal government. In 1965, brutality against activists marching from Selma, Alabama, to Montgomery further disillusioned SNCC. The group moved away from seeking integration as its primary goal and wavered on the tactic of nonviolence. Compared to the NAACP and King's SCLC, SNCC had been seen as the "youth" civil rights vehicle, sometimes working in conjunction with the "professional" or "adult" establishment groups.

In early 1966, just before its members elected Carmichael, SNCC further distanced itself from the mainstream with its most controversial stance—opposition to the Vietnam war. SNCC likened the senseless killing in Southeast Asia to the murder of one of its volunteers who'd been shot to death while attempting to integrate a gas station. Carmichael, whose personal and philosophical journeys matched those of the organization, seemed the perfect leader to take SNCC in a new direction.

Less than a month into Carmichael's tenure, James Meredith started the March Against Fear. The man who'd integrated the University of Mississippi in 1962 would travel on foot through his home state to encourage African-American voter registration and prove that black people needn't be afraid to stand up for their rights. On the second day of the demonstration, Meredith was shot and wounded.

Carmichael and two SNCC officials, traveling by car in the South, went to Memphis to visit Meredith in the hospital. They felt "tired of folks being brutalized or killed with impunity," Carmichael recalled. "Tired of the indifference and complicity of the nation. Tired of mealy-mouthed politicians. Tired too especially of half-baked, knee-jerk ideas from our side. Particularly of these wretched, pointless marches, appealing to whom? Accomplishing what? What we felt . . . was an all-encompassing anger and frustration, as much with movement futility as with racist violence."[4]

Despite this frustration, Carmichael saw potential in picking up the march where Meredith had fallen. "I wanted this march to *demonstrate* the new SNCC approach in action," he later wrote. "We wouldn't just *talk* about empowerment, about black communities controlling their political destinies. . . . We would *demonstrate* it."[5]

Carmichael and SNCC wouldn't have to hike down the highway alone. Dr. King also pledged to pick up Meredith's mission. On June 7 Carmichael and King linked arms, along with Floyd McKissick, head of the Congress of Racial Equality (CORE), and began to march down Mississippi highway 51.

No more than fifty yards into the trek, McKissick, King, and Carmichael encountered three Mississippi Highway Patrol officers. "Get off the highway," one of the troopers shouted. "We don't care if you march, but do it on the shoulder."

King said, "In Selma, we marched on the pavement."

"But you had a permit," the trooper countered. "We don't care if you march to New Orleans, but get off the pavement."

The civil rights leaders and the state troopers pushed and shoved each other, getting their arms and legs tangled up. The troopers forced King and Carmichael off the road. When the two tried to walk back onto the pavement, one of the troopers placed his hand on his holster. King reportedly asked other marchers to physically restrain Carmichael, saying, "Get Stokely, get Stokely!" Carmichael lay flat on the pavement with several people on top of him until he, and the situation, cooled off.

King convened a quick meeting near the shade of a road-side ice cream stand. Then the marchers continued their journey, sticking to the shoulder. They walked "through mud and high grass," according to a reporter, for another six miles. The march dispersed, and Carmichael, King, and the others rode back to Memphis in cars.[6]

Ernest Withers had marched with them that morning, along with Lawson. A photograph shows the pair walking one row ahead of King and Carmichael.

That afternoon the photographer stood in room 307 of the Lorraine Motel, a black-owned establishment just off the grungy, industrial south end of Main Street. The room overlooked the motel parking lot from the second-floor balcony. Dr. King reclined on a twin bed as Withers took pictures. King held up the afternoon paper, emblazoned with a headline announcing his place at the head of the march.

Withers followed King and Carmichael to Centenary Methodist, Lawson's church. He photographed the men as they relaxed in the basement, Carmichael sipping a Coke.

That night, in an address to six hundred people, Carmichael fumed not about Meredith but about Vietnam. "If I was a white man with a million dollars, I'd be fighting in Vietnam because then capitalism would mean something to me." Instead, Carmichael intoned, "I'm poor, and capitalism means nothing to me, and I'm not going [to Vietnam]. Every black brother and every black cousin and every black uncle should come home now and fight here because here is where the fight is." He grappled aloud with the central issue of his struggle: having come to the movement as a nonviolent activist, he now believed that increasingly aggressive tactics were needed. "If you don't have power, you're begging," Carmichael said. "It's time to get power that every other group has. We've got to remove them and make sure they are gone. . . . We need power."[7]

Late that night in his room at the Lorraine, King hosted a summit of civil rights leaders to collaborate on a vision for the rest of the March Against Fear. Whitney Young of the Urban League and Roy Wilkins of the NAACP had flown in. It was Carmichael's first meeting with the "big Negroes." He expected to hear them advocate the "least controversial, most conventional, media-compatible, acceptable to the establishment and administration approach possible"— exactly the approach that he wanted nothing to do with. "Could some visiting dignitaries flying in from New York to walk the last four miles and then leave help a sharecropper family overcome years of intimidation and fear?" he wondered. "Or, could a march be designed so as to give local communities the confidence to assert themselves?"

NAACP director Roy Wilkins, like his local branch leaders in Memphis, would surely champion the professional, respectable strategy, emphasizing legal challenges to segregation. He cultivated relationships with the nation's most powerful people as well as the patience that gradual change from above required. Carmichael suspected Wilkins was jealous of King and that that had motivated the NAACP's involvement in the Mississippi march. The NAACP had been the most important black organization since its founding in 1909 but had lost the spotlight since King's dramatic Selma-to-Montgomery march successfully pressured President Johnson to sign the Voting Rights Act.

Before Wilkins could set the tone of the Lorraine meeting, Carmichael launched into a broadside of tactical profanity toward the respectability-minded leader. "It was verbal abuse of the highest order," recalled Carmichael, in a 1988 interview. "We wanted to let them know it would be impossible to work with us."[8] King reportedly remained silent. Carmichael thought it was because he was amused. Ultimately, the March Against Fear would proceed without NAACP support.

Afterward Carmichael felt that Wilkins poisoned potential allies in the press and in the movement against him. Word of conflict quickly got out of King's room at the Lorraine. The FBI picked up a report that Carmichael had almost come to blows with King's right-hand man Ralph Abernathy, a leak that could have reached Agent Lawrence from any number of NAACP sources if Wilkins had had division on his mind.[9] But Carmichael wouldn't need Wilkins's help in making enemies.

Carmichael's new direction for SNCC crystallized as the March Against Fear slogged through the Mississippi heat. King came and went, tending to other commitments, but Carmichael kept marching on down the blistering road. Their numbers fluctuated and support from the establishment flagged, but Carmichael and the marchers staged voter registration efforts, held nightly rallies, and camped in public places.

Just over a week after declaring "It's time to get power," Carmichael spent six hours in a Greenwood, Mississippi, jail, locked up for assembling without permission. By the time police released him, a night rally was under way at Broad Street Park. There Carmichael sensed a spirit of self-assertion and defiance. He gazed out at field hands and shack-dwellers he'd worked with during Freedom Summer. Their valiance lifted him. "It was huge," Carmichael recalled.

And tense. Rumors circulated that Byron De La Beckwith, the man who had murdered Medgar Evers, had been deputized and was on armed patrol around the event. A local friend who'd worked in Greenwood with Carmichael during Freedom Summer told him that a sadistic cop who'd beaten her and two other women senseless was out there as well. Previous speakers at the rally had spread news of Carmichael's arrest and worked the crowd into a fever.

Stepping up on the flatbed truck that served as a stage, Carmichael passed SNCC orator Willie Ricks, who worked the crowd like a hype man and prided himself on his touch with an audience. "Drop it now," Ricks told Carmichael. "The people are ready. Drop it now."

SNCC activist Cleveland Sellers, who'd been pushed into the mud on Carmichael's first day of the march, recalled, "When Stokely moved forward to speak, the crowd greeted him with a huge roar. He acknowledged the reception with a raised arm and clenched fist."

Carmichael spoke with his trademark intensity. "The only way we gonna stop them white men from whuppin' us is to take over," he said. "We been saying freedom for six years, and we ain't got nothin'. What we gonna start saying now is Black Power!"

The crowd picked up the chant in unison: "Black Power!"

Carmichael and SNCC became synonymous with Black Power, a concept seen as encompassing independence from white society and aggressive self-defense against the violent, white supremacist counterinsurgency. Observers explained that it was a result not only of the brutality against activists but also of the failure of justice against attackers and murderers, and of the very real need for people to protect themselves where law enforcement failed.

Nevertheless, white media and law enforcement tended to perceive and portray Black Power as violent. The term "militant" stuck to Black Power advocates.

"It was nothing new," Carmichael later reflected. "We'd been talking about nothing else in the Delta for years. The only difference was that this time the national media were there. And most of them had never experienced the passion and fervor of a mass meeting before." James Meredith, for one, remarked that if he'd been carrying a gun instead of a Bible, his attacker would be dead.

Carmichael objected to how the press cast an "ideological struggle" between "Black Power" and "Freedom Now," King's slogan. But an editorialist in Memphis wrote, "The shots that felled Meredith . . . usher a new phase into the hitherto passive civil rights movement. The incident has weakened, perhaps beyond repair, the position of the advocates of passive resistance."

Black Power confused and frightened King's longtime supporters, who didn't want to be associated with the sort of violent outbreak Carmichael seemed to advocate.[10] A source with the Memphis NAACP branch hinted at widespread dissension toward Carmichael's posture, saying, "Responsible leaders of the NAACP abhor the radical extremist statements recently attributed to Carmichael . . . to the effect that they want and demand 'black power' and . . . 'the courthouses in Mississippi should be burned.'"[11]

The FBI heard discord in the movement. According to bureau intelligence, Dr. King's top adviser Stanley Levison felt that the closing rally of the March Against Fear would not be effective since civil rights had taken a backseat to Vietnam as the issue of the day. King called his inner circle together to discuss the financial woes of the march—it had run up a twenty-thousand-dollar debt, which the SCLC would have to address. Not only did SNCC have no money, but Carmichael's militancy had chilled King's fundraising efforts.[12]

Carmichael would later explain that Black Power had to do with electing black officials in majority black districts—gaining political power to fairly represent black citizens—but his true meaning got lost in the rhetorical smoke of burning courthouses.

Whatever Black Power meant, the cry soon echoed through the streets of American cities, as Carmichael's intensity resonated with African Americans whose lives remained unchanged by voting rights legislation and NAACP court victories.

Though Carmichael's statements would force King to take a stand on Black Power, the two remained firmly united on one issue: both men opposed the war in Vietnam, a stance that distanced them from the NAACP—and the FBI.

17

ERNEST WITHERS GRABBED A LEAFLET CIRCULATING right outside his office, at Handy Park on Beale Street.

> War, violence, murder and hating are the monstrous enemies of human life. Trying to cover them over with the pious mouthings of patriotism cannot cleanse them of their evil stench. . . .
>
> The war gives most Americans a chance to forget about poverty, segregation, racism, unemployment, slums, and the lack of equal opportunity. . . . Why are over 50% of the Vietnam deaths from Shelby County young and poor Negro boys? Why are we spending $30 billion in Vietnam for war and less than $3 billion to end slums and poverty here at home? . . .
>
> The American white man cannot be trusted overseas until he can be trusted in matters of prejudice, segregation, freedom, poverty, and slums here at home.

The arguments were classic Jim Lawson. The leaflet closed with three quotations. One came from Stokely Carmichael,

and one came from Dr. King, who'd publicly denounced
the war in April 1967. The third, perhaps the most poi-
gnant, was sourced to an unknown marcher in Mississippi
who'd said, "Ain't no Viet Cong ever called me a 'nigger.'"[1]

Withers vented his feelings about Lawson confidentially to his handler. He felt Lawson was climbing into "the
intellectual bed of Stokely Carmichael and Martin Luther
King, Jr., who recently gained many headlines by bitterly
attacking U.S. policy in Vietnam and urging Negroes not
to support the war."[2] On April 4, 1967, King had said, "We
have been wrong from the beginning in our adventure in
Vietnam," and named the United States "the greatest pur-
veyor of violence in the world today."[3]

By attacking the war, Withers felt, Lawson had
"demeaned himself in a most demogogic fashion," as Agent
Lawrence reported, "resorting to cheap unadulterated
demogogery [sic] and untruths in the material." To Withers, the material fell into the dangerous category of propaganda that his mentor L. Alex Wilson had warned him
about: "calculated to inflame the emotions and not the reason of the reader."

Lawson had recently appeared on a panel discussion
broadcast over local TV. A reporter asked him if he was
a Communist, and though Lawson denied party membership, he answered, "We could learn much from the Communists." That statement stuck to his FBI file entries for
years, justifying continued investigative scrutiny.

Withers was not alone in opposing King's antiwar

activism. Jackie Robinson, an influential voice in race after breaking the color barrier in major league baseball, penned a column that the Associated Negro Press syndicated to African-American newspapers throughout the country. Twenty years to the day after Robinson made his debut with the Brooklyn Dodgers, he published these words:

> Everybody has his idols.
> Dr. Martin King is one of mine.
> He is a man of tremendous ability and courage and I believe that he is a dedicated man. However, when you have an idol it does not necessarily mean that you agree with everything he says or does. It happens that I do not agree with Dr. King in his stand on Viet Nam.

Robinson believed that King's antiwar focus pulled the leader's eyes from the ghetto. He applauded King's accomplishments and defended his right as a man of God to oppose bloodshed, but he reminded him that his original mission still needed him.

"We have heard the 'black power' cries," Robinson wrote, "Let's hear more on domestic situations from Dr. King."[4]

———◆———

King needed to develop new tactics, as law enforcement learned how to "sterilize" the effectiveness of street protests. In Birmingham and Selma, police had attacked protesters, resulting in embarrassment to the state and nationwide sympathy for the marchers' cause. In Memphis, sailors and Marines, furloughed from nearby Millington Naval Air Station, turned out to peace demonstrations to heckle protesters and support the war, but police knew that any confrontation between them and antiwar demonstrators would engender public sympathy for the antiwar side. So they made every effort to keep pro-war hecklers moving along, and they refrained from making contact with the peace activists as well. Every week in the spring of 1967, Lawson organized Saturday peace vigils, and every week the Memphis police gained more experience both in defusing confrontational street activism and in protecting protesters.

Without conflict, the movement went stale. In the summer of '67 the weekly peace vigil, seldom attracting more than thirty people, dwindled as the heat rose.

For his part, Agent Lawrence was pleased. The new approach "definitely frustrated and sterilized the demonstrators," he wrote. "Further, it prevented any possible assaults of the demonstrators which could well play directly into their hands, propaganda wise, by rendering them into a martyr status."[5]

But the peace vigils fostered another worrisome development. At one of them, Withers overheard a young man talking about forming a Black Power group in Memphis. Withers began to pay close attention to his Black Power advocate, photographing him with Lawson as they demonstrated together. Withers saw that the young man tooled around town on a Honda motorcycle.

Agent Lawrence had already heard about the young radical from NAACP contacts, who told him this fellow came from a conservative local family but had quit the branch youth group. Now he talked of launching an "extremist" campus organization in its place.[6] The radical hoped to work hand in hand with Lawson on Black Power and opposition to the war.

Withers asked Lawson what was up. The minister said frustration and anger were boiling over throughout the impoverished community surrounding his church, and he could hear cries of Black Power. Police beatings were both the answer to and the cause of much of the conflict. Should a spark fly, the young people around him would explode.

After making Black Power popular in mid-1966, Stokely Carmichael shot to the top of J. Edgar Hoover's target list. The FBI director publicly maligned Carmichael as allied with the Revolutionary Action Movement, which was "dedicated to the overthrow of the capitalist system in the United States, by violence if necessary."[7] The bureau anticipated racial violence as angry young people found Carmichael and the hot rhetoric of SNCC appealing. Memphis was on high alert.

On 5/16/67 SA William H. Lawrence purchased from Ernest C. Withers, CS (commercial photographer) five copies of a photograph of the

notorious SNCC leader, Stokely Carmichael,
since this office had no slick photographs of him.
It is felt if he comes here it would be wise to have
the photographs.[8]

———•———

Carmichael never came to town, but his ideas resonated
deep into South Memphis.

A sweltering Friday night turned into the morning
of July 1 as John B. Smith cruised the neighborhood with
a couple of friends. John B. had recently come home from
two years in Vietnam and proudly wore his olive drab field
jacket. He had a job running a forklift at the defense depot,
rented his own apartment, and had bought a '63 Volkswagen
Beetle. He was twenty-four years old.

That morning Smith's old friend and high school basketball teammate Charles Cabbage rode with him. Like
Smith, Cabbage had returned home to Memphis recently,
not from war but from school. He majored in history at
Morehouse College, located in Atlanta, the same city as the
central office of SNCC.

While Smith had returned home a patriot, Cab came
home a radical. In Atlanta, he'd met Carmichael and been
steeped in the city's activist culture. Atlanta also was home to
Dr. King and headquarters of the SCLC. Cab attended a New
York City antiwar rally where King spoke in mid-April 1967.[9]

John B. and Cab had grown up in Riverside. It was a tough part of Memphis but home to tidy eight-hundred-square-foot houses where intact, working poor families lived, like their own. Smith and Cab called their section of Riverside "the Valley."

Riding in John B.'s VW bug, they sipped cans of beer, puffed cigarettes, and argued about politics. Cab ridiculed John's patriotic innocence, while John mocked the value of Cab's education.

"You don't even have a job," John B. told Cab. "Your broke Black Power ass should have learned how to make some money."

Cab countered with a diatribe about black people controlling their own destinies.

John B. held to his bottom line that America's greatness and fairness would prevail for African Americans as it had for the freedom fighters in the American Revolution and the slaves in the Civil War.

As their discussion heated up, John B. pulled into a service station at the corner of Parkway and Third, at about half-past one in the morning.

The gas tank was under the hood, but the catch on the hood was broken. He'd come up with his own way of opening it—he got out and popped it. He happened to note the cap on the gas tank. He handed the attendant a bill and got back into the car to keep fussing with Cab, while the attendant filled the tank.

Afterward the attendant approached John with his

change. "I can see you don't have a gas cap," he said. "I'll sell you one for a buck."

John B. had just noticed the gas cap on the tank when he popped the hood. This would be the second time he'd lost a cap at this filling station.

Cab saw a circular bulge in the attendant's shirt pocket that was making a greasy stain. He got out of the car. Skinny, deep-voiced, and six foot two, he pointed to the oily bulge. "Just show him that's not it, and we all leave," he said.

"I don't have to show you a motherfucking thing," said the attendant.

John B. said, "That's it, I'm calling the police." He went to the phone booth and made the call.

Other cars were waiting to pull up to the gas pump, but John B. didn't move his VW. People who'd been hanging out drinking with John B. and Cab near the gas station, at the Log Cabin, came over and stood around the bug.

A police cruiser arrived to see a line of cars stretching down the street and a large group of young black men. Fearing a riot, the cops in the cruiser called for backup.

Five more cruisers sped into the gas station lot. After hearing John B.'s complaint, an officer asked the grease monkey if he had the gas cap.

"No."

The police told everyone to clear out. John B. pleaded with them to try harder to get his cap back. When he didn't stop or move his car, the police arrested him.

"But I'm the one who called you," he said.

They pushed him into the back of a squad car. He opened the door and got out to explain his case to the lieutenant at the scene. Four cops tackled him, cuffed him, and threw him headfirst back into the car.

Cab and a bystander were arrested as well, for arguing with the police. The bystander reportedly walked away, saying he was not under arrest and would blow the officer's damn head off, at which point the police grabbed him.

A neighborhood patrolman said he'd seen all these guys drinking together at the Log Cabin. The police theorized that the young black men must have cooked up this plan to trap them.

Downtown, John B. and Cab refused to take alcohol breath tests. John's cuffs were on so tight, tears came to his eyes. He mentioned this to an officer, who further tightened them. The police took his shoes, shirt, and belt and put him in a cold cell. He thought the temperature was about forty-five degrees. They threw Cab in with him. They shivered there for two hours. John B. emerged with his forehead throbbing, his right hand stiff, and his faith in the system tested.

A few hours later in court, John B. and Cab faced charges of disorderly conduct and resisting arrest. The judge fined them $102—he suspected they had been trying to start a riot. "Why would I call police before starting a riot?" asked John B.[10] The incident nonetheless became notorious as the Gas Cap Riot.

Two hours in the cold cell and a morning in court converted John B. Smith from an American patriot to a Black
Power revolutionary.

⊢———•———⊣

The next evening two young men visited Ernest Withers's
studio. One, a tall, skinny guy with a peach fuzz mustache,
was Charles Cabbage. The other was the Black Power radical Withers had seen at the peace vigils, who drove the
Honda motorcycle: Coby Smith, no relation to John B.

Cab and Coby were on a publicity tour, hoping to spread
the story of what had happened to Cab and John B. with the
police in Riverside. The *Tri-State Defender* and the NAACP
hadn't been sympathetic, but Withers had encouraged them
to tell their story. Coby did most of the talking. As Withers
later told Agent Lawrence, the young man wanted to exploit
the Gas Cap Riot as a rallying point for Black Power.

In doing some background research on the Black Power
advocates, Withers picked up that Coby Smith and Cab
knew each other from Atlanta, where they'd both come
under the influence of Stokely Carmichael and SNCC.
Coby said he wanted to turn Memphis into an SNCC
town. This city needed a good race riot, he reportedly said,
and they were going to turn it upside down.[11]

The bureau had already opened a file on Coby Smith,
and now, after visiting Withers, Charles Cabbage got
one too.

Cab and John B. had found only trouble from the police they'd called for help in Riverside; just so, Cab, John B., and Coby unknowingly made themselves FBI targets while seeking help from local movement supporters. They told their story to the *Tri-State Defender* and to the NAACP, but Agent Lawrence had a source in both of them. The NAACP source reported to him that Coby Smith "became obnoxious, demanded immediate action by the NAACP, and indicated he was going to create Negro unrest in the city of Memphis," while the editor of the newspaper independently corroborated that Smith threatened to incite a riot.[12]

After the Fourth of July, Coby Smith returned to Withers's studio. According to a July report from the Memphis FBI to J. Edgar Hoover's office, Smith said that he and Cabbage had come to Memphis from Atlanta "in the hopes of creating racial disturbance."

Withers had already checked with local NAACP branch president Jesse Turner about these guys, and he knew Turner and his colleagues felt panicked. Withers next saw Coby at Jim Lawson's church.[13]

Lawson organized a Vietnam Summer protest in Memphis, as part of a nationwide plan of Dr. King to pressure President Johnson to end the war.[14] As with the Meredith march, the NAACP wanted no part of the antiwar movement or any other street protests, but the Memphis branch's leadership could control its board member Jim Lawson no more than it could control Coby Smith and Charles Cabbage.

Coby went to Lawson's peace vigil downtown, which was supposed to be silent, and reportedly shouted "Black Power!" at passersby. To anyone who'd listen, he claimed he'd *started* the recent race riots in Atlanta. Withers watched Lawson during all this. The minister appeared nervous. He edged away from the Black Power shouts but didn't stop them.[15]

In fact, the controversial minister did something that was unconventional even by his own standards. Far from alienating or informing on the Black Power boys, he hired them.

18

LYNDON JOHNSON HAD DECLARED WAR ON POVERTY IN his 1964 presidential campaign. Following his election, he launched a series of domestic programs known collectively as the Great Society, which included the establishment of the Office of Economic Opportunity (OEO).

Led by Sargent Shriver, a brother-in-law of the late president Kennedy, the OEO funneled federal dollars into local antipoverty efforts. One such was Memphis Area Poverty–South, which deployed seven social workers and fifty neighborhood aides over an area extending five miles south from Beale Street.[1] The aides went door to door, surveying the living conditions of poor families and informing the residents about available benefits.[2] Rev. James Lawson was a co-chairman of MAP-South.

Days after the Gas Cap Riot, Lawson hired Charles Cabbage, John B. Smith, and Coby Smith as part-time neighborhood aides. Paying a dollar fifty an hour for twenty hours per week, the jobs didn't exactly win the young men's personal wars on poverty. But it got them traction in the slums, where their faces became familiar, and they honed their organizing skills.

In mid-July 1967, riots broke out in Newark, New Jersey, followed by smaller disturbances in Cairo, Illinois, Durham, North Carolina, and Minneapolis. Rochester and Birmingham soon flared up. On July 23, Detroit exploded into the year's deadliest racial conflict. Police and African Americans exchanged gunshots, transforming the city into an urban war zone and resulting in an estimated forty-three deaths. From Havana, Stokely Carmichael urged a militant uprising, while SNCC leader H. Rap Brown incited a riot in Cambridge, Maryland. Brown justified black militant revolution with his infamous phrase, "Violence is part of American culture and is as American as apple pie."[3]

On the night of July 27, as Detroit smoldered, rumors of a potential riot surfaced in Memphis, and four thousand National Guard troops assembled. No real action erupted. Police arrested two people for tossing a Molotov cocktail onto the roof of Pancho's Mexican Restaurant, not exactly a bastion of white power. Local NAACP executive A. W. Willis commented that riot talk had rippled through the city now for three weeks—in other words, since Coby, John B., and Cab had started making the rounds. The Detroit situation gave credence to the local rumors, resulting in hysteria if little damage. There were still only three people in all of Memphis known to advocate turning the city upside down.

The next week a report to lawmakers on Capitol Hill about urban unrest suggested that federally funded community workers throughout the country might be agitating on the job—that the OEO's local programs could be, in effect, "subsidizing rioters."[4] OEO chief Shriver suspected that the OEO's enemies were fomenting the "riot subsidy" controversy to harm the chances that an OEO funding bill would pass. Only seven out of more than six thousand people arrested for rioting, he noted, were employed in OEO "community action programs."[5]

An investigator for the Senate Judiciary Committee visited Memphis to look into the possibility that MAP-South was employing people who identified with organizations, like SNCC, that advocated violence. The next day the investigator turned over some names to Senator James Eastland, a jowly, florid, ancient Mississippian with a fat cigar, and to Senator Ted Kennedy, the fresh-faced heir to the Massachusetts mane and name.

"We have some information on some people in Memphis," Eastland told Kay Pittman Black, the *Memphis Press-Scimitar* race reporter. "I don't know whether they will be called to testify or not. We'll have to study the information and see."[6] Though the senator would not reveal their names, the reporter had an idea who he meant. She went out and got to know them.

Cab and John B. showed Black around the slums. Standing on a street lined with rickety two-story shanties, she asked Cab about rumors of his involvement with the most controversial and feared civil rights group, SNCC.

"Sure I'm sympathetic toward SNCC," Cab said. "They

are dealing with this poverty problem at the grassroots, and that's where you've got to deal with it."

He had touched on an uncomfortable truth. White people high in government, like the OEO, were making the rules of engagement with black poverty, but the white way might not be the right way to solve the problem. When ordinary black people got a voice, as in MAP-South, high-powered whites intervened in opposition. In Nashville, a federally funded "liberation school" had come under congressional scrutiny, and members of a grassroots group in Kentucky even faced sedition charges.

Cab pointed out that hang-ups over organizational affiliation created another obstacle for the problem of solving poverty. "If the newspapers would report it like it really is, if they'd come into here and really look at poverty, and stop worrying about inconsequential things like whether you're a Snick or a Communist, maybe we wouldn't have to burn it down," he said. Reporter Black took down every militant word.

"Just look at these people, the shacks they have to live in," Cab said, "the bitter, angry young men. Sure they're angry. They can't find jobs. They can't earn a decent living."

What about riots? "Riots are started by just this sort of mess. These people feel like their backs are up to the wall. What does a man do when his back is up to a wall? He fights back."

Cab wondered, "Why can't all of this be worked out in a gentlemanly manner? Why must the people, the city officials, continue to ignore these folks' plight? Why must the people of Memphis refuse to look at what is in their city?"[7]

Cab informed Black that he and his friends had been fired from the War on Poverty on suspicion that they were SNCC sympathizers. It was a paradox as ugly as the Gas Cap Riot. The gas cappers had called for help, yet they had been the ones arrested. When the OEO-ers talked about poverty solutions, they lost their jobs fighting poverty.

Cab, John B., and Coby still had one local advocate: Jim Lawson held a closed-door meeting at his church to try to get them back their jobs. He had publicly blistered the local War on Poverty committee for firing his neighborhood aides. "This represents, in my judgment, that the WOPC is not concerned with ending poverty," he said. "They are not concerned with waging an effective war. If this is their attitude, they might as well close up."[8]

———+———

As darkness fell on August 10, 1967, Ernest Withers stood on the sidewalk outside Centenary Methodist, Jim Lawson's church. He sported a fresh haircut, a gold-plated watch, and a neat short-sleeved shirt. A camera was slung around his neck.

Inside the church, a closed meeting of MAP-South leaders deliberated whether to give Cab and Coby their jobs back.

As Withers watched, fifty bouncing, ebullient children

and teenagers stormed into the church vestibule. Lawson poked his head out to see the cause of the ruckus. One of the kids told him, "We want to show our support," for Cab and Coby.

"No one knows that better than I," Lawson replied, but he asked the boys for quiet and shooed them back out front, where he could address everyone.

He stood on the front steps and asked the crowd, "Who hired Coby?" Practically every face in the crowd looked up to Lawson. "I did," he said. "And I hired Cabbage, too."

He let that sink in.

"As long as I'm in there," he said, pointing at the crowd, "you know the battle's being fought." Heading back inside, he snapped, "I've been marching since before you even thought about it."

The kids sat on the stairs and on windowsills. They stood around in circles talking. Police cruisers rolled by, and the officers eyed the youthful crowd.

Withers heard that Coby Smith had organized this group to protest the firings, though the support appeared spontaneous and natural.[9]

After an hour and a half, Lawson came back out to announce the decision: the War on Poverty Committee would give the neighborhood aides a hearing to fairly determine whether they could have their antipoverty jobs back.[10]

At his hearing, Cabbage admitted he'd discussed with impoverished residents the tactic of carrying out rent strikes against landlords, saying, "If this is the only way a slum landlord can be made to improve his property then a poverty agency should direct itself to that."[11]

Advised that MAP-South couldn't condone rent strikes, Cab replied that he worked only thirty hours a week for the organization but lived in poverty twenty-four hours a day.

A. W. Willis, an attorney who represented Cab and Coby, sympathized. "We need more people concerned with the ghettos," he said. "I didn't ask [anyone] if he was a member of SNCC, and I don't care. I'm a member of some organizations I'm ashamed of," he continued. "One of them is the Chamber of Commerce." [12]

Cabbage and Coby earned a hollow victory. The committee reinstated their jobs and restored their back pay, but they had been funded only as temporary work for the summer. The positions expired shortly after the ruling.

One important result of MAP-South was to inflame the reputation of the already controversial Jim Lawson. According to Agent Lawrence, "As of August 9, 1967, several of the responsible NAACP leaders in Memphis, Tennessee, felt that Rev. JAMES MORRIS LAWSON, JR., was the most dangerous Negro in Memphis as he had been the mentor of Charles Cabbage and [Smith] and had obtained for them their jobs on MAP-South."[13]

The MAP-South episode also radicalized the thinking of Charles Cabbage. To Cab, the SNCC hunts and hearings merely distracted the city and the nation from addressing the reality of poverty. The system's true priority was to avoid it. He questioned, as Stokely Carmichael had before him, how sincerely a white society could ever engage with Negro problems. The MAP-South flap galvanized Cab to work around the establishment. He and his friends felt a sense of clarity and purpose, even liberation, after their dismissal from the War on Poverty. "A group of us got together," he said, "decided that there was a dire need for community action, independent community action, by members of the black community who had a free hand to operate without controls from any outside forces."[14]

But Cabbage was too late. The establishment already had him.

———————

While the MAP-South hearings were under way August 25, 1967, FBI headquarters circulated a letter to twenty-two field offices, including Memphis, announcing a new objective: the "Counterintelligence Program, Black Nationalist-Hate Groups" investigation that most people know now as COINTELPRO.

The letter outlined COINTELPRO's goal, "to expose, disrupt, misdirect, discredit, or otherwise neutralize the activities of black nationalist, hate-type organizations . . . their leadership . . . membership, and supporters, and to counter their propensity for civil disorder."[15]

The letter instructed that each office assign supervision of the program to "an experienced and imaginative Special Agent, well-versed in investigations relating to black-

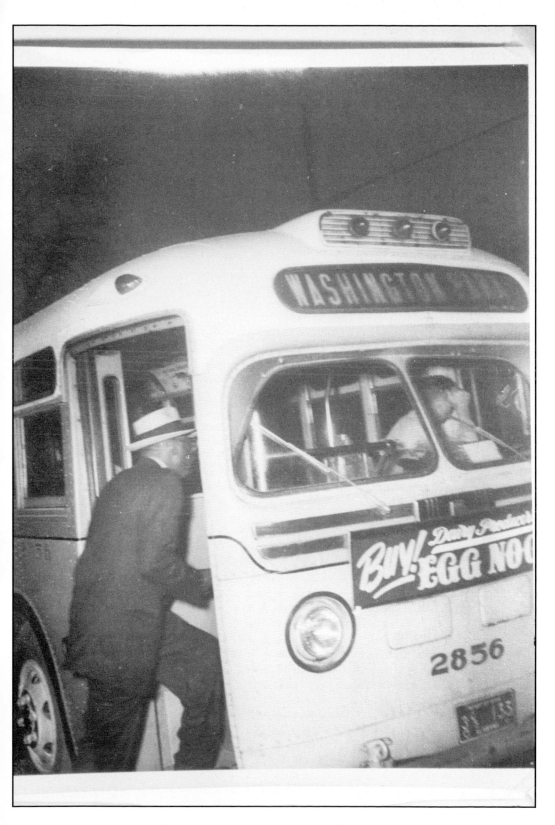

L. Alex Wilson, left, Montgomery, Alabama, December 21, 1956.

Main Street, Memphis, 1960.

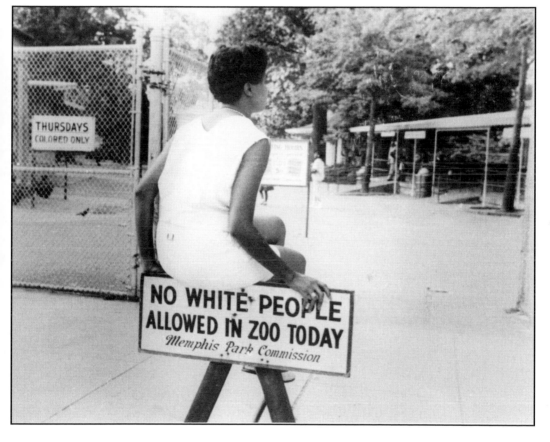

Overton Park, Memphis, ca. 1960

Muhammad Mosque 55, Beale Street, Memphis, 1964.

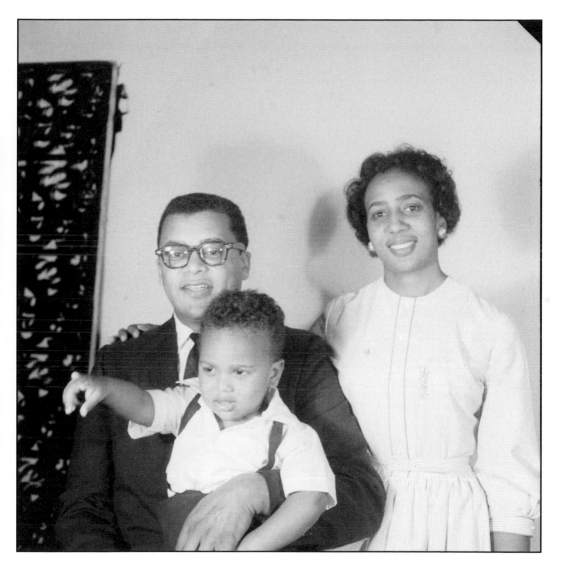

Rev. James Morris Lawson, Jr., with family, Lawson home, Memphis, ca. 1965.

West Tennessee Voters' Project activists, Withers's studio, Beale Street, Memphis, 1965.

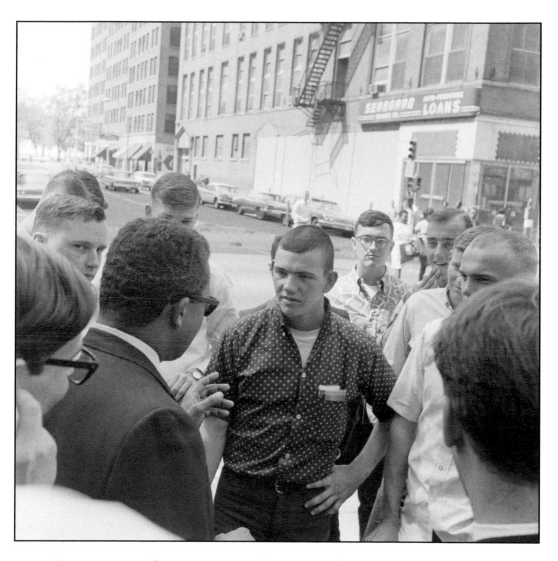

Lawson engages with counterprotestors during antiwar demonstration, Memphis, 1966.

Charles Cabbage, left, and Coby Smith, Withers's studio, Beale Street, Memphis, 1967.

nationalist, hate-type organizations." They were to use the power of negative publicity in neutralizing the target groups. They should exploit personal conflicts among members and between leaders, and "through the cooperation of established local news media contacts . . . careful attention must be given . . . to insure the targeted group is disrupted, ridiculed, or discredited . . . and not merely publicized."

In closing, the letter urged the field offices "to take an enthusiastic and imaginative approach to this new counterintelligence endeavors and the Bureau will be pleased to entertain any suggestions or techniques you may recommend."

The program would require intensive focus. Informants would be essential.

In October 1967, in the spirit of COINTELPRO, the bureau also initiated the Ghetto Informant Program. In black neighborhoods all over the country, agents would enlist entrepreneurs like liquor store owners and barber shop operators—and perhaps a commercial photographer here and there—to report to the bureau on the target groups. The grapevine of inside informants would grow to over three thousand.[16]

Withers got a new code name—ME-338 R (Ghetto).

———————•———————

Back in early August, as news of the MAP-South controversy was breaking, *Press-Scimitar* reporter Kay Pittman Black alerted the FBI to her findings about Lawson's men-

torship of Charles Cabbage. She contacted SNCC headquarters in Atlanta and asked if Cabbage and his colleagues
were members. SNCC replied that it had no members in
Memphis, as she also advised the bureau. Agent Lawrence,
in his report on Cabbage, listed Black as an informant, noting that her identity was "protected at her request."[17]

In September, two weeks after the FBI launched its
COINTELPRO mission to disrupt, ridicule, or discredit
targets in part by using cooperative local news media, an
article by Kay Pittman Black in the *Press-Scimitar* brought
Jim Lawson's image problems to the broad public.

Knowing that MAP-South and Black Power were
mingled in the public mind, Black opened the story by
stating that MAP-South officials "are planning even bigger activities next year to follow this year's initial program
that drew attacks ranging from Memphis to the halls of
Congress."

In the second paragraph, she characterized Lawson
as a man "not afraid to get embroiled. To use his words,
he's 'violence prone.'" This was a misquotation of what
Lawson had said in the interview and a distortion of his
intended meaning.

Farther down the page, Black provided Lawson's full
"violence prone" statement, in which he lamented the very
misperception Black encouraged with the story, that "any
Negro man who has virility today is violence prone, including myself." He was attempting to highlight the absurdity
of the suggestion that a pacifist minster, who'd been jailed

for his nonviolent principles, would instruct people to take up weapons and fight.

Nevertheless, Lawson's photograph appeared, over the caption " . . . I'm violence prone . . ." (ellipses in the original).

Continuing, Black wrote that Lawson "has shown he's not afraid to defy Uncle Sam—one such encounter having put Lawson in prison for 13 months."[18] Here she referred to Lawson's stance against the Korean War, without saying so until deeper into the story.

Kay Pittman Black was neither a typical white media hatchet-person, nor a typical gritty city reporter. The local NAACP probably considered her sympathetic.

In the coming months, she would be almost as ubiquitous as Ernest Withers on the local civil rights beat, and like Withers, she was an FBI asset. In fairness to Black, every hot race topic in Memphis did lead back to Jim Lawson: he publicly expressed Communist sympathy, he provided Black Power a safe haven, and he advocated as much civil disruption and public protest as possible, while local leadership preferred negotiation. And in a place where people don't answer straight, Lawson spoke bluntly, showing his penchant for "hardheaded calculation" that *The New Republic* had noted back in 1960, rather than the dangerous politeness and sticky charisma that permeates the Memphis atmosphere. None of this violated any law, of course, but Jim Lawson was guilty of being different.

Labor leader Jerry Wurf summarized the man out of place: "What Lawson never understood was the degree to which he was hated in Memphis—far out of proportion. . . . They feared Lawson for the most interesting of all reasons. . . . They feared him because he was a totally moral man, and totally moral men you can't manipulate and you can't buy and you can't hustle . . . and that's why they hung the label of super radical on him."[19]

19

THE CITY'S RIOTOUS SUMMER OF 1967 BEGAT ITS political fall.

In September, A. W. Willis became the first African American to run for mayor of Memphis, entering the wide-open Democratic primary. At the opening of Willis campaign headquarters, Ernest Withers noticed the presence of Charles Cabbage, John B. Smith, and Coby Smith, as well as Willis's pastor, Rev. James Lawson. The candidate and the minister had both stood up for the three young Black Power activists throughout the MAP-South controversy. With his pastor's blessing, Willis had now hired them as campaign workers.[1] Agent Lawrence's NAACP sources told him that Lawson and Willis hoped to control the disruptive outsiders by employing them.

But the three activists seemed to take their employment as an endorsement of their Black Power philosophy.

Only the FBI knew that two days before the Willis campaign launch, a private meeting had taken place at John B. Smith's apartment. Fifteen people, including one FBI informant, had gathered to hear Cabbage lay out his plan. Black people needed to burn and riot *strategically*, he reportedly said, in order to force the white power structure to address racial inequities in housing, small business, and jobs. He regretted that such a plan had become necessary, but people with power had failed to respond to reasonable requests for help, and he saw no alternative. The time for action was fast approaching.

Cabbage offered an idea of how to start a race riot: stage an assault. Have a white male attack a black woman in a crowded place. A group of Black Power men would rush to her defense and attack all the whites in the area. Cab predicted that Black Power would control Memphis by the summer of 1968.[2]

A few nights before the election, an African-American community leader hosted a rally at Club Paradise for a white mayoral candidate, Hunter Lane. Cabbage and some friends, who were present, heckled the candidate with a chorus of "Uncle Tom!" and "Sell-out!"[3] Withers, who observed them, felt that a black nationalist theme was creeping into Willis's rhetoric, probably to racially shame any black voters considering voting for a white candidate. Withers thought the tactic would doom Willis's chances.

According to many black voters and black political analysts, African Americans' paramount goal in this race must be not to elect one of their own but to defeat Henry Loeb. Thousands pledged support to a lesser-evil white candidate, the incumbent mayor, William Ingram. The mayor could not claim to have a spotless record on their behalf, but Loeb had built his career on a platform of white supremacy.

In 1967 the most powerful and inescapable name in Memphis was Loeb. Two brothers, Henry and Bill, were a pair of handsome high achievers in their prime.

Henry Loeb, tall and commanding, was an Ivy Leaguer and Navy veteran, like Jack Kennedy—he had captained a PT boat in World War II. Bill Loeb was a big family man. He operated, and expanded, the family's laundry chain and added a fast-growing circuit of barbecue and fried chicken restaurants. He featured his highly photogenic, squeaky-clean kids—eight of them—in print advertisements for the chicken and rib joints. The Loeb name overshadowed the city as Bill's ads ran daily in the newspapers, Henry's latest political maneuvers typically made front-page news, and Loeb's Laundries and Loeb's Bar-B-Q stands sprouted on busy streets.

Henry Loeb had served as a city commissioner during the 1958 Glenview controversy. He had antagonized black Memphis when he reacted to demand for new black neighborhoods by saying, "We ought to go out to the Penal Farm . . . to find more suitable locations for Negro homes."[4]

In 1959 Loeb made his first mayoral run, as a Democrat, calling for white unity in government. He had thereby helped inspire a massive black political uprising. The city's black population united across party lines—African Americans were still split fifty-fifty in this longtime Party of Lincoln stronghold—to support a slate of

African-American office candidates known as the Volunteer Ticket. The ticket backed bipartisan candidates and men of different faiths and backgrounds. Dr. King gave a keynote address to one of the many massive Volunteer Ticket meetings. Black voters turned out in record numbers, hoping to keep Loeb from the mayor's office. Their urgency frightened a record number of whites to the polls, who succeeded in electing Loeb.

The rancor remained high in '67. Rumors circulated that Loeb had bribed Willis to run in order to divide the black vote. "No one can buy me," Willis stated on a WDIA radio forum. "I don't need Loeb's money. I have no respect for Henry Loeb at all." He referred to Ingram and Loeb, both white candidates, as segregationists.[5]

In November, on primary election night, Cab rode around in a loudspeaker car proclaiming that Black Power meant voting for a black mayor. Withers observed that this had a chilling effect, scaring and confusing would-be Willis supporters.[6]

When Willis lost, Cab said he planned to make Memphis suffer.[7]

NAACP branch president Jesse Turner interpreted Willis's defeat as a product of history. "The years of physical slavery followed by subsequent years of economic slavery have left the scars of their wounds," he wrote. "These include lack of confidence in one another and the belief of white superiority." Turner feared that empty promises made in exchange for black votes would sow the seeds of racial unrest. "The next twelve months will be crucial for race relations in our community," he predicted.[8]

———◆———

Withers did nothing to discourage Cabbage, Smith, and Smith from visiting his studio throughout the fall of '67. As he had done with Nation of Islam members, Withers made the young Black Power activists feel welcome, and he discussed issues with them. Associating with this controversial group risked his reputation as a sound member of the community, but he gained their sympathy. Meanwhile he monitored each incremental phase of the group's development.

Twenty-four-year-old Vietnam veteran John B. Smith had himself been a photographer in the army. Smith believed in the power of pictures to tell the story he saw in South Memphis, the story of poverty and slums cordoned off from the rest of the world. He regarded Withers, twenty years his senior, as a mentor. As John B.'s gray VW bug chugged around Beale with no hubcaps, Withers waved.

He watched their numbers grow to ten committed Black Power supporters. Cab told him that Coby Smith had gone back to school.[9] Cab went on an impromptu speaking tour of local college campuses, where he exhorted his listeners to read *Muhammad Speaks* and called school officials and powerful leaders like Thurgood Marshall Uncle Toms.[10] On November 20, John B. and Cab dropped by the Withers studio at 327 Beale. They said they'd been at Memphis State, recruiting. In studying the young men's clothing, the middle-aged Withers struggled with counterculture symbolism, mistaking a peace sign around John's neck as an upside-down Y in a circle. And he noticed the back of John B.'s army fatigue jacket, where in all capital letters, Smith had patched on the word INVADERS.[11]

Withers asked if they'd adopted a new tag. No, John B. said, a few of the kids they'd recruited around the Valley liked to call themselves the Invaders. The bunch of them threw house parties and record hops. One of the kids had picked up the name from a TV series about space aliens secretly mixing in with earthlings.

———•———

On January 2, 1968, as Henry Loeb moved back into City Hall, Charles Cabbage visited the Withers photography studio. Cab demanded to know, "Has the fuzz been around here looking for us?"[12]

Withers said he didn't think so.

Cabbage clarified, "I mean someone such as the FBI."

Withers said that back during the riot rumors, some of the black beat cops on Beale Street had asked what he knew about Cab and company, since they had hung out so regularly.

Cab prowled around the Withers studio and talked nervously. After he left, Withers alerted Agent Lawrence to the visit.[13]

Lawrence feared that the Black Power boys were on to Withers. He decided to take a risk to protect his informant and at the same time deepen the bond between Withers and Cabbage. Lawrence explained the tactic in a memo:

> It was felt wise to conduct a "fake" interview with ME 338-R (Ghetto) [Withers's code name], particularly in view of the fact that Charles Cabbage recently queried ME 338-R as to whether or not the "fuzz" (a term utilized by him to refer to the FBI) had been by.

Lawrence instructed Withers to tell Cabbage, next time, that two FBI agents had come to see him. The agents had heard about how much time the Black Power group spent with Withers, he was to say, and they wanted to see what the photographer knew. Lawrence told Withers to say the agents wanted his photos of the group, but that he told them he'd sent off the photos to *Jet* and didn't think they would be returned.

Meanwhile FBI agents actually did interview the owner of the pool hall where Cab and John B. hung out. Word got back to Cab, who went to the FBI office himself and confronted Agent Lawrence. He was simply trying to "contact young black cats to establish dialogue with them and educate them as to their black heritage," Cab said. But the FBI interrogating community people hurt his outreach efforts. Nobody wanted to join a group under FBI surveillance.

Cab told Lawrence that the NAACP were a bunch of Uncle Toms, chained to white ideology by the dollar. Smart blacks were forming their own political and financial networks, independent of white liberal support. His and other Black Power groups around the country were "soul brothers," Cab said.

Lawrence noted Cab's attire, a leather jacket with tong fringe at the neck and chest. Cab spoke in grandiose, roundabout terms, much to Lawrence's amusement: "We want a programmatical approach to the programs. We must take a problematical approach to the problem." Lawrence asked about Cab's recent inflammatory speeches. Had he said that Memphis needed a good race riot, that Memphis should be burned?

Cab admitted making those statements but explained that he was being allegorical, trying to shock Memphis people into helping poor black people. He didn't literally mean to burn the place. His goals were to uplift and educate and to not wait around for white support or the white system to do the work for them.[14]

A week later Withers met with Cabbage and his friend Clifford Taylor and told them that two FBI agents had interviewed him. Cab remarked that he had been interviewed by "a tall cracker," meaning Lawrence, and a bald one, Orville Johnson. Withers said he didn't know the agents' names but they sounded like the same pair who had come to see him about Cab and the Black Power boys.

Cab replied, "The FBI is sneaking up on us."

Withers said he had covered for Cabbage and his friends all the way, telling the agents that the Black Power movement was legit and hadn't incited violence. Cabbage and Taylor particularly appreciated Withers deceiving the agents about their photos.

Afterward Withers described the deception to Agent Lawrence, who noted, "Cabbage and Taylor seemed to 'fall' for this story, and this seemed to further endear informant to them."[15]

Six months later the Civil Rights Documentation Project conducted an oral history interview with Cabbage that verifies that judgment. Cabbage offered local authorities' treatment of Withers as an example of heavy-handed tactics. "I mean take Mr. Withers here if he don't mind me using his name. He's a photographer. He earns his living taking pictures. They come in and bust him down while he's in his shop, with the door closed, staying there because you know if he goes out in the streets it would be unsafe, and they come in and get him. You couldn't even classify him, not in the traditional sense, of what you might call a militant. But they come bust down on him."

In any case, Withers maintained his cover. He had developed steadily since passing Agent Lawrence a picture of a Tent City activist in December 1960. He shared the government's skepticism of Communist sympathizers and countercultural figures from beatniks to Black Power advocates. Yet he developed far-reaching connections throughout these groups. He had gained the trust of his handler and become a resourceful asset. He had felt both the anger growing within the movement for his people and the violence escalating against that movement. Now, with local powers moving against racial progress, and federal power closing in on the civil rights movement, Withers stood on the verge of the most explosive phase of his secret career.

IV

I AM A MAN

20

FROM 1949 TO 1959, BEFORE ERNEST WITHERS GOT involved with the FBI, the inspector in charge at FBI head-quarters in Washington had been Frank Holloman. In 1959 Holloman left Washington to become special agent in charge (SAC) in Memphis. That gave the Memphis office an unusually strong connection to J. Edgar Hoover.

Back in Washington, Holloman had read virtually every memo and seen virtually every visitor who entered Hoover's office. He had marveled at the Boss's remarkable memory, extremely high intelligence, inexhaustible energy and indus-try. Hoover also awed Holloman with his temperament, idiosyncrasies, and wrath. The Boss struck Holloman as an emotional man, given to elation over achievement and despondence over setbacks. "As all of us, he had his own moral code by which he lived," Holloman recalled, adding, "his might not have fitted someone else's." Holloman recog-nized one motive above all driving Hoover—"safeguarding the heritages of America."

Running Hoover's Washington office required Holloman to work a seven-day week of pleasing a notorious perfectionist.

Over the intercom, Hoover would interrupt Holloman's tasks to request the instantaneous delivery of some esoteric data. Holloman had to satisfy Hoover's intense desire for an attractive lawn, a virtual impossibility considering the amount of shade over his front yard and the dogs Hoover dearly loved. Holloman would reflect, "It was a rare occasion that I ate my evening meal before 9:00 p.m."

But Holloman trusted Hoover, and Hoover looked out for Holloman. During their last year cohabiting in the Washington office, Holloman sought Hoover's advice on a personal matter. A relative of Holloman's was spending an increasing amount of time in the company of a Christian youth group coordinator. The youth group leader hosted regular gatherings at his home, and Holloman became suspicious upon learning that two high school boys were living there. He checked bureau files and found a record showing that the youth group leader had been arrested in a park at three-thirty one morning along with a male who admitted being a sexual pervert.

Holloman wrote a message to Hoover asking for advice on how he might invisibly break up the relationship between his relative and this purported pervert running Christian youth meetings. He had already hatched a convoluted plot, he told Hoover, involving his personal physician. He was thinking of suggesting that the physician check the youth group coordinator's police record and "then take any action necessary independently without my appearing in the picture." The doctor, Holloman wrote to Hoover, "will be

vitally interested in this character as [his] daughter belongs
to the organization. There are a number of sons and daughters of quite reputable people . . . who belong to this organization and I believe something should be done to stop this
character . . . before the boys and girls are hurt. I realize
there is no direct evidence of sex perversion . . . but the cir-
cumstantial evidence is quite strong."[1]

Hoover's handwritten reply reads:

I think it is alright to do as you suggest.

H.

Determining outcomes "without appearing in the picture" was all in a day's work at the Washington office.

The Memphis SAC job suited Holloman well. He was
born in Mississippi, and his recollections suggest that he
needed to lengthen the leash Hoover had on him. Having a
little distance from the director, and being closer to home,
would be a good thing for Frank Holloman.

But an employee could escape Hoover's power only by leaving the bureau. In early 1960, a letter arrived for Holloman
from his old Washington colleague Cartha "Deke" DeLoach,
a member of Hoover's inner circle and head of the bureau's
crime records division. DeLoach was headed down South, he
wrote. Addressing Holloman by the nickname "Preacher,"
he continued, "I am certainly looking forward to my visit in
'Rebel territory' and I know it will not take any time at all for
me to be reoriented in Rebel ways with you riding the reins."[2]

"Preacher" showed "Deke" around Memphis, though Holloman would apologize that it "is considered a 'closed city' and places of amusement and things to do here are very limited."

The two men refreshed useful contacts, including editor of the *Memphis Commercial Appeal* newspaper, Frank Ahlgren, whom Holloman described as "an ardent and close friend and supporter of the Director and the Bureau over the years," while noting that the paper "has always been one of our greatest boosters."[3]

In mastering public perception for the bureau, Hoover and Holloman could have had no better friend than Ahlgren. The *Commercial Appeal's* area of circulation extended from the Missouri boot heel, through Arkansas to the Mississippi Delta and the city itself.

In a letter to Hoover, Holloman noted, "Getting the Bureau favorably before the public on a regular basis . . . will certainly be of inestimable value in the event that the Bureau should come under attack from whatever source." He added, "I have found no evidence of any outward or under-current feeling of animosity whatsoever toward the Bureau in this area," and more importantly, "the people in this area have a very deep admiration and respect for you personally."[4]

The bureau's only PR problem in Memphis, according to Holloman, was with regard to civil rights and election law investigations. "There is still a very deep seated segregationist viewpoint on the part of practically all white people, including the most prominent citizens," he wrote in 1960, two months into Henry Loeb's first mayoral term.

DeLoach's visit had been more than social. Something was up. During Holloman's early months as Memphis SAC, he had received an imperfect performance rating from Hoover, and the DeLoach visit may have been designed to check on him. A few months later Hoover demoted Holloman, knocking him down to the rank of special agent.

Holloman was devastated. "The mere thought of having to restrict my activities is, to say the least, the greatest shock, heartache, and disappointment of my life," he wrote to the Boss. "I cannot quite visualize myself not being in the thick of the battle on the front lines."

The ostensible reason for Holloman's demotion was a health exam that had discovered a possible heart condition. The exam had taken place at a government hospital in Washington, well within Hoover's purview. But Holloman's personal physician would soon find him in good health and clear him to return to full duty. Holloman, at forty-five, kept right on smoking and would live another thirty-seven years.

Commercial Appeal columnist Jack Carley—"who writes all of the favorable editorials that appear in this paper concerning the FBI," according to Holloman— wrote to Hoover to express his distress at Holloman's demotion, but added, "We are delighted that he is going to remain in Memphis. Despite the physical handicap which has overtaken him he can be of invaluable service to the Bureau and to this area. . . . He knows the people, their mores and their problems."[5]

Holloman still yearned to get back on the front lines, writing Hoover on the day of Senator John F. Kennedy's presidential campaign stop in Memphis:

> The racial situation continues somewhat tense, although we have not had as much violence in this area as I had expected. I am convinced the white people . . . respect us and will continue to support us, although to them Civil Rights and Election Law investigations are a source of irritation . . . You are a symbol of integrity, honesty, and patriotism to them and they look to you as someone they can trust and have complete confidence in.[6]

Despite such persistent flattery, Hoover never restored Holloman to authority. Holloman would hang on as special agent at the Memphis office until he retired in 1964.

Thereafter Holloman settled in Memphis but never quit working. A thin man with wavy white-gray hair and sleep-deprived eyes, he still yearned to return to the front lines.

In 1968 newly reinstalled Memphis mayor Henry Loeb gave Holloman the opportunity to become the city's director of police and fire. Holloman accepted the job, partially on condition that the mayor "would have no influence whatsoever in the police department," he recalled. "He could not recommend anyone for hiring, firing, or for any administrative action." Likewise, Holloman would not attempt to influence Loeb's leadership of the city. Agreeing to stay out of each other's official business they developed a positive relationship.

Though Holloman had clout and a sterling reputation as a lawman, many rank-and-file police resented him from day one. His predecessor, Claude Armour, had risen from the ranks, and the cops in the street had seen Armour as one of them. Armour was gruff and tough and kept his men in line. When the Memphis schools integrated in 1961, Armour had told them to put their feelings aside and make sure it went peacefully, to avoid the embarrassment that had happened over in Little Rock a couple of years before. If they fouled up, he said, he'd run them out of town. They chose not to test him. The outsider Holloman would have to earn this level of respect.

Budget cuts didn't help Holloman in the cops' estimation, though some of the boys dealt good-naturedly with the situation. A prankster among them circulated photos of a half-bushel of corncobs sitting beside an empty toilet paper dispenser in the headquarters' restroom.

Holloman did little to smooth the transition. He publicly stated that the force needed more college-educated officers—which threatened the livelihoods and insulted the intellects of those currently on the books. His first day on the job, he wrote to his division chiefs, "It has come to my attention through members of the Negro race that occasionally personnel of the Division of Fire and Police address Negroes as . . . 'Boy,' 'Girl,' 'Nigger' and 'Nigra.' . . . I have publicly stated that the policy of this Division would be that there would be only one class of citizens and that all citizens would be treated alike regardless of race, creed, or economic status."[7]

Despite the department's budgetary issues and Holloman's management trouble, the new police director updated the force's intelligence division. He instituted Hoover-style strategies and tactics. He borrowed his old colleague, Special Agent William Lawrence, to help set things up.[8]

The revamped intelligence force would be challenged right away. Only a month into Holloman's tenure, a note crossed his desk: the city garbage men were going on strike.

21

THE MEMPHIS SANITATION STRIKE GAINED SUPPORT from the local NAACP and from the American Federation of State, County, and Municipal Employees (AFSCME). The workers demanded a raise, plus rainy-day pay when bad weather canceled a shift, implementation of some safety measures, recognition of their union as their collective bargaining agent, and a dues check-off, or automatic contribution to the union straight off the top of each worker's paycheck. They pushed for medical and life benefits in memory of the two workers who had been crushed to death on February 1 while eating lunch in the back of their garbage truck—the last straw for the disgruntled thirteen hundred who walked out on their jobs a week and a half later.

The sanitation men had regularly threatened strikes throughout the 1960s, but the threats never escalated beyond talk. Mayor Henry Loeb didn't think the men could last without their wages. He wasn't about to sign a contract with a labor union. "City employees can't strike against their employer," Mayor Loeb told the sanitation men. "Go back to work!"[1]

Frank Holloman's new police intelligence force had its first big assignment. Loeb's stubbornness and inaction with regard to the strike undoubtedly complicated Holloman's life, creating challenge after challenge for the police.[2] But true to his word, Holloman did not interfere: "I did not at any time participate in the policies pertaining to the labor strike," he said.

Holloman canceled days off for the entire force and instituted rolling twelve-hour shifts, nine to nine, for the strike's duration. He squeezed habitual offenders in the sanitation department as potential strike informants. He dispatched African-American police detectives Ed Redditt and Willie Richmond to strike meetings, and black radio stations WDIA and WLOK were monitored throughout their broadcast schedules. A patrolman noted vehicle descriptions and tag numbers outside the Gay Hawk, a diner at the edge of downtown, where the strikers gathered on the morning of February 12, 1968.

Holloman foresaw a lengthy fight. Considering the city's budget shortfall—a projected $2.2 million deficit by the end of the fiscal year in June—combined with the workers' demands for higher pay, Loeb's attitude toward African Americans, and the skin color of the strikers. Furthermore, he sensed the strike's potential as a racial conflict and, even more frighteningly, as a vehicle for Black Power.

Detectives Richmond and Redditt were well known in the community. At early meetings, strikers heckled and publicly outed them so strike sympathizers wouldn't let anything slip out around them.

Four days into the impasse, the Memphis Police Department (MPD) sent a recent police academy graduate to attend a strike meeting under cover. He was an African American in his early twenties. He had a car and attended classes at Memphis State. He wore his hair long and natural. The police hid him in deep cover, assigning him the code name Max. "I moved to a new location and accepted an employment, a fictitious employment, and in that way established a total, separate identity from the one I had with the police department," Max explained. He kept using his real name, though—Marrell McCullough.

The same day Max mixed into the strike, Agent Lawrence and another agent, Howell Lowe, knocked on the door of an apartment in the Riverside neighborhood of South Memphis.

"I let them in," recalled John B. Smith.

Lawrence, in his skinny black tie, specs, and dark suit, interviewed several young men in torn jeans, worn sneakers, gray sweatshirts, and army surplus gear. The apartment had no heat.

"They questioned us about our organization, what our intentions were," said John B.

They said that Mr. Cabbage . . . had registered some
concern about the harassment we were receiving
from the Memphis Police Department dating back
to July 1967 and that he had come down to explain
to the FBI who we were in order to establish some
official record what type of organization we were,
what our intentions were, so that if the harassment
continued we would be able to launch some type of
complaint against the Memphis Police Department.
In response to Mr. Cabbage's request, the FBI said
that they had come by to see for themselves what
type of organization we were, and that's essentially
what happened at that meeting.

Lawrence was following up not out of concern for Cabbage
but on orders from the top. FBI headquarters had become
interested in this ragtag group of guys sitting around a cold,
tiny apartment. It must have had something to do with that
name. "A black power movement, known as The Invaders,
is developing in the Memphis Division," read the memo
from J. Edgar Hoover's office. "Keep the Bureau informed
concerning the progress of this organization," it concluded.
The Invaders got their very own case file.[3]

That little piece of intel that Ernest Withers had gathered about John B. Smith's jacket seems to have triggered
upper-level interest. John B. insisted that the Invaders were
merely part of a larger organization known as the Black
Organizing Project (BOP). Lawrence met several BOP

board members at the apartment, but that name, the Invaders, was too catchy.

As the sanitation strike unfolded, Withers attended meetings and rallies, and during the first weeks, he noticed no Black Power activity. Every day a couple hundred striking sanitation workers marched quietly down Main Street and around City Hall. Meanwhile scabs collected the trash in East Memphis, where the prosperous whites lived.

The new city council, with three African-American members, struggled to resolve the conflict speedily but instead passed a measure that recognized Loeb as the sole city authority with the power to end the strike—the one that Loeb himself remained stubbornly against settling. Frustrated and bitter, hundreds of striking workers stormed out of City Hall on February 23—and headed straight into a police cordon. The cops were there in numbers to block a destructive rampage from the strikers. "They was blocking us, standing up against us pushing," sanitation man Ed Gillis explained. "We wasn't pushing. We was just standing there and singing, 'I'm planted by the waterside like a tree planted by the roots.'"[4]

Leaders of the strike began lining up the sanitation men for a march. The police, on their tenth day of twelve-hour shifts, pulled on gas masks. Word of the coming showdown reached Frank Holloman, who ordered his men back and permitted the strikers to march down the west side of Main Street. He instructed his officers to create a moving wall of squad cars separating the lane of marchers from auto traffic.

As the march began, the squad cars, rolling five officers deep, tightly guarded the border along the traffic stripe down the middle of Main.

James Lawson, in ministerial garb, marched up and down the column of strikers, urging them to remain calm despite police provocation and warning the police not to escalate the situation.

Some of the cop cars slowly crossed the line, nudging into the marchers. A woman named Gladys Carpenter decided to step forward and stop them. She had marched from Selma to Montgomery in 1965 and had experienced police disrupting a demonstration. Now she put herself between the line of sanitation men and the squad cars inching into the march.

On the busiest corner of the shopping district, Carpenter shouted, "Oh! He runned over my foot!" A group of strikers moved to rock the car, to push it off her foot, while an officer provided Holloman with a play-by-play over the walkie-talkie.

The police director's focus shifted from avoiding trouble to limiting trouble. "We could be another Detroit," he thought. "We could be another Watts."[5] He had a half-million people to protect. "I could actually hear on the radio what sounded to me as if it was the breaking of windows," he recalled. "I thought that for the protection of everyone involved, the citizens as far as the demonstrators and others, that the crowd should be dispersed."[6]

Policemen crushed against the driver's side of the squad

Memphis police break up the sanitation strike march of February 23, 1968. Special Collections Department, University of Memphis Library.

car, while demonstrators crowded against the passenger side. On orders from Holloman, officers reached into their holsters, pulled out handheld aerosol cans, and squirted the strikers. As an FBI memo summarized the moment: "The Mace generally worked most satisfactorily."[7]

A stream of the chemical hit Lawson on the side of the head. He refrained from rubbing his eyes and didn't touch his glasses, but as he looked back toward the police, a blast of Mace hit him straight in the face.

Dozens of demonstrators fell to the sidewalk incapacitated and staggered blindly through the street. One collapsed in an alley, where he groped around on his hands and knees until he felt a chunk of ice at the end of a drainpipe. He broke off a piece to wash his eyes. The scattered marchers reassembled at Clayborn Temple, the strike headquarters located off Beale Street.

That night Lawson conferred with Holloman. Prior to the strike, the two men had met on several occasions to discuss methods of improving relations between the police and the black community. Back then Lawson had felt some hope for Holloman, but no longer. Peaceful demonstrators had been provoked and brutalized—on Holloman's order. The police director apologetically assured the minister that Mace worked better than bullets. Nevertheless the two would remain in regular contact during the coming weeks.

Dorothy Withers recalled her husband arriving home from the march with a bloodied head. "He came in that evening as tired and discouraged as I ever saw him," she said. "He sat a while but didn't talk much. Then he got up and washed his head and went out to a meeting. Those were hard days."[8]

———◆———

After the Main Street clash and his meeting with Holloman, Lawson got a call asking him to chair the strike strategy committee. He accepted. He declared a strike boycott of the white newspapers and began pickets at the city dump, as well as at the Loeb's Bar-B-Q and Loeb's Laundry locations in African-American districts. He coordinated daily marches downtown.

To better organize the strike, he formed Community on the Move for Equality (COME). It was headquartered at Clayborn Temple, a block south of Beale Street, built in the nineteenth century as a grand cathedral for elite Presbyterians. After they vacated it for digs in the fashionable suburbs, an African Methodist Episcopal congregation had moved in.

Now the neighborhood, the heart of the community at large, was home to weathered and dilapidated blocks, cold-water flats, slum houses, and penal colony-style projects. Prostitutes, boosters, and pickpockets hung outside the Harlem House and Avalon Pool Room.

Next door to Clayborn Temple, on the corner of Hernando and Vance, stood the boxy, modern AME Minimum Salary Building, another hub of strike activity.

Ernest Withers joined COME, through his allegiance to H. Ralph Jackson, another minister prominent in strike planning.[9]

The day after the Mace incident, the MPD sent an undercover man to the Labor Hall in North Memphis. Strikers recognized the officer and manhandled him. From the speaker's platform, a union man denounced him as a "dirty black son-of-a-bitch" and sellout. They confiscated his pistol and Mace and removed him from the union hall.

That night a raucous crowd, six hundred strong, gathered at Mason Temple, the Church of God in Christ headquarters. As Lawson began, "We are here to discuss very serious business that will determine the fate of the city," a rumble came from the crowd. "I know there are no policemen here, they should have learned their lesson at the union hall," he quipped. But he soon heard there were two cops in the building. "Just remove them," he reportedly said, and two informers voluntarily departed.[10]

The police violence further motivated African-American citizens to back the strike. "It was a sort of mystic thing," explained Benjamin Hooks. "There was some movement around which we could gather our energies, for certainly the response to the strike was out of all proportion to the issues involved. . . . It can only be explained in terms of a long feeling of frustration."[11]

Withers, from his studio at 327 Beale, had watched the young militant set recruit followers from among the low-lifes and derelicts on the street. He lost count of the young people he saw with INVADERS stitched across their T-shirts, sweatshirts, and jackets.

Since the fake interview the FBI had conducted with him, the emerging Black Power movement had drawn closer to Withers. He handed out a few dollars to Cab, here and there, and listened as John B. sought his help. Coby Smith, he learned from John B. and Cab, had let the middle-class Negroes get to him and he didn't want to be involved anymore. John B. and Cab were now publishing an underground Black Power newspaper, the *Afro-American Brotherhood Speaks*, and planning to expand it.

Just before the strike began, John B. had asked Withers for a job, but the photographer said he couldn't afford to hire an assistant. John B. needed proof of income to get a home loan and reportedly asked Withers to write a letter anyway, vouching for him as his thirty-five-dollar-per-week employee. Withers consulted Agent Lawrence, who nixed the phony letter of employment, telling Withers it could get him a fraud charge. Withers said it might be possible to give John B. some part-time work later on. That way he could further ingratiate himself to him and Cab and infiltrate the Invaders.[12]

On the night of February 26, Withers tailed John B. to the COME meeting around the corner at Clayborn Temple. The tone of the meeting turned militant. Rev. Malcolm Blackburn, pastor at Clayborn Temple, took the microphone and said, "I see Brother John Smith is here, and I'd better let him speak a few words."

Wearing his Invaders uniform—Afro, amulet, and shades—John B. delivered a fiery, impassioned speech. He accused the white power structure of sending scab garbage men to pick up in white neighborhoods in East Memphis, while the stench built on the streets of black South Memphis. He also denounced "We Shall Overcome," sit-ins, and getting your head bashed.

"Get your guns," John B. told the crowd. "You're going

Withers's photograph of John B. Smith addressing a sanitation strike rally at Clayborn Temple. Copyright Dr. Ernest C. Withers, Sr., courtesy of the Withers Family Trust, Thewitherscollection.com.

to need them before this is over. . . . You preachers do the praying and we'll do the other work."¹³

Local informants had been on high alert for Black Power involvement in the strike, but up to this point they had seen no evidence of any. Now Withers surmised that Lawson had invited the Black Power element in, just as he had with MAP-South's War on Poverty and the Willis for Mayor campaign.

Lawson's COME and the local NAACP branch had been struggling over control of the strike, Withers told Agent Lawrence. Perhaps allowing John B. to speak had been a shrewd calculation on Lawson's part to wedge out the NAACP. Considering the NAACP's bitter opposition to Black Power, Lawson must have known that the organization would want nothing to do with the Invaders.

As Lawson well knew, however, the Invaders could cause more problems than they solved.

The morning after John B.'s "get your guns" speech, Capt. Earl Clark inventoried the MPD's crowd control equipment: 124 Remington 12-gauge pump shotguns with 20-inch riot barrels, 24 Stevens double-barrel 12-gaugers, 75 Winchester .30-.30 long range rifles, 17 Thompson .45 caliber submachine guns, a pair each of Mauser .30 machine pistols and Smith and Wesson .38 revolvers, 300 batons, 45 nightsticks, a dozen tear gas grenade launchers, hundreds of tear gas and sickening gas grenades, 450 helmets, 115 gas masks, 1,500 Mace canisters, 31,000 rounds of ammunition, three straitjackets, and two sets of leg irons.[14]

The number of militant activists in the street increased, and a new face mixed in with the many surrounding the Invaders. But unlike everybody else in the crowd, he had his own car. So Cab and John B. made Marrell McCullough the group's minister of transportation.[15] For forty cents, McCullough bought some letters to sew across the back of his jackets: INVADERS.

22

AS THE INVADERS GREW IN NUMBER, SO DID GOVERN-
ment anxiety over Black Power. On March 4, 1968, the FBI
director's office issued a document that expanded the counterintelligence program against so-called black-nationalist
hate groups, outlining five major goals.

1. Prevent the coalition of militant black-nationalist
   groups. In unity there is strength . . . An effective coalition of black-nationalist groups might be . . . the beginning of a true black revolution.
2. Prevent the rise of a "messiah" who could unify, and
   electrify, the militant black-nationalist movement. . . .
   Martin Luther King, Stokely Carmichael, and Elijah
   Muhammad all aspire to this position. . . . King could
   be a very real contender for this position should he
   abandon his supposed obedience to white, liberal doctrines (nonviolence) and embrace black nationalism.
3. Prevent violence on the part of black-nationalist
   groups. . . .
4. Prevent black militant nationalist groups and leaders

from gaining respectability, by discrediting them to three separate elements of the community. . . . First, the responsible Negro community. Second, . . . the white community. . . . Third, . . . the Negro radicals, the followers of the movement. This last area requires entirely different tactics from the first two. Publicity about violent tendencies and radical statements merely enhances black nationalists to the last group; it adds "respectability" in a different way.

5. . . . Prevent long-range growth of militant black-nationalist organizations, especially among youth. . . .

J. Edgar Hoover asked FBI field offices to provide a summary of local black nationalist activity, a list of potential targets for COINTELPRO operations, and suggestions for action. "These should not be general . . . but should be specific as to target, what is to be done, what contacts are to be used." Each field office was to file a progress report with Hoover's headquarters every ninety days.

With this memo, Hoover's office put maximum pressure on field agents throughout the country to find and counteract militant groups. While local offices were to carry out the program at the grassroots level, the instructions urged, "We should emphasize those leaders and organizations that are nationwide in scope and are most capable of disrupting this country."[1]

As the COINTELPRO document arrived at the federal building in Memphis, Rev. James Lawson invited a leader who was "nationwide in scope" to come support the strike in Memphis: Dr. Martin Luther King, Jr.

Hearing about Lawson's invitation to King, reporter Kay Pittman Black of the *Press-Scimitar* contacted the Atlanta headquarters of the SCLC to see when King might make it to Memphis. She learned that he had speaking engagements elsewhere through March 15 and passed on this information to the FBI.[2]

As news of a possible visit from King circulated, Lawson assembled the strikers for a sit-in at City Hall. They had regularly gathered to fill the public building and demand attention, sometimes even spreading out bread and cold cuts on a long table to make their lunches. Lawson told the workers and their supporters, including Black Power advocates, that the situation had reached a crisis point. If they continued their sit-in at City Hall and refused to leave, they would be arrested and taken to jail. "I am ready to be arrested," Lawson said.[3]

John B. Smith was not. He walked out of City Hall with another Invader. Memphis police captain Jewell Ray noticed the Black Power boys and told two uniformed patrolmen to tail them and find a reason to arrest them.

Out on the street, the two Invaders flagged a ride. A young African-American man picked up the pair. He didn't know them.

Within a few blocks, the police stopped the car. They arrested the motorist for reckless driving and took the

Invaders to jail on the granddaddy of all trumped-up charges, disorderly conduct.

The police threw the three young men into a holding cell that was already cramped with more than a hundred sanitation strike supporters who'd heeded Lawson's call to sit in at City Hall. A press photographer snapped a picture of John B. looking cool on the other side of the bars.

The next day's news coverage of the sit-in and the mass arrests lumped the Invaders in with Lawson and the strikers. John B.'s picture appeared in the *Press-Scimitar*, straightening his sunglasses, seemingly unimpressed, over the caption:

> "INVADER" BOOKED
> John Smith, wearing a jacket with the word "Invaders" on the back, was one of 118 strike supporters arrested.[4]

The press story gave the impression that John B. had gone to jail in solidarity with the sanitation men. Covering up the police's sham arrest of the two Invaders, it also gave the impression that the Invaders had been part of the strike. That could be useful for the strike only as long as Black Power presence scared up some productive negotiations. But Invader involvement could also harm the strike, linking the nonviolent direct action with the much-feared militant revolutionary threat.

Though the core Invaders had been under surveillance

since the previous July, they had so far been all talk and no violence. The police had no evidence to charge them with any crime. Cab had even stood eye to eye with Agent Lawrence in the FBI office and explained that he didn't mean his violent rhetoric literally, and that assurance seemed to be playing out as hard fact.

The MPD's Invaders infiltrator, Marrell McCullough, would say, "During that time, in the sixties, there was a lot of talk of violence, and this group was no different—a lot of young people getting together, making violent statements and doing a lot of violent talk but actually committing no acts of violence."[5] According to McCullough, the Invaders' armaments consisted of a Saturday-night special—a light-caliber six-shooter—not exactly the tool to wreak widespread havoc.

The FBI even admitted that John B.'s arrest for disorderly conduct had been a "put-up." After the subsequent press coverage, Agent Lawrence wrote that his assets Ernest Withers and Kay Pittman Black

independently advised they regretted the arrest of John B. Smith and the attendant publicity . . . as all this did was to make a martyr and hero of Smith in the eyes of the young impressionable Negroes to whom he and Charles Cabbage have been trying to peddle their Black Power philosophy. . . . In other words, the Memphis Police Department gave him the publicity he so badly wanted, and in order to

satisfy an emotional wish to see him arrested, the
Police Department may well have helped to create
an irresponsible militant agitator whose actions
may create a series of incidents which may later
haunt them.[6]

Despite having an informant and an infiltrator covering
the Invaders, law enforcement had no proof to show that
the Black Power group planned any action to match its violent talk.

This evidence problem would soon change.

John B. got out of jail, feeling resentful of Lawson. Smith
sensed that the minister was merely using the Invaders.
Lawson wanted the fearsome Black Power group involved
so that the city would feel threatened, but he didn't want
the young men making any real decisions.

John B. reasoned that if Lawson wanted the Invaders to bring the hot rhetoric, they would deliver. He put
together the seventh issue of *Afro-American Brotherhood
Speaks*, subtitled *Black Thesis*. The cover carried the slogan "Black Power!!" over an illustration of a clenched fist
in militant salute.

The lead article, written in preacher rhythm, tallied the
dues of being black:

Rents are high, apartments are filthy, and white
policemen patrol your community ready to crack
heads at any moment. Dues are what we pay when

this country will not enforce law to protect us, but rather laws to keep us under control. When these same police beat us half to death and the policemen are promoted and given a raise. Dues are what we pay when the city we live in spends millions of dollars on riot control and nothing on trying to alleviate the conditions that cause them.

A piece on the strike criticized its direction: "The preachers have got us so busy singing praying and marching that we aren't doing anything . . . Why has the community let the preachers take over, and tried to lead in a fight which [t]here must be some real fighting[?]"

By circulating the newspaper outside a strike meeting, the Invaders could purposefully give the impression that it carried some official sanction.

Meanwhile Lawson, after getting out of jail himself on the night of March 5, called together the striking sanitation workers and their supporters at Clayborn Temple. The next day, he announced, they would gather at the temple for a twelve-thirty march, down Beale and up Main to the police station they'd all just come from. They would, Lawson reportedly said, create incidents to cause further mass arrests, a Gandhian tactic that Lawson learned of while working in India.

Charles Cabbage picked up a pile of *Afro-American Brotherhood Speaks* from the office where his girlfriend worked on Beale Street and went over to Clayborn Temple.

Outside he was surrounded by Black Power kids—maybe forty by Ernest Withers's count. One of them handed Withers a copy of the paper.

While putting together the issue, John B. had felt that words weren't enough. He had had an idea. He got in touch with an artist he knew, in fact, the kid who'd named the Invaders: Donnie Delaney.

Donnie drew up the idea, and John B. tacked the illustration on as the last page of the new issue. It looked hastily drawn, but on its full page, it depicted the clearly labeled components of a homemade explosive device under the heading MOLOTOV COCKTAIL.

23

AFTER THE CLAYBORN TEMPLE MEETING, WITHERS HAD
a conversation with Cab, who said he felt the FBI watching
him. He knew the white man was dedicated to the destruction of the Negro, and he expected the white power structure to try to kill militants like him. He wouldn't take it
lying down. He said: "This is a revolution and now is the
time for militant, and, if necessary, violent action."[1]

Cab savored public panic. If white people feared him,
they would know how he had been taught to feel.

Swarms of kids in the streets had bought letters and
sewn INVADERS onto their jackets, enhancing the illusion
of a Black Power revolution. White people and the press
suddenly thought Invaders were everywhere. "The Invaders" summed up white paranoia toward Black Power. "The
Invaders" had captured J. Edgar Hoover's imagination.
"The Invaders" sold papers—as the strike became the con-
suming local drama, people needed heroes and villains.
"The Invaders" verified MPD director Holloman's early
suspicion that through the strike, Black Power could take
hold in the city. Flames and blood in Newark, Watts, and

Detroit primed Memphians for a battle. "The Invaders" stepped straight out of their nightmares.

The FBI and the Memphis police teamed up to track the Black Power group. The police "were as interested in the Invaders as we were," Agent Lawrence recalled. "So in this sense it would probably have been a joint interest—and a joint investigation. We were sharing information as we developed it on almost a daily basis."[2] Every day the FBI's Memphis office sent thick reports on the strike to Director Hoover.

Hoover's old colleague, Memphis police director Frank Holloman, could feel the emotions simmering to a new, volatile level and was concerned about the possibility of violence. "Uppermost in my mind was the knowledge, which I had of what had happened at Watts and Detroit," he recalled, "what had happened in New Jersey, which had happened in other places, in which massive destruction was caused, and that was the one thing that was uppermost in my mind, to prevent a full scale riot and destruction of property and the loss of life and injuries to people in the city of Memphis."

Only a few hundred people at most participated in the marches, and they were more boisterous than threatening, but still the police director deployed tactics designed to keep them in line. "You have to anticipate problems at any type of a large crowd, but particularly one in which emotions are prevalent, and emotions were prevalent at that time," Holloman recalled. He denied counterdemonstrators' permit requests. The strike leadership kept him informed of their march schedules and routes. And of utmost importance, Holloman pushed to keep sidewalks clear during the marches.[3]

As the Invaders attracted more young people to the strike, Holloman noticed a difference between the morning marches, composed entirely of striking sanitation workers, and the afternoon marches, conducted after school let out. This observation didn't require great detective work. The morning marches of older workers proceeded peaceably, without incident. The youth march brought a coffin to City Hall one day and conducted a funeral on the steps, declaring justice dead.

⊢——◆——⊣

On March 14 two speeches at Mason Temple, the COGIC home base, finally made clear the extent of the sanitation strike had great support in the city. First, NAACP director Roy Wilkins and Bayard Rustin, known for organizing the March on Washington, addressed an audience of nine thousand people (according to Memphis police estimates, which skewed toward minimizing strike popularity).

Four days later Dr. King came to town.

"At my first conversations with him," Lawson recalled, "he was at a point of exhaustion, and had been ordered by the doctor to rest absolutely." His doctor feared that he would collapse and prescribed a vacation. So King had taken a few days off to go to Mexico, Lawson recalled.

On the night of March 17, Lawson called King at the hotel in Los Angeles where he was staying. "Did Andy tell you that tomorrow night you'll be speaking to maybe ten thousand people or so in Mason Temple?" he asked.

King said he didn't realize that.

Wilkins and Rustin had recently packed the temple full, Lawson said, and King could plan on drawing a crowd just as big.

King liked the idea of speaking at COGIC's international headquarters and remarked favorably on the legacy of founding bishop Charles Mason. The South didn't have many buildings that could hold a mass meeting of that size, nor had many movements gathered such multitudes.

King asked Lawson to be sure to pick him up at the airport, and the two bade each other fond goodbyes until they met the next day.

The plane touched down after seven that night. Driving to the airport to pick up Dr. King, Lawson and union leader Jesse Epps passed Mason Temple and found it already packed to capacity.

Lawson and Epps decided to tease King a little at the airport. Epps told King, "Jim was wrong. He told you you'd be speaking before ten thousand people, and we found out just tonight that that was a mistake."

King said, "Well is that right?"

Epps said, "You're going to be speaking now before *fifteen thousand* people, because no one else can get in there."

King laughed. "This is really some movement."

They arrived to the temple after nine and entered through a side door. The audience stood and gave King a deafening ovation.

Not every speech makes history, but in Mason Temple, King linked the local strike to his new nationwide Poor People's Campaign and thereby increased the size, urgency, and importance of both. The realization seemed to come to King as he spoke. "Now, you're doing something else here," he said. "You are highlighting the economic issue. You are going beyond purely civil rights to questions of human rights. That is distinct."

The sanitation strike, he explained, exemplified his redefinition of the civil rights movement, beyond integration and voting. "Now our struggle is for genuine equality," he said, "which means economic equality. For we know, that it isn't enough to integrate lunch counters. What does it profit a man to be able to eat at an integrated lunch counter if he doesn't have enough money to buy a hamburger?"

King told the strikers, "This is the way to gain power— power is the ability to achieve purpose. Power is the ability to effect change. . . . I want you to stick it out, so that you will be able to make Mayor Loeb and others say yes, even if they want to say no."[4]

The Poor People's Campaign, he said, would bring poverty out of isolation in places like South Memphis, the

Mississippi Delta, and Alabama's Black Belt and deliver the issue to Washington, where the nation's leaders could not ignore its human costs. They'd build a shantytown on the Mall and assemble a Mississippi sharecropper shack on the front lawn of the Smithsonian.

Behind King on the stage sat Lawson, Andrew Young, and SCLC staffers Ralph Abernathy and James Bevel. Sensing the power of King's connection with the strike, through his spontaneous, impassioned encouragement, Lawson and Young whispered about a new plan—for King to lead a mass march in support of the workers. Lawson passed Young his handy yellow pad, and Young scribbled a note to King.

At the podium, King became even more excited, declaring that all African-American citizens, not just the sanitation men, should go on strike if the mayor wouldn't meet the sanitation department's demands.

Young sneaked the note up in front of King, just as the crowd's cheer built to a roar.

"They will hear you then," King said. "The city of Memphis will not be able to function that day."

He stepped away, without seeing the yellow slip Young had passed him, as the audience gave him another standing, screaming ovation.

Lawson and Young immediately told him their idea that he lead a mass demonstration. King agreed, and Young checked the calendar. They could do it that Friday, March 22.

King turned right back to the podium and told the

crowd to stay away from work and keep the kids out of school on Friday because he'd be back to lead them all in a mass march. Together, King said, they would "make this the beginning of the Washington movement."[5]

Lawson recalled, "And of course there was great general hysteria when he made this announcement."[6]

Now the local movement and the national scene were connected.

King stayed that night at the Lorraine Motel, in room 306, before heading to Mississippi to organize for the Poor People's Campaign.

A police captain in attendance at King's speech characterized the message as "a demagogic appeal to the baser emotions of a predominantly Negro audience." Agent Lawrence included this assessment in the "urgent" report he sent to Director Hoover's office the next day.[7]

Lawrence kept tabs on King's location and phoned the Jackson, Mississippi, office to say that King would be in their territory. Just two weeks after the FBI rolled out its national initiative to neutralize King, he seemed to be building momentum.

24

FRIDAY, MARCH 22, ARRIVED, BRINGING A PARALYZING snowfall. Lawson canceled the march. Heavy snow remained piled on the streets over the weekend, while the FBI scrambled to learn what would happen next.

On Monday night, March 25, a COME meeting set out plans for Dr. King's return. On March 27 Rev. Ralph Abernathy would come to Mason Temple and reinforce King's call for a citywide strike of African-American workers and a walkout of black students from city schools the next day. On the morning of March 28, at ten o'clock, King would lead a mass march from Clayborn Temple to City Hall.

Ernest Withers noted the information. Late that night, after the meeting, he told Agent Lawrence of the mass march schedule. The next morning he and Lawrence conferred again. Afterward Lawrence transmitted the schedule for King's upcoming demonstration to Hoover's office via "urgent" teletype and a letterhead memo.[1]

The march schedule Withers provided was a significant piece of information that the bureau previously had wrong. The papers and police sources reflected misinformation and confusion about the time, date, and route of the march.

King, for his part, was now calling the sanitation strike march a dress rehearsal for his forthcoming Poor People's Campaign in Washington. On the streets of Memphis, he would preview the unity and nonviolent discipline he'd show the world in late April from the nation's capital.

———◆———

At FBI headquarters in Washington, King's plan to bring thousands of poor people from around the United States to the capital vexed his nemesis Hoover. Ten years later, George C. Moore, head of the FBI's racial intelligence division, would describe the Washington's power structure's concerns about the campaign.

> [The] Bureau's attitude toward that proposed
> march on Washington or poor people's campaign,
> Washington spring project, or whatever it might
> have been called at the time, was that there would
> be thousands of people coming into Washington
> and that the situation in the country was becoming
> quite volatile as far as disturbances and riots were
> concerned, and the fact that there could be such a
> mammoth, large march would be a matter of con-
> cern from a violence standpoint, and I believe—and
> it is also my recollection—at the time it was not

only the Bureau's feeling but it was also a feeling of other people, including the Department of Justice as well as—in the back of my mind, I think—the President of the United States was concerned about this sort of thing.[2]

On March 12 the bureau issued a monograph, "Martin Luther King, Jr.: A Current Analysis,"[3] warning that participants in the forthcoming Poor People's Campaign would "conduct sit-ins, camp-ins, and sleep-ins at every Government facility available including the lawn of the White House." King's strategy, according to this document, was not only "massive civil disobedience" but "dramatic confrontation." It quoted King himself as saying, "To dislocate the function of a city without destroying it can be more effective than a riot, because it can be longer lasting, costly to society, but not wantonly destructive."

COINTELPRO had recently formulated the FBI objective of preventing "the rise of a 'messiah' who could unify, and electrify, the militant black-nationalist movement," and it identified King as "a very real contender for this position should he abandon his supposed obedience to white, liberal doctrines (nonviolence) and embrace black nationalism." Now "A Current Analysis" suggested that King and Black Power would unite. "King has met with black nationalists and attempted to gain their support," and had gained the support of Stokely Carmichael. The "danger," the monograph warned, was that "black nationalist groups . . . plan to attempt to seize the initiative and escalate the nonviolent demonstrations into violence." King planned to use this potential for violence to press Congress into taking action "favorable to the Negro."

On March 14, the bureau sent copies of "A Current Analysis" to the president and the attorney general, and within a few days it circulated throughout federal government offices.[4]

The FBI sought to pressure King to abandon the Poor People's Campaign and to keep himself and his three thousand demonstrators away from Washington. The task of counteracting King fell to Moore, head of racial intelligence, who devised the bureau's strategy.

On March 11, at a "racial conference" in Washington, he had introduced a rumor campaign to dissuade potential participants from traveling to Washington. "We could use our informants," Moore wrote, "without their knowledge, to spread the story about lack of funds and organization." Other rumors could spread fear of impending violence, or alternatively mislead supporters into believing that if they came to Washington to participate, their names would be taken down and reported to the government, resulting in their welfare funds being discontinued. Finally, "we would point out also that the Project is strictly for Martin Luther King's benefit which is actually the case."

The bureau encouraged participating agents to "tie in any rumor of this nature to your local problem. Also think of other counterintelligence methods and secure telephonic approval from the Bureau prior to utilization."[5]

On March 26, with King's campaign less than a month from reaching Washington, Moore proposed planting a misleading editorial in FBI-friendly newspapers, "designed to curtail success of Martin Luther King's fund raising for the Washington Spring Project."

———•———

In Memphis, during a lull in strike activity around the March 22 snowstorm, Agent Lawrence caught up on his paperwork, probably in response to Director Hoover's new COINTELPRO directive.

He prepared a lengthy report on Charles Cabbage, summarizing the young Black Power leader's previous nine months, his rise from nonentity to the FBI Rabble Rouser Index. He catalogued Cab's comments—"Memphis should burn," "This city needs a good race riot," "The black man must overthrow capitalism by any means necessary"—and recalled his draft dodging, his founding of the Invaders, and his distribution of a Molotov cocktail recipe.

Lawrence also typed formal reports on his meetings with Withers from early March, describing the atmosphere of violence that had developed through the Invaders' growing physical presence and increasingly brash bombast.

The agent would explain, years later, how he and his top

informant on this mission worked together to maintain the flow of information amid secrecy. "I would call him if I had occasion to alert him to something," Lawrence said. "Otherwise I would hope that he would call me, which he frequently did. Then periodically we would meet in person under what we hoped were safe conditions, to personally exchange information, go over descriptions, any photographs, things of that nature." At his busiest, Withers earned two hundred dollars per week in cash, about $1,500 in current value. This level of income probably made the bureau his top client at the time.

As Memphis thawed and King's return visit approached, Lawrence felt exhausted, having worked around the clock on the sanitation strike and the Invaders for a month and a half.

He wasn't the only man in the city with raw nerves. The anticipation for King's march brought a sense of highwire suspense. Violence and vandalism peppered the city, especially wherever a sign said Loeb's. The mayor's stubbornness toward the strike only made things harder on his brother's businesses. Every night angry young people hit the laundries and barbecue stands with rocks and Molotov cocktails, shattering windows.

Withers connected the steady increase in tension to Charles Cabbage. "Cabbage said he has a master plan," Lawrence wrote of Withers's observations,

> namely to quietly but effectively organize a Black Power militancy in Memphis, a sort of para-

military party. . . . He hopes that its existence will
scare and unnerve the Negro as well as the white
community . . . to the point where the political
power structure of Memphis will fear possible
riots and disruptive tactics on the part of the Black
Power movement. Then, Cabbage will step in and
convince the power structure that only he, Cabbage,
can "keep the lid on" and prevent trouble by controlling the militant Negro groups. He feels that in
this manner, he can become funded . . . to organize
and direct the young Negro militants into nonviolent channels.[6]

Withers called Cab's gambit "verbal blackmail," noting
that the leader had set his sights on gaining an annual salary
of $12,000 for performing the service of controlling local
militants. The streetwise informant felt Cab had based his
plan on the principles of a long con—selling a mark on a
story to extort him. He was working in the spirit of the
Beale underworld rather than racial uplift.

Both Withers and Lieutenant Eli Arkin of the MPD
estimated that ten to twenty thousand people would participate in King's march, based on the huge turnout for
King at Mason Temple and the leader's call for a total
strike and school boycott by the city's African-American
citizens. At Mason Temple, King had seen only the dig-
nified workers sitting in the front row for his talk and the
thousands of adult supporters who had cheered him. He

might not have been aware of the volatility in the street, or the possibility that calling for student participation virtually promised to concentrate the city's violence and anger near downtown.

As militants raced through the city, Withers noticed an offshoot group, younger than the Invaders, led by eighteen-year-old Willie James Jenkins and twenty-year-old John Henry Ferguson, with maybe a dozen followers. Lawrence wrote that "in [Withers's] considered opinion from this group will come those who will engage in sporadic acts of vandalism."

Cab's plan seemed to be working.

On March 27, the day before King's appearance, COME sent a letter to business owners who'd supported the strike, touching on the historical drama and tension of the moment.

> You already know that Dr. King will return to lead the march on Thursday, March 28, 10:00 A.M....
> We want you to march with us that day....
>
> While we understand the fear in which some of you approach Thursday, we also know that to be a man or woman means to push through our fears in order to serve our brothers.

The letter closed, "May the grace of God with love and justice be with us during these momentous days."

COME's list of instructions for the march began with "Be peaceful and non-violent," and urged demonstrators to maintain two car lengths between themselves and the marcher in front of them, and to keep the sidewalk clear. The instructions provided telephone numbers one could call if arrested.

A separate Community on the Move handout flooded the housing projects and schools, speaking to the students Dr. King called on to walk out and join him—

> Be cool, fool,
> Thursday's march is King's thing.
> If your school is tops, pops, prove it.
> Be in the know,
> Get on the go,
> Thursday at 10.
> See you then.
> Together we stick.
> Divided we are stuck, Baby.

As MPD plainclothes detective Ed Redditt canvassed Beale Street, he heard talk that downtown stores would be looted during the march. He passed this tip along to the head of the MPD's inspectional bureau, which furnished it to Chief James MacDonald.[7] The top-level police brass knew the possibilities the next day held.

That night Dr. King's second-in-command, Ralph Abernathy, gave a speech at Mason Temple to motivate the people for the mass march. While Abernathy exhorted the crowd, King mingled at a fundraiser for the Poor People's

Campaign in Harry Belafonte's New York apartment. He drank sherry and padded around in sock feet, talking late into the night.

At the Minimum Salary Building, next door to strike headquarters at Clayborn Temple, Ernest Withers and two other men put together signs for the mass demonstration. "I remember that J. C. Brown and myself and one other fellow named Reverend Grant Harvey were the men that Reverend [H. Ralph] Jackson sent down . . . to rent a saw to cut the sticks for those signs," Withers recalled. "And J. C. Brown printed those I AM A MAN signs right over there at the Minimum Salary Building. I had a car, so we went and rented the saw and came back that night and cut the sticks. We cut them and nailed those I AM A MAN signs on them."[8]

Withers and the two men worked past midnight. The march with Dr. King would mark the first time in the six-week-old sanitation strike that demonstrators would carry mounted picket signs—a minor change that would have dire consequences.

Though Withers knew well the threats and acts of violence soaring through the city, he seems to have missed the potential for mayhem in those sticks. The sight of those garbage men with signs held high would make one hell of a picture, though. As Withers would later explain, he believed at the time that his photographs of the I AM A MAN signs would help people all over the country to understand what was happening in Memphis.[9]

25

AN HOUR AND A HALF BEFORE START TIME, REV. HAROLD Middlebrook asked the sanitation workers to assemble on Hernando Street, outside Clayborn Temple. Ernest Withers turned up in his black-rimmed glasses, a dark jacket, and a white striped sport shirt. He carried two Rolleiflex cameras on straps around his neck.

The garbage men gripped their signs and gathered on the asphalt beside the temple. Withers peered down into the viewfinder of his camera, looking at a miniature mirror image of the scene before him. The sanitation men stood shoulder to shoulder, from curb to curb, several rows deep. They hoisted their signs, blocking the sky with their message: I AM A MAN.

Over three hundred MPD officers began taking their places throughout downtown. Mobile tactical units made up of state highway patrolmen, sheriff's deputies, and city cops cruised through their assigned territories. Pairs of officers stood guard at twenty street corners. Six cruisers each containing four criminal investigators looped through three-block zones. Three pairs of officers had rooftop

detail, with binoculars and walkie-talkies atop tall buildings. Frank Holloman paced his office with the radio on
and Chief MacDonald by his side. Assistant Chief Henry
Lux waited at the airport for Dr. King.

One area of the city was conspicuously uncovered. The
first five blocks of the march route, north on Hernando
Street, turning west on Beale, had no assigned police.[1] This
was a change in strategy. Given the tension surrounding the
strike and the bad precedent of the Mace incident on Main
Street the month before, Holloman opted "to not have a
show of force or to have a large number of policemen in
sight," he later said. "We felt it would be better to depend
upon [organizers of the march] and they assured us of their
ability to marshal the marches themselves and we did rely
on that."

Local police and the FBI's Memphis office now had years
of experience with street marches. Law enforcement had
successfully prevented violent disruption of civil demonstrations going back to the antiwar marches of 1966. Of
course, city authorities had never dealt with a mass march.
March 28 in Memphis would measure up to the Selma-
Montgomery campaign of 1965 and the closing ceremonies
of the March Against Fear in 1966. The largest sanitation
marches until then drew around a thousand protesters, but
most topped out in the low- to mid-hundreds.

One of Holloman's strategies for keeping peace during
the sanitation marches had been to clear the sidewalks, in
order to protect civil demonstrators, ordinary citizens, and

property. Clear sidewalks prevented marchers from getting tangled up with innocent passersby—or malevolent counterdemonstrators—and established a buffer between the marchers and the businesses they passed.

Rev. James Lawson, as the key local organizer, had made his own preparations for the big day, circulating the leaflets to get out the word and coordinating the parade marshals. COME had recruited volunteers to keep marchers off the sidewalks and spaced safely from one another. They wore white armbands to identify themselves.

"Well, Thursday was a very beautiful day as I remember," Lawson said. "Warm, bright, and as I made my way down toward the Minimum Salary Building around eight-thirty or nine, I knew that it would be quite a great event because people were already beginning to gather."

Black Power activists wearing sunglasses, amulets, and army jackets stood on the Clayborn Temple steps. John B. Smith came, but Charles Cabbage stayed away. Plainclothes detectives Ed Redditt and Willie Richmond attempted to blend in but might as well have worn ten-gallon hats and shiny brass stars.

As Withers snapped his classic picture of the sanitation men and their signs, hundreds of students charged out of nearby high schools to join the march. An officer in a police helicopter spotted a group and alerted patrol cars. The kids armed themselves with bottles, bricks, and rocks, and when the cops arrived, the students attacked. The police called for backup and requested clearance to use tear gas. After a thirty-minute standoff, the students overwhelmed the cops and bolted out into the street. They blocked traffic as they skipped and bounded toward Clayborn Temple.[2]

The crowd got jittery with the arrival of the schoolkids. As ten o'clock approached—start time for the march and arrival time for Dr. King—they received picket signs like everyone else, but some turned I AM A MAN around and with lipstick or markers wrote FUCK YOU MAYOR LOEB and LOEB EAT SHIT.

Outside the temple, local NAACP president Jesse Turner and city councilman Fred Davis felt the pressure build as the crowd swelled into the thousands. Teenagers tore off and discarded the I AM A MAN placards and began fencing with the two-by-two signposts.

Davis asked, "Do you believe we can conduct this march and go all the way around [City Hall] and come back . . . without anything happening?"

Turner shook his head. "No chance."[3]

During this juncture, an FBI source reportedly advised Agent Lawrence of the potential problem these sticks presented.

The route of the march was to first lead right through the haunt of pickpockets and pool sharks, pimps and boosters, to the corner of Beale and Hernando. There a number of known Beale Street criminals, Withers would report, mixed in with the strike supporters. He reportedly saw a female leader of the Invaders drinking Robitussin, beverage of choice for the Beale underworld. The two African-

American plainclothes detectives at the scene watched kids passing bottles, downing wine and whiskey.

The march's ten a.m. start time arrived, but King didn't. The temperature broke seventy degrees, less than a week after a record snowfall. Marchers sang and beat drums. The police chopper buzzed overhead. Five to six thousand demonstrators were now jammed into a few narrow streets around the temple. Parade marshals struggled to keep everyone under control.

Voices in the crowd threatened, "We gon' tear this sonofabitch town up!" and "We're gonna get some white bastards today."[4]

"It was very clear from the beginning," Lawson noted, "that all kinds of people were milling in every which way and all kinds of directions. The sidewalks stayed filled, and in spite of my various attempts to get the marshals to function, to clear the sidewalks and get people to march in the street, the sidewalk stayed pretty full. Especially Hernando . . . the sidewalks there were just completely filled with people all the way up and down."

Lawson and Holloman both wanted clear sidewalks, but no police were present to help control the crowd, and the parade marshaling was insufficient to handle the job. Several strike leaders felt the march just needed to begin in order to release tension.

At ten-thirty, word reached the temple that King's flight had finally arrived—the SCLC leader would head straight for the scene. A white Lincoln Continental soon drove up and stopped near the head of the parade. Lawson recalled, "When the car from the airport got there at the Hernando-Linden intersection, well, pandemonium broke out. By that I mean everyone was excited and hysteria reigned."

Even inside the car, Dr. King felt the volatility. Faces and hands pressed against the windows. Abernathy tried to cut the mood, kidding that he'd got the crowd *too* excited at his speech last night.[5]

Lawson cleared his way to the Lincoln and opened a door. King stepped out, dressed in a dark double-breasted suit, white shirt, and shimmering slim tie.

A group of young men made a break through the crowd as they moved toward King.[6] Now at the head of the march, King linked arms with Abernathy and another preacher and began walking toward Beale Street.

Assistant Chief Lux would remain with the front line of the march, the only cop in sight. He had a radio to Holloman's desk and a bullhorn in his hand. As King and the human chain advanced, the kids from farther back in the march jostled him, patted his shoulder, and reached for his hand. King got unnerved.

Now before King stood a man with a camera, the same man who had taken his picture on the bus in Montgomery twelve years before. King had been twenty-seven that day in 1956. Now he was crowding forty. He looked fifty.

Withers peered down into the camera viewfinder. The leader looked edgy.

Between the late night at Belafonte's place and the

morning flight, plus the overwhelming atmosphere crackling around him, King had reason to feel unsettled. He seemed to try to slow down but couldn't with the feisty crowd of thousands pushing him forward. The churning crowd stretched back at least three blocks, bouncing and hefting their signs. King could have lifted both feet and been propelled by the great momentum behind him.

Lawson, marching near King, saw that the sidewalks were fully crowded.

The column headed west on Beale toward the Mississippi River.

At the tail end—three blocks behind King—an FBI informant listened to a young man associated with the Invaders tell a group of fifteen to twenty teenagers and college kids to smash windows and loot.[7]

Another informant saw this group carrying two-by-two signposts with no signs attached.[8]

Officers aboard the two police choppers overhead saw this group make its move.[9] Near the corner of Beale and Hernando, a boy no older than fifteen wielded his two-by-two, swung at the front display window at Quality Liquors, and shattered the glass.[10] Looters flooded the place. The woman working there shouted, "You can have anything you want so you don't harm me." A looter picked up the cash register and carried it out.[11] Practically every bottle in the store soon followed.

Within moments, the young men swung their two-by-twos and shattered the glass at Paul's Tailoring, across

Withers's photograph of Dr. Martin Luther King, Jr., leading the sanitation strike demonstration of March 28, 1968. Copyright Dr. Ernest C. Withers, Sr., courtesy of the Withers Family Trust, Thewitherscollection.com.

Beale from the liquor store. Paul's employees retreated from the front of the shop and clung helplessly to the back wall as the crowd streamed in through the broken panes and pulled out handfuls of suits and swaths of cloth, and spilled back out like water through a busted dam.

Looters with two-by-twos smashed windows all along Beale Street, breaking glass of pawnshops, shoe stores, and Schwab's dry goods, anywhere stuff could be grabbed.

At the head of the march, King flinched. The window pops sounded like gunshots. He kept moving forward, turning north up Main Street.

Merchandise piled on sidewalks and in gutters: broken bottles, a fractured violin, a trampled fedora, a dismembered mannequin. The cry "Burn it down, baby!" soared above the clash.

King had stood in the eye of extreme violence before, withstanding a police attack in Selma, a racist mob attack in Cicero, and a bomb explosion at his home in Montgomery. But never before had one of his marches turned violent from within.

The first assigned police guard, just a pair of officers, stood at the corner of Second and Beale. They radioed for backup.

The cops had been concentrated, per Holloman's plan, along Main Street, the heart of the white shopping district. The head of the march turned right onto Main, toward a line of officers, who already wore gas masks.

Looters rushed from the tail to the front of the march and smashed into the police. Around Dr. King, rioters clubbed police with their signposts, and police struck back with nightsticks. A looter shattered a window. No plot to harm King physically could have been better orchestrated. He stood exposed in the middle of a riot. He had to find safety or take his chances in a street battle. The march was hopeless.

His top men, Ralph Abernathy and Bernard Lee, remained by his side. They flagged down a car, the last one allowed across Main as police closed the street. The driver recognized the three men. Lee opened the driver-side door, and the driver slid over to let him take the wheel. King and Abernathy got in back.[12]

King had been downtown for less than half an hour.

Lawson would say that he urged King to get away from the march but that King refused until practically forced into the car.

Assistant Chief Lux, however, would say that King abandoned the march, fearing for his own safety, without attempting to stop any of the violence or property destruction. Lux would quote King as saying, "I've got to get out of here." The quote would form an important part of the smear campaign to come.

A police motorcyclist escorted King from the scene. Assistant Chief Lux had already informed headquarters that windows were being broken. With King safely away, he ordered the march to be dispersed and handed his bullhorn to Lawson.

Lawson ordered the marchers to turn around and head

back through the melee to Clayborn Temple. But before they could reach safety, police cars began arriving from City Hall on Beale's cross streets, alongside the riot. Officers engaged with rioters and launched tear gas canisters as soon as the order came to disperse.

Legitimate protesters—the sanitation men, ministers, and peaceful demonstrators—were herded into the battle, where police indiscriminately clubbed and gassed them along with rioters and looters.

Ernest Withers, once he heard windows shatter, had broken away from the front of the march. In a day of conflicting reports and warring agendas, he performed a vital function. He roamed through the mess, camera drawn. He snapped pictures of police standing in a circle around a young man who lay on the sidewalk as they beat him unconscious with their nightsticks. Published in the local black press, the image would contradict the cops' denials that there had been police brutality. A policeman swung his nightstick at Withers and got his picture in *Time* magazine.

Gas-mask-wearing officers marched up Beale in a line of battle toward Clayborn Temple. Lawson, with a slight head start, had gotten many peaceful marchers to move toward safety. The police arriving at Clayborn Temple, however, learned that rioters had arrived first. A shower of bricks and rocks rained on officers from the temple roof.

At twelve-thirty, Patrolman L. D. Jones, clutching his sawed-off pump shotgun, and with eyes streaming from the

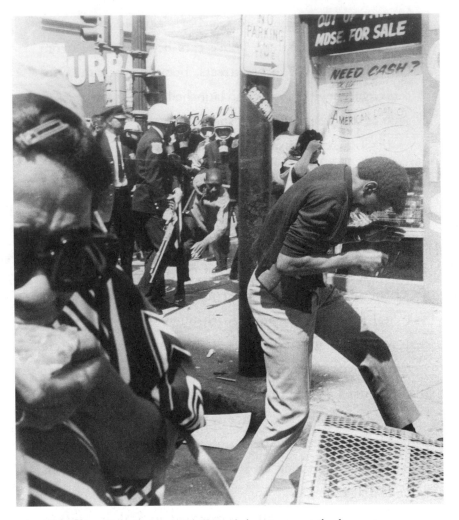

Memphis police officers stop the King-led sanitation strike demonstration of March 28, 1968. Special Collections Department, University of Memphis Library.

gas, told a group of reporters, "We're trying our damndest. Write that down. We're trying our damndest. The police didn't start this. Write that down. Treat us fair."[13]

Fifteen minutes later Patrolman Jones and his partner, C. F. Williams, caught a call that a looting was in progress at the Sears, Roebuck on South Third—the riot had spread a mile from its epicenter. They drove to the store and saw the windows busted out. Glimpsing a teenager carrying a TV set, they followed.

They chased the boy to the Fowler Homes apartments. Williams stopped the cruiser. Jones got out and pushed through a crowd that had rushed from the courtyard to block the police car. Sixteen-year-old Larry Payne, the boy the police had tailed, hid in a boiler room. Patrolman Jones went down the steps after him, as neighbors moved in tight on the police. Jones would say that fifteen or twenty people closed in on him, shouting threats. He drew his shotgun and yelled for Payne to come out with his hands up. Payne cracked the door.

Patrolman Jones would say that Payne put his left hand out, holding it up in surrender, but when Payne's right hand came out, it held "the biggest knife I have ever seen."[14]

Numerous other witnesses would contradict the cop's account. Payne "threw up his hands," John Nolan said. "He had them up before he came out the door. Larry stood there. The policeman put a gun in his stomach and pulled the trigger. It was a shotgun. Larry's hands were still above his head." At 1:20 p.m., Payne was pronounced dead at John Gaston Hospital—the riot's only fatality.[15]

A photograph published the next day shows Payne among a group of three young African Americans outside a Main Street tailor shop. The shop's windows are all broken, and a policeman is beating one of the three, while another lies dazed nearby. Payne stands behind the cop. Beside each young man, a two-by-two signpost lies on the ground.

A phone call came in to Frank Holloman's office from Lawson at Clayborn Temple. "The black power boys are here trying to stir up the crowd," the minister reportedly said. "We have to get the women and children out of here."[16]

Withers made his way to the temple. Police charged into the sanctuary and launched tear gas, the grenades arching high under the vaulted ceiling, trailing fumes. Though they would deny resorting to such tactics inside a church, Withers's photographs tell the truth, showing officers leaving the building in gas masks, some carrying gas grenade launchers.

At City Hall, Holloman hung up with Lawson and rushed to an emergency city council session. He told the council, "We have a war in the city of Memphis."[17]

The first bulletin from FBI Memphis went to Washington D.C. at 1:14 p.m.:

> Rev. Martin Luther King Jr. arrived Memphis around ten a.m. and proceeded to Clayborn Temple, located heart of Negro area, Memphis, and headed the scheduled downtown mass march in support of Memphis sanitation strike with marchers estimated by police to be five to six thousand in number, leaving temple area at approximately eleven a.m. cst The parade marshals were unable to form any orderliness to marchers and as crowd moved in Negro

neighborhood it began breaking windows and engaging in sporadic looting. King remained with crowd . . . until it reached south end of Main . . . which put it into the downtown business area. At this point King dissociated self from march.[18]

Just as the wire was crossing Director Hoover's desk, a Molotov cocktail blew out the windows of the Loeb Laundry a block south of Clayborn Temple.[19]

At two in the afternoon, Mayor Loeb instituted a seven p.m. curfew, authorizing the arrest of anyone who couldn't furnish an official business or emergency reason for being out. The governor of Tennessee mobilized the National Guard, but not before Molotov cocktails crashed through store windows all over the city as the action scattered.

The police made three hundred arrests that day and shot four alleged looters, including Larry Payne. Sixty people, including five police, sought hospital treatment for their injuries. Approximately 150 fires were reported. Glass shards, fractured two-by-twos, and torn cardboards bearing the slogan I AM A MAN choked the gutters along Beale Street.

Despite the riot, injuries, property damage, and death, and despite the tanks crunching through the city enforcing the curfew, nothing could stop a party planned for that night. Shortly after seven, when Mayor Loeb's curfew began, guests began arriving at his brother Bill's home. Bill had brought a shiny new investor into his local barbecue business and wanted to introduce him to friends.

As the city smoldered, sixty elites stood on the back lawn at Bill's palace and watched Pat Boone play doubles tennis.[20]

26

SEVEN MILES WEST OF THE LOEB CELEBRATION, MARTIN
Luther King, Jr., lay despondent.

After leaving the scene of the riot, he and his group had
checked into the Holiday Inn—Rivermont, a high-rise
hotel overlooking the Mississippi River, about a mile and a
half from where the march began. They took a suite on the
eighth floor. King had got into bed fully clothed and pulled
up the covers.[1]

While burning through a chain of Salems, he spoke
to Ralph Abernathy, who'd been his adviser so long, he'd
posed for Ernest Withers's camera next to King on the
front seat of the first integrated bus in Montgomery.

"Maybe we just have to admit that the day of violence
is here," King said. "Maybe we just have to give up and let
violence take its course."

Abernathy had never seen King like this nor heard him
talk this way. In his depression, King contemplated calling
off the Poor People's Campaign.

To lift King's mood, another aide arranged for an

important friend to get in touch. Stanley Levison phoned King's room from his home in New York City.

An adviser and fund-raiser for King's SCLC, Levison had been a faithful friend for many years. Formerly an affiliate of the Communist Party–USA, Levison had been Hoover's justification for investigating King, as a possible Red influence of the civil rights movement.

The bureau tapped Levison's phone and picked up his conversation with King in Memphis. Agents heard King tell Levison that a local Black Power group called the Invaders had incited the riot.

———◆———

In the confusion of March 28, 1968, it's easy to lose sight of the day's key issue—the possibility that the FBI sabotaged Dr. King's march. The riot happened during a month of increasing federal anxiety over the Poor People's Campaign and two days after the FBI proposed smearing Dr. King to curtail support among potential supporters. If the bureau had indeed encouraged the riot, it would need someone else to blame. Creating a wedge between King and Black Power fit the bureau's COINTELPRO objective of preventing the rise of a black messiah who could electrify and unify the black nationalist movement, beginning a true black revolution. The conduct of Ernest Withers's longtime handler, William Lawrence, in documenting the riot, provides clues of treachery.

While King smoked in bed, Ernest Withers conferred with Lawrence. The next day Lawrence finished a long memo about the riot, which the Memphis office sent on to Hoover.

Lawrence had three sources of information about the demonstration: Ernest Withers, *Memphis Press-Scimitar* reporter Kay Pittman Black, and a third party whose observations closely match those of MPD undercover officer Marrell McCullough, who had infiltrated the Invaders. Addressing the factors that contributed to the violence, Lawrence wrote that Lawson's COME strike support group had unwittingly armed anyone who showed up to march.

> The COME group handed out literally hundreds of prepared placards made of cardboard and carried on long 4-foot pine poles. It was apparent to these three sources prior to the march that many of the youngsters were planning to use the placards as sticks and clubs because they were indiscriminately ripping the cardboard away, leaving a 4-foot pole in their hands which many of them waved in a threatening manner.[2]

Lawrence was referring here to the I AM A MAN strike support posters. Addressing how the two-by-twos became weapons, Lawrence's "source one" for this memo—Withers—made the most specific accusation against an Invaders leader in provoking the riot.

Source one pointed out that prior to the start of
the March 28, 1968 march that John [B.] Smith
and some of his associates were in his opinion inciting to violence in that they were indiscriminately
giving out the 4-foot pine poles to various teenage
youngsters in the area and John Smith was heard
by source one to tell these youngsters, identities not
known, not to be afraid to use these sticks. He did
not elaborate as to what he meant.[3]

Later in the summary, Lawrence wrote, "Source one
[Withers] pointed out that as mentioned . . . these individuals [the Invaders] had done much by their previous statements and actions . . . to incite some of the more ignorant
and greedy youths who were in the march."[4] By "previous
statements and actions," Withers reportedly meant the
Molotov cocktail handout that the Invaders had distributed three weeks before the march.

Lawrence's—and the FBI's—explanation for the origins
of the riot was that COME had handed out the sticks, the
Invaders had instructed youths in using them as weapons,
and a nonviolent march had become a riot.

But there are problems with this formulation. For one,
Invaders leader John B. Smith denied that he had handed
out signposts to youngsters at the march or encouraged
their use as weapons. Such a denial is what one would
expect, but Smith got some pretty strong backup from
the police officer who'd infiltrated the Invaders. In 1978

Marrell McCullough testified to the House Select Committee on Assassinations (HSCA), which was conducting an inquiry into the King assassination. McCullough corroborated Smith's claim:

> I was with the Invader group, and they never joined the march. They were just walking around the temple here talking. . . . John [B. Smith] spent most of his time right around the door of the temple. . . . I never saw him [remove the sticks from the placards and pass them to youngsters,] and I never saw anyone passing sticks out to the youngsters, other than the sticks with the placards on them.

Asked about Lawrence's March 29 memo stating that Smith had urged people to commit violence, McCullough replied, "I would characterize [Smith's statements] as rhetoric of violence but nothing specific as to 'take this stick and break a window.'"

Another point in favor of John B. Smith came out of the HSCA inquiry itself. The committee conducted a thorough investigation of the riot, using its power to subpoena FBI files and gain access to confidential sources. It studied Lawrence's March 29 memo to headquarters, and his source's accusation that Smith had handed out the two-by-twos and told people to not be afraid to use them. HSCA took testimony from that confidential source, and found discrepancies between the informant's testimony and the statements in Lawrence's memo, concluding: "The informant denied having provided certain information that had been attributed to him and placed in his informant file."

When Lawrence himself testified before the committee, he stated that his sources of information on the riot and the Invaders had been accurate. Afterward he contacted Withers and told him "that committee had asked me if info attributed to him—in my letterhead memo [of March 29] had actually been furnished by him—and I had to reply that it had been."[5]

Lawrence acknowledged that he couldn't tell Withers what to say to the HSCA, but warned that "denying that he had ever furnished info which I attributed to him . . . would nevertheless create a situation indicating that He or I had perjured ourselves in that I said one thing and he another."

The HSCA leveled no perjury charges but concluded that "the discrepancy tarnished the evidence given by both the Bureau and the informant, and it left the committee with a measure of uncertainty about the scope of FBI involvement with the Invaders."[6]

As Lawrence said, *someone* perjured himself about the Invaders in the riot. All the evidence indicates that it was Lawrence who fabricated the story of Smith inciting violence and misattributed this version of events to his "source one" informant, Withers.

In the months following the 1968 riot, Lawrence would repeat the story of Smith inciting it with greater embellishment. In a lengthy report dated May 6, 1968, he upgraded the statement about the sticks to a direct quote: "Source two [Withers] . . . recalled hearing John B. Smith tell some of the youngsters, 'Don't be afraid to use these sticks if you have to.'"[7]

Perhaps the strangest thing is that Lawrence never pursued the matter further, indicating that his case against Smith must not have been very strong. The FBI never arrested or prosecuted Smith on charges associated with the riot, despite the evidence in its files that he had incited it. The evidence shows that the FBI used Withers falsely as a source of untrue information—a revelation, if not one that clarifies the bureau's role, or Withers's, in spoiling the final march of Dr. King.

———•———

While Lawrence inaccurately held Smith responsible for inciting violence in his March 29 memo, he failed to disclose his informant's own proximity to the signposts used that day as weapons.

In a May 6, 1968, report, Lawrence wrote, "[Withers] pointed out that the COME group had organized the march and had made a bad mistake by giving out several hundred pre-constructed pasteboard placards which had been stapled onto long pine poles or sticks."[8] The distribution of the poles appears here as a "bad mistake" on the part of COME, according to Withers, the person who brought the lumber to the strike.

Lawrence rehashed the story of the two-by-twos even more flavorfully later in the report.

> On the night of March 28, 1968, source two [Withers] advised that the biggest definite contributing factor to the violence in his opinion was the fact that the COME group had for the first time in any of their numerous daily marches furnished wooden sticks to the marchers, as previously they had merely used cardboard placards which could not become lethal weapons. He pointed out that giving out several hundred hard pine sticks was tantamount to giving out an equal number of baseball bats which could easily be used to break windows and which could be used as weapons by the participants in the march.[9]

Again, it seems strange that the person who supervised bringing the sticks to the march could so quickly claim that what he had done "was tantamount to giving out an equal number of baseball bats."

In neither instance did Lawrence note Withers's role in putting the two-by-twos into play, though he seems to have been aware of it. In a memo to the Memphis office dated April 2, 1968, Lawrence provided deeper detail on the origin of the sticks.

> [First name unknown] Harvey, brother of Fred Harvey, and who is a teacher at Jeter High School, earlier in the week . . . rent[ed] a Skil

saw which was taken to the Minimum Salary
Office of AME Church next to Clayborn Temple,
where J. C. Brown cut the pine wood into four-foot
lengths for the placards.[10]

Much of this memo has been redacted. But those names—
Harvey and Brown—corroborate what Withers told a
German sociologist in 1982: "If anybody is . . . responsible for that riot up there, as anybody, I might be responsible, . . . because I and Harvey and J. C. Brown back here
went down . . . there to rent the saw to cut the sticks that
was used in the riot and we certainly wasn't doing it by plan."

Also on April 2, J. Edgar Hoover may have directed the
use of FBI funds for some yet unknown endeavor. A teletype from him to the Memphis bureau that day reads in
part (the document is heavily redacted):

> In the event it is necessary to [name redacted]
> for actual expenses incurred, authority is granted to
> pay him up to seven five dollars. If payment is made,
> obtain itemized accounting of his expenses.[11]

Agent Lawrence's signature appears, acknowledging receipt
of Hoover's memo.

Perhaps the FBI Memphis memo describing the construction of the signs and the teletype with Hoover's pay-
ment authorization also contain information linking the
FBI to the two-by-twos. But until we are able to view unre-
dacted copies of both, we'll never know.

27

ERNEST WITHERS WAS WELL AWARE OF THE ATMOSPHERE of violence permeating his city, so it's hard to excuse his help in distributing the lumber on March 28 as a miscalculation, and it's especially difficult to accept that a longtime, well-compensated FBI operative made such a mistake innocently.

Withers the photojournalist, however, had a vested interest in getting a picture that would tell the story of the sanitation strike. The I AM A MAN signs positively met L. Alex Wilson's guidelines about depicting civil rights : *Does it hurt? Is it true? What good does it do?* The photographer had followed these principles to Montgomery, Tent City, and Medgar Evers's funeral, and he had pursued many dangerous leads over the years to tell the story. On the day of the riot, he had walked through tear gas across the shattered glass of the neighborhood where he'd done business for twenty years, calmly documenting cases of police brutality and misconduct that would be seen in local papers and across the country. His conduct as a photojournalist never changed during the years of his informant work, and his courage and commitment through the most physically threatening and emotionally trying times of his life are beyond reproach. As a small businessman, he had a market for strike photography and an incentive to create a powerful image. Throughout the strike, he sold his work to the *Tri-State Defender* and the *Memphis World*. The two-by-two sticks were an important prop, and he had a legitimate motive for hands-on involvement in the assembly of the signs.

But the secret Withers, the spy, also had reasons to spoil the march. Rev. James Lawson, a target of Withers's espionage and his personal enmity, had orchestrated the march and invited Dr. King. A disaster had the potential to ruin Lawson in local civil rights circles and to demote him in King's esteem. Withers had often spoken to Agent Lawrence of Lawson's unpopularity among NAACP leaders and the minister's own flock, once implying that African-American leaders wanted Lawson out of Memphis. In an interview in his later years, Withers damned Lawson as an egotistical attention-seeker, the type of figure whom both L. Alex Wilson and William H. Lawrence cautioned Withers against.

Scapegoating the Invaders for causing the riot had the potential to discredit a group for whom Withers had no respect. Invaders had been calling for a riot in Memphis for the past nine months. Though Withers knew better than anyone how likely—or unlikely—Invader threats were to be carried out, pinning a riot on the group would destroy the credibility of Black Power in Memphis. This concept may have appealed to Withers the civil rights conservative, forcing the movement's alpha leader away from fringe elements.

Of course, Withers may have seen the I <u>AM</u> A MAN signs as good for both causes, helping the strike and the FBI.

———◆———

There are other factors to consider in the March 28 violence.

Frank Holloman's strategy, as we have seen, was to keep police out of sight for the first several blocks of the march. In this respect, he broke from tactics that had been used to protect civil demonstrations from unrest in Memphis going back to 1965. But in so doing, he failed to keep the sidewalks clear to protect citizens' property during demonstrations. The absence of police in those blocks played directly into the hands of the looters and others who carried the widely distributed two-by-twos.

If the Invaders had nothing to do with inciting the violence or acts of looting, who did?

Lawson investigated immediately after March 28 and concluded that some encouragement to loot had come from a "combination playboy crook." This individual had allegedly stood on the corner of Beale and Hernando and vocally encouraged theft. "These were not Invaders," Lawson said in an interview two years after the riot, "and the fact is, the Invaders were nowhere to be seen at this time." Lawson, like Invader John B. Smith and undercover men Marrell McCullough and Ernest

Withers, exonerated the Invaders, countering the FBI's conclusion that Smith had fomented the riot.

During his investigation, Lawson obtained pictures of the action, showing "people in the march and people who were in the sidewalk. We found a number of pictures of guys who were fairly well known as small-time shoplifters and thieves in the Beale Street area. . . . In doing some talking to various people, it became clear that this main strategy was planned essentially by these kinds of persons. . . . Helping to get windows busted they had certain plans to replenish their stocks."

He added, "This is the way that one person that worked on this said that it happened. And he put his report together from a number of people that were working in the streets."

Lawson did not divulge the names of those who provided photographs and observations linking the looting to the underworld. There were at least four African-American professional photographers on the scene. Of course, one photographer had impeccable knowledge of the Beale Street underworld and knew very well about Hayes Riley, the criminal chieftain on Beale whose political connections went back to the turn of the century. Many years later Withers told me as we meandered up Union Avenue, "you oughta look into a fellow named Hayes Riley, Beale Street hustler."

Of the looters, Lawson said, "I wouldn't say this is a formal clan, but we do know for example that there was systematic looting of stores, and that automobiles did pull up to certain stores on Beale Street and take out everything in the windows very quickly."

He explained, "We had people on the streets working on this, particularly after we saw many of the photographs and particularly after those photographs were identified for us."[1]

Withers connected Lawson to a bigger theory. In an interview for the 1981 documentary film *Beale Street*, he said, "Jim Lawson says that there was infiltration by people, elements, provided by some agency in America. Without indicting any agency by name, he said that there was a heavy influx of out-of-town troublemakers. Plus, a heavy group of mad young people, that were really not a part of the real interests of the march."

Pressure mounted on King to curtail the Poor People's Campaign in light of the Beale Street disturbance.

On the evening of the riot, two U.S. senators called on him to cancel his march on Washington. "If this self-seeking rabble-rouser is allowed to go through with his plans here," said Harry Byrd of West Virginia, a segregationist, "Washington may well be treated to the same kind of violence, destruction, looting, and bloodshed."

Edward Brooke, the nation's highest-ranking African-American official, said, "He [Dr. King] has a difficult task to keep it nonviolent. I don't believe that riots and looting like we had in Memphis will serve the cause of civil rights."[2]

In Washington, FBI racial intelligence chief George C. Moore contacted assistant director William Sullivan, noting that the Memphis riot "clearly demonstrates that acts of so-called nonviolence advocated by King cannot be controlled. The same thing could happen in his planned massive civil disobedience for Washington in April."[3] Moore alerted the Memphis FBI office to find out if King had done anything to trigger the violence, if he had made statements to incite the crowd, or if he had attempted to get the marchers under control and prevent violence.[4]

At 7:22 p.m. on March 28, Memphis sent a teletype to Washington, relaying police intelligence official Lieutenant Eli Arkin's account of King's actions during the riot. "Arkin stated King was obviously scared and stated, 'I've got to get out of here.' When the trouble started . . . King made no effort to quiet the mob . . . his only concern was to run and protect himself."[5]

The next day, based on this information, Moore proposed to Sullivan that the FBI "publicize hypocrisy on the part of Martin Luther King."[6] He composed a two-paragraph editorial that stated, "Like Judas leading lambs to slaughter, King led the marchers to violence, and when the violence broke out, King disappeared." He headed, the piece declared, to the white-owned Holiday Inn, despite the strike's boycott of white downtown businesses, instead of to the African-American-owned Lorraine Motel, where he usually stayed.

An FBI-inspired editorial against King ran in the March 30, 1968, *St. Louis Globe Democrat.* That same day the Memphis *Commercial Appeal*—where editor Frank Ahlgren had long supported Hoover and the FBI—called the civil rights leader Chicken à la King, accusing him of fleeing the scene of the trouble he'd brought. A *Commercial Appeal* editorial echoed the bureau's theme, that violence followed the nonviolent leader and that Washington, D.C., would not be safe if the Poor People's Campaign took place. "Dr. King's pose as a leader of a nonviolent movement has been shattered. He now has the entire nation doubting his word when he insists his April project—a shanty town sit-in in the nation's capital—can be peaceful."[7] A caricature illustration showed the leader standing in a pile of broken glass, saying, "Who? Me?"

Just before Dr. King left Memphis the day after the riot, Stanley Levison called him again, with the FBI listening via its bug on Levison's end.

"I think that we have to face the fact that from a public relations point of view and every other way we are in serious trouble," King said. "I think as far as the Washington campaign is concerned it is in trouble."

Levison disagreed, but King countered that other African-American leaders would seize the news from Memphis to discredit him. They'd say, "Martin Luther King is dead," King explained. They'd say, "He's finished. His nonviolence is nothing, no one is listening to it."

He continued, "Let's face it, we do have a great public relations setback where my image and my leadership are concerned."

Levison replied, "That is only if you accept their definition, and this, I think, is a profound error you are making."

"But I'm saying I don't accept it myself," King said.
"What I'm saying is that many people will accept it."

Levison said, "And I say the people will accept it for a few
days, but if events prove otherwise, they will not accept it."

"That's the point," King said, "if events prove otherwise."

King said the riot showed a failure of leadership in
Memphis. The Invaders started trouble, he said, to get
revenge on Jim Lawson. "They were too sick to see what
they were doing yesterday was hurting me much more than
it could hurt the local preachers."

Levison argued that perfect adherence to nonviolence
would always be a problem for King's demonstrations. "The
other side can always find a few provocateurs to start violence no matter what you do."

"So I've got to do something," King said, "that becomes a
kind of powerful act . . . of unifying forces and refuting the
claims that would be made by the press."

"I'm just very bothered by the idea that you would be
accepting the logic of the press," Levison countered, "which
is that if you can't control 100 percent and only 99 percent, you are a failure. This kind of arithmetic makes sense
nowhere else, but they have imposed this on you."

"Well, you watch your newspapers," King said. ". . . I
think it will be the most negative thing about Martin
Luther King that you have ever seen."

"The first reaction will be exactly what you are describing," said Levison, "but I don't think that it is absolutely inevitable that the truth is going to get buried."

"It will stay buried, Stan, unless I do something now."

To King, it would not be enough to control his followers in Washington. He needed to show that he could unite the turbulent elements of the movement. At a news conference on the morning of March 29, 1968, he declared, "We are going to have a massive nonviolent demonstration in Memphis."

———————•———————

Returning to Memphis less than a week later, King would be murdered. The assassination overshadows the riot, but it highlights the significance of the event. If the windows on Beale hadn't been broken, King would have had no reason to come back.

Withers observed King and his top SCLC associates closely during the final two days of King's life. Withers photographed King's arrival to Memphis airport on April 3. Withers hung around the Lorraine Motel, where King's party and several Invaders were staying. With the city under a tornado warning, Withers followed King's party to Mason Temple and heard King address a mass meeting of two thousand. Late that night and into the next morning, Withers attended a meeting of COME, SCLC, and the Invaders. He reported to Agent Lawrence on the high tension among Charles Cabbage, members of the local movement, and King's SCLC advisers. King, however, remained patient and conciliatory toward the militants.[8]

Withers spent April 4, 1968, in court. Federal judge Bailey Brown had issued a temporary restraining order to prevent the SCLC from leading a mass march in Memphis, and King's attorneys argued for the removal. That evening Withers returned to the Lorraine but then left for his Beale Street studio. That was where he heard about the shooting.

28

THE FIRST FBI MAN ON THE SCENE OF THE KING ASSASSI-
nation was Special Agent Howard Teten.

He had simply been agent on call for that particular shift, but he of all agents was a fateful choice. Teten was a criminal scientist, at that moment developing the types of psychological profiling and forensic crime scene analyses that would launch a thousand TV shows but had yet to become standard investigative procedure. Teten is known today as the godfather or grandfather of criminal profiling, for developing and teaching his technique of reading the psychological makeup of a criminal based on the crime scene. The bureau neither supported nor stood in the way of his research, which he based on solved homicide case files, and the bureau probably didn't know he was working on such a thing.

His role in the Memphis office was weapons instructor, and his input on the assassination case would not have been major. But he did catch the call.

Teten and two MPD officials processed the crime scene. "I went to the autopsy," Teten said, "which is the reason I know the path of the bullet."

He would say only that there had been forensic problems with respect to collecting the evidence, including the alleged murder weapon, without going into detail.

As the investigation proceeded, and the case against alleged assassin James Earl Ray picked up steam, Teten's psychological profiling tactics kicked in, and he felt doubts about the conclusion that Ray had acted alone in killing King. "I recall being very upset because no one would listen to what I thought were very important things," he said.

Teten learned that Ray had initially purchased a certain type of rifle from a Birmingham sporting goods store and had had it fitted with a scope. The weapon, Teten felt, was an excellent choice for "hunting humans."

But then Ray returned to the store and exchanged the rifle "for what I consider a total piece of trash," Teten said, "but had a heavier caliber. And I felt it suggested that he really didn't know what the hell he was doing, but someone told him to use a different caliber gun."

For Ray to make the swap on his own made no sense. "And I thought, um boy, somebody else is involved here."

The shot was not that of a pro, which certainly fit Ray. The assassin had aimed for King's head and missed by four inches, Teten determined—two things an experienced sniper would not have done.

"But there's been books written about Ray not being the killer," Teten said. "I processed that bathroom he shot out of, and I looked at those angles, and that shot couldn't have come from anyplace else. They tried to say it came from down in the bushes. It couldn't have come from down in the bushes. The angle was wrong.

"And the bullet had to have come from an angle. I laid out that angle. Simple trigonometry. I just laid it out and there it was. It landed right on that window [where the shot originated]. And we measured it. We triangulated it. We did get down and cast footprints in all the weeds and brush down in there [beneath the flophouse], but they didn't turn out to be anything.

"I still feel that he was not alone in that. I can't help it. I think there was something, and I don't know what. And I couldn't figure out why he would go out of his way to do this at that time, unless somebody talked him into it."

Teten recalled that after the disturbance of March 28, King talked to somebody in New York, "then he came back to do another march."

The case went quickly from the Memphis office to higher up. "Sullivan or somebody came out from the Bureau and that turned the case into a special," Teten said.[1]

The man Hoover sent to take over the King murder investigation was Cartha DeLoach, who back in 1960 had come to tour "rebel territory" with then Memphis special agent in charge Frank Holloman.

———◆———

Thirty minutes after the shot, Ernest Withers arrived at the scene of Dr. King's murder, the Lorraine Motel.

He reached a police barricade.

At the scene, he met a young South African man, Joseph Louw, who'd been taking pictures of King for a public television special. Staying at the Lorraine, Louw had heard the shot and rushed out of his room with two cameras to find King laid out on the balcony, wounded.

Louw quickly expended two rolls of film. His hands were still shaking when he met Withers.

"I could tell from his anxiety he must have something," Withers said.

The two got into Withers's car and headed for the Beale Street darkroom. "He said he wasn't sure if the exposure was good because the light was bad," Withers said.[2]

At Withers's studio, Louw tried to develop the film, but Withers heard him struggling and offered to help with the processing. "He didn't know how to develop his film!" Withers recalled. "He didn't know anything about the darkroom and he was so nervous and shaky that I finally just took it from him and developed it myself."[3]

Despite shaky hands and poor light, the photos turned out.

Louw recalled, "The first picture I looked at was Dr. King laying behind the railing."[4]

Life magazine purchased Louw's photographs and published the image of King lying wounded while witnesses point toward the direction the fatal shot came from. One figure kneels beside King's body—undercover police officer Marrell McCullough.

After developing Louw's film, Withers returned to the Lorraine. He photographed King's briefcase. He took a picture of King's blood pooled on the balcony. He saw motel owner Walter Bailey clean up King's blood into a glass jar.

An impulse got ahold of Withers. He found a medicine bottle in King's room, then knelt at the dark red puddle, dipped the bottle in, and scooped out a bit of King's blood. He didn't know if it was right or wrong.

——•——

Dr. King understood moral complexity.

He had delivered one of the two triumphant speeches of his career on the eve of his death. While a storm rattled the Mason Temple shutters, King gave an impromptu sermon, mixing his feelings at this powerful moment with some classic King motifs. Distinctive for the stunning prophecy delivered in its words, as well as the soaring sound and imagery of its climactic verses, it became known as the "Mountaintop Speech."

> We've got some difficult days ahead.
> But it doesn't matter with me now.
> Because I've been to the mountaintop.
> And I don't mind—Like anybody, I would like to live a long life.
> Longevity has its place.
> But I'm not concerned about that now.

I just want to do God's will.

And He's allowed me to go up to the mountain.

And I've looked over.

And I've seen the Promised Land.

I may not get there with you.

But I want you to know tonight, that we, as a people, will get to the Promised Land.

So I'm happy, tonight.

I'm not *worried* about anything.

I'm not fearing any man.

Mine eyes have seen the glory of the coming of the Lord!

Before taking his crowd to the summit, however, King had tackled the dark matter of humanity. He reminded everyone that he himself was a sinner. "There is a schizophrenia, as the psychologists or the psychiatrists would call it, going on within all of us," he said. "And there are times that all of us know somehow that there is a Mr. Hyde and a Dr. Jekyll in us.

"And we end up having to cry out, with Ovid, the Latin poet, 'I see and approve the better things of life, but the evil things I do.'"

———◆———

Four hours after King's death, Withers phoned a tip to Agent Lawrence. On the previous day, an eccentric private investigator had visited Withers's photography studio insisting that Withers divulge King's location. Withers put the man off and didn't think much about it. Then he heard after the assassination, radio reports that the suspect had driven away from the scene of the shooting in a newer white automobile. The eccentric PI had driven a white car.

The PI had come to see Withers many times over the years. He had told Withers at one point that he planned to join the Ku Klux Klan as an infiltrator. He also shared that he'd been hospitalized for schizophrenia.

Withers told Lawrence he didn't feel good about informing on this man, but he had to. The lead went nowhere, as the FBI's manhunt quickly focused on a man who had registered at a flophouse near the Lorraine under the name John Willard. This suspect's real name was James Earl Ray.

———◆———

April 8, 1968, the date Dr. King had chosen for a peaceful demonstration in Memphis, instead saw a memorial march through the city.

At eleven a.m., two thousand people left Clayborn Temple and headed toward City Hall, avoiding riot-torn Beale Street. On Main, Coretta Scott King and Ralph Abernathy joined the march. The number of marchers grew to fourteen thousand, including Harry Belafonte and Bill Cosby.

That afternoon, after participating in the memorial march, Memphis police and fire director Frank Holloman sat in his downtown office and wrote a letter to Mrs. King, asking her forgiveness. The Memphis Fire Department had billed her for the ambulance transportation of her husband from the Lorraine Motel to St. Joseph Hospital. For Holloman, the letter fittingly punctuated a catastrophic introduction to a job he'd held for less than three months.

As the King assassination was scrutinized over the years, Holloman defended his position as a public servant unwittingly dragged into crisis. "There apparently has been a persistent effort to prove a theory or allegation that the FBI engaged in a conspiracy to assassinate Dr. King and that I, because of my past association with the FBI, was a party to that conspiracy," Holloman said. "It is unbelievable to me that the FBI would even entertain such an idea. It is ludicrous and preposterous that I would be a party to such a thing either directly or indirectly. . . . Proving those theories or charges with truth and facts is another matter and has not been accomplished."[5]

———◆———

On April 16, 1968, the city of Memphis and its Sanitation Department settled the strike. It still took Mayor Henry Loeb nearly two weeks after an international tragedy struck his city to sign off on essentially what the workers had wanted all along. Loeb agreed that the city would recognize AFSCME as the sanitation department's union and allow a payroll deduction from each worker's check to pay union dues. Workers would receive a pay raise of fifteen cents per hour.

AFTERWORD

IN 1970 SPECIAL AGENT WILLIAM LAWRENCE RETIRED TO a small mountain town in North Carolina.

Lawrence's top racial informant, Ernest Withers, continued to supply information to the FBI after Lawrence left, until the FBI stung Withers himself.

Ray Blanton, elected Tennessee governor in 1975, appointed Withers to the state alcoholic beverage control board. Beyond his duties as a licensor of nightclubs and liquor stores, Withers functioned as a liaison in Blanton's wide-ranging corruption network. Tennessee employees sold state-owned vehicles and kept the cash, and they accepted bribes from illegal businesses. The FBI investigated and caught Withers on tape as he helped make arrangements to have a prisoner released from the state penitentiary in exchange for money, a cash-for-clemency scheme. The bureau arranged the whole 1978 operation as part of a wider sting of the Blanton administration. Results included arrests of several top aides, the premature ouster of Blanton from the governor's office, and a major motion picture, *Marie*, starring Sissy Spacek as Marie Ragghianti, the whistleblower in the governor's cabinet who prompted the investigation.

Withers can be heard on the FBI tape complaining that he'd received no money for running bag in the operation. The episode again highlights Withers's knack for getting into compromising situations. This late 1970s scandal and his removal from the police force back in 1951 bookend his public life with instances of corruption. But growing up in the brutal Crump regime, this was simply how he had learned to survive. And as with certain aspects of his FBI career, particularly monitoring Communist influences, or translating the uplifting features of the Nation of Islam for a suspicious government, you can see some positive in Withers's pay-for-parole involvement. He helped free a young African-American man who faced a lengthy prison term for a first offense.[1]

The tenacious pursuit of action that fueled Withers's singular journalistic contributions also kept him near trouble for most of his adult life. He personifies the flawed hero.

By the time his association with the FBI ended, he had sent his eight children to college, achieving his major family goal. In another ten years, his photography would gain appreciation as an important body of work, historically and artistically, and he would enjoy his last two decades as a living legend, publishing books, delivering lectures, and seeing his pictures exhibited all over the country.

As of this writing, Rev. James Lawson is nearly ninety

Ernest Withers on Beale Street. 2002, Bill Chapman.

years old and still leading nonviolence workshops in Los Angeles.

The Invaders would receive attention from Withers and the FBI until 1972. Of the key members, Charles Cabbage died in Memphis in 2010, and John B. Smith lives in Atlanta. Coby Smith still lives in Memphis.

More than a decade after I met Ernest Withers at his office, I interviewed his daughter Rosalind there. Since her father's passing, Roz had led a total transformation of the building, opening her dad's old studio into a bright gallery showcasing his photography, and adding a café.

The place buzzed with positive energy, as family members guided tours, while in a nearby archive, undergrads chattered as they cataloged the millions of images the photographer left behind.

Roz and I sat in a banquet room outfitted with tables and a podium.

The FBI revelation had hit her hard. Because her father never talked about it, she has had to grapple with what it meant. She doesn't shy from the FBI questions, she just doesn't have many answers. She stands by her father's one statement about FBI work: that he never tried to learn any high-powered secrets, it would have been trouble. Roz never knew the FBI operative. She only knew the loving, funny, hard-working father.

Roz's excavation of her father's history has brought her close to the sister she didn't grow up with. Now the two women are driving forces of the Withers Family Trust, a nonprofit that encompasses the famed photographer's vast intellectual property. As the fiftieth anniversary of the King assassination approached, Roz Withers directed a digitization of twelve thousand of her father's civil rights photos. Many have never been published, many more haven't been seen for years. The Ernest Withers legacy is still in process.

People from all over the world roam Beale Street and drop in to the Withers Gallery. They see the images of Dr. King on the bus, Elvis and B.B., Moses Wright at the Emmett Till trial, the Little Rock Nine.

I've wrestled with what writing this book will mean to Withers's photography—his ability to continue telling the story, to continue supporting his family, and for us to celebrate his work. I think we have to embrace him for all he was. It's not as if the most famous, successful, appreciated artists are also the purest, simplest people. And we can't simply drop people, great people especially, who don't fit our standards of purity. This is particularly true of how we treat African-American historical figures. Is it our task now to decide how a black person should have navigated a racist world? Without institutional American racism, Withers would never have become involved with racial espionage. But he still would have been a great photographer.

While we sat and talked, I told Roz about how her dad busted me looking through his pictures. I glanced up and saw his name in reverse, printed on the plate-glass window,

ERNEST C. WITHERS BUILDING, 333 BEALE. I realized that Roz and I were in the exact room where he'd stuck me.

Looking back on that day, knowing so much more about him now, I wonder if there was a part of Withers that sort of appreciated me sneaking through his things. Could he not sympathize?

I remember how his charisma had me totally at ease and speaking freely. His small-talking Memphis charm, I figure, must have been a great asset for an intelligence gatherer, allowing him in with Nation of Islam brothers, idealistic college students from up North, an activist minister like Jim Lawson, and the militant Black Power advocates the Invaders. I wish I had known to ask him how it felt to be in that courtroom with Emmett Till's murderers, or on that fluorescent-lit balcony looking at a puddle of Dr. King's blood.

I wonder what the photographer-hero-spy thought, standing among the crowd at Mason Temple on the last night of Dr. King's life, listening as the leader said, "There's a tension at the heart of human nature, and whenever we set out to dream our dreams and to build our temples, we must be honest enough to recognize it."[2]

A bright and upbeat Withers Gallery feels like the right place for this dark path to end. Through a window that the Withers story had opened, I saw the FBI COINTELPRO documents outlining what my government had planned to prevent a great man from improving

America. I'd had to consider if this rightfully celebrated journalist had been part of the program. I wondered— should I just have followed what the great photographer said when he closed me into this room?

"Don't touch anything."

ACKNOWLEDGMENTS

AS I MENTIONED IN THE INTRODUCTION TO THIS BOOK, the revelation of Ernest Withers's FBI work came from the reporting of Marc Perrusquia at the *Memphis Commercial Appeal.* Perrusquia broke the story in 2010 and continued publishing stories about Withers's casework based on FBI files. The newspaper sued the FBI to open the Withers informant file, and the parties reached a settlement. I obtained copies of the files released as a result of that settlement through the National Archives and Records Administration in the spring of 2017. I'm grateful to Perrusquia and archivist James Mathis for bringing these documents to light.

Other useful primary source material came from a variety of outlets. In response to my FOIA request, the FBI archives provided a case file on the 1958 Glenview housing discrimination incidents, and the National Archives provided FBI case files on the 1966 James Meredith march and on the security investigation of Charles Cabbage; thanks to David Sabonya, Mary Kay Schmidt, Noah Shanklin, and Laurel Macondray. The Centers of the Southern Struggle series, edited by premier FBI civil rights historian

David Garrow, published FBI files on the Invaders and the Memphis sanitation strike that were generated during 1968. Thanks to my former editor and always friend Ralph Eubanks for help in D.C. and with softshell lunches. Suzanne Bonefas, director of special projects at Rhodes College, provided tremendous help with critical information in the Crossroads to Freedom collection.

Plenty of Withers's professional associates and Beale Street contemporaries generously shared their time and insight, to the betterment of my understanding of this fascinating man and his place, including Rev. Harold Middlebrook, Tony Decaneas, Moses Newson, D'Army Bailey, Mike Cody, Adrian Miller, Sr., Clifford Miller, Jr., Calvin Newborn, Minister Sukhura Yahweh (aka Lance "Sweet Willie Wine" Watson), Coby Smith, Charles Cabbage, John C. Smith, and John B. Smith.

It's hard to overstate the importance of Rosalind Withers to her father's afterlife. Roz has shown courage and kindness in dealing with difficult matters to find the truth. The Withers Collection has been an important resource and major ally, especially Connor Scanlon.

Bill Chapman has told many a fond tale of Ernest Withers and generously shared his own portrait of the man.

Utmost appreciation goes to my team, agent Paul Bresnick and editor Tom Mayer—ten years and three books together—plus W. W. Norton & Company assistant editor Emma Hitchcock and copyeditor Janet Biehl.

Closing this book is a bit like saying goodbye to two dear

people who made my time in Memphis the most rewarding experience of my career.

Nathaniel "Pedro" Lewis, Beale Street's great hustler, harmony singer, and outlaw Muslim, knocked me on my ass when I interviewed him. I've never heard more in-depth, incisive talk on race than what he told me. He has gone on, but his warmth and wit are constant sources of energy and true inspiration for me. His honesty makes me push harder to find the truth, yet wonder if I'll ever get there. Pedro was working on a memoir at the time of his death, and I hope his story will get out.

My beloved friend Emerson Able, Jr., died while I was working on this book. He's alive to me every day, though. This story began when I met Able, right around the time I met his fellow Manassas High alum Ernest Withers.

But maybe it really, really began with Scott Barretta at the Hard Luck Café.

Thanks to everyone at the Virginia Foundation of the Humanities, except Jerry, for supporting my work, promoting my work, and doing much excellent work for the humanities in my home state.

Retired FBI special agents Howard Teten and Bob Fitzpatrick worked in the Memphis office during the period of the assassination and shared what they could about their experiences.

I'm blessed that people have sustained and supported my work in Memphis and lifted my spirit with their friendship. Wayne Dowdy, with whom I've shared many laughs and impassioned discussions at the Memphis Public Library, and Chris Ratliff, formerly of special collections at the University of Memphis, are two of my best archival buds. I cherish my friendship with the man whose rhythm is this city's heartbeat, Howard "Bulldog" Grimes, and I appreciate Scott Bomar's love for the music and history of this city. Hi Records friends and family, Sylvester "Blade" Sartor, the late Mabon "Teenie" Hodges, Leroy Hodges, Charles Hodges, and Hubby continually inspire and amaze me.

I hope Majorie won't threaten to sue me if I thank photographer Justin Fox Burks for much fun at the Boss Lounge, One Block North, the Blue Worm, CC Blues Club, and even Club Hughes. Belated thanks to Graham Burks for help on a dream that didn't quite come true.

I miss my neighbors and friends Alex Turley, Mindy Turley, Calvin Turley, Henry Turley, and Lynn Turley; yes, I like the Turleys. Speaking of neighbors, my closest and dearest was John Underwood, and the legendary Melbo who done gone on. Robert, it was fucked up of us to call the cops and tell them you were cooking meth—I don't even know what that was about. Scott and Sarah Newstok made me writer-in-residence of their beautiful home for consecutive summers while I worked on this book, and their family is my family, I love you guys. Charles Crawford, Aram Goudsouzian, John Bass, Jonathan Judaken, Charles Hughes, and Russ Wigginton (who may not remember introducing me to Cab and Coby a while ago), have been supportive of my career and are major benefits to the community. Speaking of which, much love to Kacky Walton, Darrell Cobbins, Anna Mullins, Larry Robinson, Kevin Cubbins, Pat Mitchell Worley, the late Sid Selvidge, Eddie Hankins, and POWer to tHA ARTivist BROther Ron Herd and his mother Callie Herd, all of whom help to get this city's story straight. I don't really like other writers, but Robert Gordon's cool. My friendship with Frank Murtaugh outlasted our time working under the same roof and our opposite sentiments in a nasty football rivalry. The Cowboys can still suck it, though.

Alexis Krasilovsky in Los Angeles shared her wonderful *Beale Street* documentary, and I pop it on whenever I need to hear somebody talk Mrmph to me. Prichard Smith made a stunning documentary on the Invaders and has been incredibly generous to me with his insights and research.

Many of the city's unsung musical heroes have helped me see the place, including the late Polly Walker, the lady who managed B.B. King in the 1960s, and her son, the late Cato Walker III, Alfred Rudd and Kurl McKinney, plus outsider with inside knowledge, the late Sir Lattimore Brown, with thanks to Red Kelly for the introduction. Likewise, Warren Lewis of New Chicago in North Memphis helped build a Black Power organization with Isaac Hayes, knew how to cut hair with fire, and patiently imparted some of his vast knowledge of the community.

My three children share a legacy of their storied hometown and spycraft. To MG, Sax, and Liv, I lovingly dedicate this book and every beat of my heart. Nothing is possible without Elise.

NOTES

CHAPTER 1

1. Ernest Withers, interview on robertfranklin.org.

CHAPTER 2

1. Ernest C. Withers, *Pictures Tell the Story* (Norfolk, Va.: Chrysler Museum of Art, 2000), p. 82.

CHAPTER 3

1. Ernest Withers, interview by Marshand Boone, n.d., http://knightpoliticalreporting.syr.edu/wp-content/uploads/2016/08/Ernest-Withers-oral-history.pdf.
2. Ernest Withers, interview by Pete Daniel and Charlie McGovern, August 11, 1992, Smithsonian Rock 'n' Soul Collection, Washington, D.C.
3. Ernest Withers, interview in documentary film *Freedom's Call*, dir. Richard Breyer (2007).
4. J. B. Martin to R. R. Church, Jr., March 25, 1941, Robert Church Family Papers, University of Memphis Special Collections.

CHAPTER 4

1. Roger Biles, *Memphis in the Great Depression* (Knoxville: University of Tennessee Press, 1986), p. 45.
2. Ernest C. Withers, *Pictures Tell the Story* (Norfolk, Va.: Chrysler Museum of Art, 2000), p. 42.
3. Ernest Withers, in documentary film *Beale Street*, dir. Alexis Krasilovsky (1982).
4. Pedro Lewis, interview by author.
5. Lawrence to SAC Memphis, LHM, February 7, 1961.

CHAPTER 5

1. Nat D. Williams, "Dark Shadows," *Tri-State Defender*, June 5, 1954, p. 5.

CHAPTER 6

1. Ernest Withers, interview by Pete Daniel and Charlie McGovern, August 11, 1992, Smithsonian Rock 'n' Soul Collection, Washington, D.C.

2. Calvin Newborn, interview by author.

3. Notice of the Crayton-Newborn guitar battle first appeared in the June 4, 1954, issue of the *Memphis World*. The Newborn ensemble with Crayton appeared in action at the local veterans' hospital, *Memphis World*, June 11. The June 25 *World* publicized the weekly Barn Dance at the Flamingo, with no mention of Crayton.

4. The Miller version of events was handed down to Cliff Miller's son Adrian, who shared it with me in an interview I recorded in June 2014. Newborn told me about his side of getting Elvis to the Flamingo in 2005.

5. Lewie and Morris Steinberg, interview by David Less, December 5, 1999, Smithsonian Online Virtual Archives.

6. "Flamingo Room's New 'Barn Dance Nite' Is Big Hit" (photo caption), *Memphis World*, June 25, 1954, p. 5.

CHAPTER 7

1. Theodore Coleman, "Latest Atrocity in Mississippi Arouses Nation." *Pittsburgh Courier*, September 8, 1955, p. 1.

2. Simeon Booker, *Shocking the Conscience: A Reporter's Account of the Civil Rights Movement* (Jackson: University Press of Mississippi, 2013), p. 74.

3. Wallace Terry, ed., *Missing Pages, Black Journalists of Modern America: An Oral History* (New York: Carroll & Graf, 2007), p. 139.

4. "L. Alex Wilson, Defender Editor in Chief, Dies," *Daily Defender*, October 12, 1960, p. 1.

5. Dorothy Gilliam, quoted in documentary film *Freedom's Call*, dir. Richard Breyer (2007).

6. Alex Wilson, "Defender Reporter Beaten by Mob Tells His Story," *Daily Defender*, September 25, 1957, p. 22.

7. Booker, *Shocking the Conscience*, p. 11.

8. Ibid., pp. 19, 55.

9. Clark Porteous, "Newly Subpoenaed Witnesses Heard for Two Hours," *Memphis Press-Scimitar*, September 21, 1955, p. 1.

10. Booker, *Shocking the Conscience*, p. 74.

11. Clark Porteous, "Mrs. Bryant on Stand," *Memphis Press-Scimitar*, September 22, 1955, p. 1.

12. Clark Porteous, "Till's Mother Tells of Viewing Body," *Memphis Press-Scimitar*, September 22, 1955, p. 2.

13. L. Alex Wilson, "Reveals Two Key Witnesses Jailed," *Tri-State Defender*, October 1, 1955, p. 1.

14. "Jailed To Bar Them From Trial," *Tri-State Defender*, October 1, 1955, p. 2.

15. L. Alex Wilson, "Tells Inside Story of Trial," *Tri-State Defender*, October 1, 1955, p. 2 and photograph on front page.

16. Ernest Withers, interview by Marshand Boone, n.d., http://knightpoliticalreporting.syr.edu/wp-content/uploads/2016/08/Ernest-Withers-oral-history.pdf.

17. Ernest Withers, interview by Pete Daniel and Charlie McGovern, August 11, 1992, Smithsonian Rock 'n' Soul Collection, Washington, D.C.

18. Ernest C. Withers, *Pictures Tell the Story* (Norfolk, Va.: Chrysler Museum of Art, 2000), p. 17.

CHAPTER 8

1. "Rev. M.L. King, Jr. Asks Changes in Treatment on Ala. Buses," *Memphis World*, December 13, 1955, p. 1.

2. Melvin Greer, "Elvis Presley Visits Fairgrounds on Tuesday," *Memphis World*, June 23, 1956, p. 3.

3. Louis Cantor, a WDIA deejay who had attended Humes High School with Elvis, asked the singer to come perform at the revue. Elvis could not perform due to contract issues, but agreed to appear onstage. Louis Cantor, *Wheelin' on Beale* (Seattle: Pharos Books, 1992), pp. 192–96.

4. "B.B. King Hears How Presley Copied His Style," *Tri-State Defender*, February 2, 1957, p. 12.

5. B.B. King, *Blues All Around Me* (New York: Avon Books, 1996), p. 186.

6. This recollection is in the highly informative appendix to Ernest Withers and Daniel Wolff, *The Memphis Blues Again: Six Decades of Memphis Music Photographs* (New York: Viking Studio, 2001), p. 163.

7. Thomas and Williams quotes are from Cantor, *Wheelin' on Beale*, p. 194.

8. Nat D. Williams, "Down on Beale: 'Pied Piper' Presley," *Pittsburgh Courier*, December 22, 1956, p. 14.

9. King, *Blues All Around Me*, p. 186.

CHAPTER 9

1. L. Alex Wilson, "Defender Writer Tells of Ride with History," *Chicago Defender*, December 24, 1956, p. 1.

2. L. Alex Wilson, "In Montgomery: An Exciting Day for Thousands," *Tri-State Defender*, December 29, 1956, p. 1.

3. Ernest Withers, interview at robertfranklin.org. For a more thorough version of the Montgomery story, see Ernest Withers, interview by Pete Daniel and Charlie McGovern, August 11, 1992, Smithsonian Rock 'n' Soul Collection, Washington D.C.

4. L. Alex Wilson, "Defender Writer Tells of Ride With History," *Chicago Defender*, December 24, 1956, p. 8.

5. L. Alex Wilson, "Riders Tell Reaction to New Pattern," *Tri-State Defender*, December 29, 1956, p. 2.
6. "Gets a Report" (photo caption), ibid.
7. The profile was that of Methodist minister Glenn Smiley, according to the photo caption, ibid., p. 1.
8. Imogene Wilson, Behind the Veil Oral History Collection, Duke University, Durham, N.C.

CHAPTER 10

1. "Throng to Hear Rev. King April 19," *Memphis World*, April 29, 1957, p. 1.
2. "Noted Rev. Martin Luther King Jr. Urges Realistic Look at Race Relations Progress," *Memphis World*, April 24, 1957, p. 4.
3. L. Alex Wilson, "For the Record: No Turning Back Now," *Tri-State Defender*, September 21, 1957, p. 5.
4. United Press, "Ike to Use 'Whatever Force Necessary'," *Memphis Press-Scimitar*, September 23, 1957, p. 2.
5. Alex Wilson, "Defender Reporter Beaten by Mob Tells His Story," *Chicago Defender*, September 25, 1957, p. 22.
6. Relman Morin, "After Violence Negroes Go," *Memphis Press-Scimitar*, September 23, 1957, p. 2.
7. Wilson, "Defender Reporter Beaten by Mob," pp. 22, 25.
8. William Theis, "Describes Mob Attack on Defender Reporter," *Chicago Defender*, October 5, 1957, p. 12.
9. Morin, "After Violence Negroes Go," p. 2. Reportedly, this version of events was read to Eisenhower over the phone as he deliberated his course of action.
10. "Dr. T.R.M. Howard" (photo caption), *Memphis World*, October 4, 1955, p. 1.
11. Francis Finley and William H. Lawrence, "Moses J. Newsom," file # 44-341, FBI Interview Report, September 24, 1957.
12. Robert C. Hickam and Milford C. Runnels, "Clarence Malcom Whitehead," file # 44-341, FBI Interview Report, September 30, 1957.
13. Quoted in *Memphis Press-Scimitar*, September 25, 1957, p. 4.
14. Nat D. Williams, "Down on Beale: Witch Hunt on Beale," *Pittsburgh Courier*, November 9, 1957, p. 24.

CHAPTER 11

1. Elton H. Weaver III, *Mark the Perfect Man: The Rise of Bishop C.H. Mason and the Church of God in Christ*, Ph.D. diss, University of Memphis, 2007, p. 125.

2. Ibid., p. 128.

3. C. H. Mason to Franklin Delano Roosevelt, December 14, 1939, FBI file number 25-286284-6.

4. Richard T. Allen, "Investigation Is Under Way in Fire at Negro Church," *Memphis Commercial Appeal*, February 15, 1958, p. 1.

5. "Church of God in Christ Hit by Mystery Fire," *Memphis World*, February 19, 1958, p. 1.

6. "Glenview Plan Directors Say Difficulty Lingers," *Memphis Press-Scimitar*, February 19, 1958, p. 26.

7. "Commissioner Loeb's Grave Blunder" (editorial), *Tri-State Defender*, March 15, 1958, p. 1.

8. Ibid.

9. "Police Praised for Action in Tension Area," *Tri-State Defender*, March 8, 1958, p. 1.

10. "Rev. Charles H. Mason Harassed by Another Fire," *Memphis World*, March 8, 1958, p. 1; "Fire Breaks Out in Negro's Home on White Street," *Memphis Commercial Appeal*, March 4, 1958, p. 1.

11. "Rev. C. H. Mason Denies 'Prostitution Charge,'" *Memphis World*, October 18, 1958, p. 8; "Woman Took Over Domestic Chores," *Tri-State Defender*, October 18, 1958, p. 1.

12. Warner Dickerson, interview by author, February 11, 2015.

13. "Editor Wilson Back Home—To Stay," *Tri-State Defender*, October 22, 1960, p. 1.

CHAPTER 12

1. Special Agent (SA) William H. Lawrence to Special Agent in Charge (SAC), "Ernest Columbus Withers PCI," February 7, 1961.

2. "Cold War in Fayette County," *Ebony*, September 1960, p. 29.

3. Trezzvant W. Anderson, "The Biggest Question: How Will Demo. Att'y-Gen'l Handle Rights?" *Pittsburgh Courier*, January 28, 1961, p. 12.

4. Joseph A. Canale, FBI report, November 19, 1958, Department of Justice file no. 72-72-34.

5. John F. Kennedy news conference, January 25, 1961, *Public Papers of the Presidents of the United States: John F. Kennedy, 1961*.

6. Lawrence to SAC Memphis, "Freebus RM," July 21, 1961.

7. Lawrence to SAC (137-907), "Ernest C. Withers," July 28, 1961.

8. Lawrence to SAC, "Ernest Columbus Withers PCI," February 7, 1961.

9. Lawrence to SAC, "Southern Conference Educational Fund," April 18, 1961.

10. SAC Memphis to Director FBI, "James Rufus Foreman aka James Forman, Racial Matters," September 6, 1961.

11. Lawrence to SAC Memphis, December 8, 1961.
12. Lawrence to SAC Memphis, November 6, 1961.

CHAPTER 13

1. Nathaniel Lewis, interviews by the author in early 2011.
2. William Fleetwood to Lord Treasurer Cecil, 1585, excerpted in Gamini Salgado, *The Elizabethan Underworld* (New York: St. Martin's Press, 1992), p. 33.
3. "Hob-Nobbing in Memphis, by Ann and Mable," *Pittsburgh Courier*, December 18, 1954, p. 16.
4. J. Edgar Hoover, "Racial Tension and Civil Rights," March 9, 1956, p. 13.
5. SAC Memphis to SAC Little Rock " . . . NOI," November 13, 1963.
6. Lawrence to SAC, "Ernest Columbus Withers CS (R)," June 10, 1964.
7. Lawrence to SAC, "Nation of Islam," January 28, 1964.
8. Lawrence to SAC, "Ernest C. Withers Confidential Source (Racial)," February 14, 1964.

CHAPTER 14

1. Ernest Withers, interview in documentary film *Freedom's Call*, dir. Richard Breyer (2007).
2. Dorothy Gilliam, interview ibid.
3. Dorothy Gilliam, "Mississippi Negroes happily Stunned by Meredith," *Washington Post*, October 7, 1962, p. 1.
4. Ibid.
5. Ernest C. Withers, Sr., "Defender Photographer Held in Jail 4 Hours After Beating by Police," *Tri-State Defender*, June 22, 1963, p. 1.
6. Elaine Woo, "John Doar Dies at 92; Key Justice Department Civil Rights Lawyer," *Los Angeles Times*, November 12, 2014.
7. John Salter (aka Hunter Gray) to author, November 15, 2016.
8. Ernest C. Withers, Sr., "Defender Photographer Held in Jail 4 Hours After Beating by Police," *Tri-State Defender*, June 22, 1963, p. 4.
9. Ibid.
10. Ernest Columbus Withers, Sr., signed statement from FBI interview, June 24, 1963.
11. John Salter to author, November 15, 2016.
12. SAC Memphis to Director FBI, "CP, USA—Negro Question, Communist Influence in Racial Matters, IS–C" (LHM), November 15, 1963.
13. John Salter, identified in "the Southern Conference Educational Fund, Inc.: Its Planned Activities and Financial Requirements, 1964," attached to Lawrence to SAC, "Ernest Withers CS (R)," May 14, 1964.

CHAPTER 15

1. Helen Fuller, "Southern Students Take Over: The Creation of the Beloved Community," *New Republic*, May 2, 1960, clipping in Ernest Withers Collection, Howard University, Spingarn Library.
2. Lawrence to SAC Memphis, "Ernest C. Withers, PCI," July 17, 1962.
3. Lawrence to SAC, "Ernest Columbus Withers CS (RAC)," July 12, 1963.
4. "Hinds Is Endorsed and Others," *Tri-State Defender*, October 26, 1963, p. 1.
5. Lawrence to SAC Memphis, April 8, 1964.
6. Lawrence to SAC, "West Tennessee Voters Project (WTVP), RM," August 24, 1965, p. 4.
7. SAC Memphis to Director FBI, "West Tennessee Voters' Project (WTVP) Racial Matters" [marked Personal Attention: Assistant Director William Sullivan], September 3, 1965.
8. SAC Memphis to Director FBI, "West Tennessee Voters' Project (WTVP)" (LHM), September 10, 1965, p. 38.
9. Ibid., p. 34.
10. Lawrence to SAC, "West Tennessee Voters' Project (WTVP) Racial Matters," October 18, 1965.
11. SAC Memphis to SAC Milwaukee, February 7, 1966.
12. Lawrence to SAC, "West Tennessee Voters' Project (WTVP) Racial Matters," October 26, 1965.
13. Lawrence to SAC, "West Tennessee Voters' Project (WTVP) Racial Matters," November 19, 1965.
14. Lawrence to SAC Memphis, March 17, 1966.
15. Lawrence to SAC, "International Days of Protest SM-C," October 22, 1965.
16. Lawrence to SAC, "Ernest C. Withers, CS," April 13, 1966.

CHAPTER 16

1. Lawrence to SAC, "Logos, IS-PLP," May 26, 1966.
2. "FBI Warns of College Unrest," *Memphis Press-Scimitar*, February 7, 1966, p. 3.
3. Lawrence to SAC, "Liaison With Groups Sponsoring Integration, RM," January 2, 1968, p. 3.
4. Stokely Carmichael with Ekwueme Michael Thelwell, *Ready for Revolution* (New York: Scribner, 2003), p. 489.
5. Ibid., p. 490.
6. K. W. Cook, "King Leads Marchers on Meredith's Route," *Memphis Commercial Appeal*, June 8, 1966, p. 1.
7. K. W. Cook, "Negroes Urged to Leave Vietnam," *Memphis Commercial Appeal*, June 10, 1966.
8. Aram Goudsouzian, *Down to the Crossroads* (New York: Farrar, Straus, & Giroux, 2014), p. 40.

9. "March to Jackson, Mississippi," July 1, 1966 (LHM), p. 3, file no. 157-147.

10. "Demonstrations Protesting Shooting of James Meredith—RM" (FBI teletype), June 23, 1966.

11. "RE: March to Jackson; Racial Matters; Election Laws, Memphis" (LHM), June 25, 1966, p. 4.

12. Ibid.

CHAPTER 17

1. SAC Memphis to Director FBI, "Spring Mobilization Committee to End the War in Vietnam; Student Mobilization Committee, Internal Security—C" (LHM), May 9, 1967.

2. SAC Memphis, to Director FBI, "Spring Mobilization Committee to End the War in Vietnam, Information Concerning Internal Security; Student Mobilization Committee, Internal Security—C," (LHM), May 5, 1967, p. 9.

3. Ibid., p. 4.

4. "Jackie Robinson . . . Wants to Hear From Dr. King," *Tri-State Defender*, April 15, 1967, p. 7.

5. SAC Memphis to Director FBI, "Spring Mobilization Committee to End the War In Vietnam; Student Mobilization Committee, Internal Security—C," April 27, 1967, p. 11.

6. Lawrence to SAC, "COMINFIL of Southern Student Organizing Committee (SSOC), IS-C," November 29, 1966.

7. "Hoover Colors Stokely Pink," *Tri-State Defender*, May 20, 1967, p. 11.

8. Lawrence to SAC, "COMINFIL, Student Nonviolent Coordinating Committee (SNCC) RM," June 2, 1967.

9. Michael Honey, *Going Down Jericho Road* (New York: W.W. Norton, 2011), pp. 229–30.

10. "Three Get Heavy Fines as 'Would-Be' Rioters," *Tri-State Defender*, July 8, 1967, p. 1.

11. William H. Lawrence, "Charles Laverne Cabbage," FBI case report, September 29, 1967, p. 7.

12. SAC Memphis to Director FBI, "COMINFIL, Student Nonviolent Coordinating Committee (SNCC) IS-C" (LHM), July 17, 1967, pp. 4–5.

13. SAC Memphis, to Director FBI, "Demonstrations Protesting United States Intervention in Vietnam, IS-C; Vietnam Summer, IS-C" (LHM), July 11, 1967, p. 6.

14. SAC Memphis to Director FBI, "Demonstrations Protesting United States Intervention In Vietnam, IS-C; Vietnam Summer, IS-C" (LHM), June 16, 1967, p. 6.

15. SAC Memphis to Director FBI Memphis, "COMINFIL, Student Nonviolent Coordinating Committee (SNCC) IS-C" (LHM), July 17, 1967, pp. 15–16.

CHAPTER 18

1. The MAP-South leadership structure is a mystery to me. A news story in the August 16, 1967, *Memphis Press-Scimitar* identifies Lawson as "chairman of the MAP-South Citizens Association," while noting that Hershel Feibelman was local War on Poverty Committee chair. Lawson ended up being the go-to leader for reporters seeking quotes on MAP-South matters.

2. "'Poor' Will Speak at MAP South Meet," *Tri-State Defender*, April 22, 1967, p. 2.

3. "Brown Aims Blast at Pres. Johnson" (UPI), *Memphis Press-Scimitar*, July 27, 1967, p. 3.

4. "Report Stirs Capitol Hill," *Memphis Press-Scimitar*, August 4, 1967, p. 1.

5. William Steif, "OEO Chief Defends Workers' Record in Summer Riots," *Memphis Press-Scimitar*, August 11, 1967, p. 15.

6. Kay Pittman Black and Bill Evans, "Senate Prober Checks in Memphis," *Memphis Press-Scimitar*, August 10, 1967, p. 1.

7. Ibid., pp. 1, 10.

8. Charles A. Brown, "Two 'Angry Young Men' Kicked Out," *Memphis Press-Scimitar*, August 8, 1967, p. 3.

9. Lawrence to SAC, "Communist and Black Power Infiltration, Poverty Program, Memphis Area Project-South (MAPS), RM; IS-C," August 25, 1967, p. 2.2

10. Charles A. Brown, "Anti-Poverty Group Demands Hearing for Two Controversial Workers," *Memphis Press-Scimitar*, August 11, 1967, p. 9.

11. Charles A. Brown, "Decision Expected Tonight in Case of Two Dismissed Poverty Workers," *Memphis Press-Scimitar*, August 24, 1967, p. 12.

12. Ibid.

13. William H. Lawrence, "Charles Laverne Cabbage," FBI case file, September 29, 1967, p. 15.

14. Charles Cabbage, interview by James Mosby, Ralph Bunche Collection, Moreland-Spingarn Archives, Howard University.

15. SAC Albany to Director FBI, "RE: Counterintelligence Program, Black Nationalist Hate Groups," August 25, 1967.

16. Kenneth O'Reilly, *"Racial Matters": The FBI's Secret File on Black America, 1960-1972* (New York: Free Press, 1989), pp. 267–68.

17. Lawrence, "Charles Laverne Cabbage," cover page C, p. 11.

18. Kay Pittman Black, "MAP South Men Defend Controversial Anti-Poverty Work," *Memphis Press-Scimitar*, September 11, 1967, clipping in University of Memphis Special Collections, *Press-Scimitar* morgue file 5446.

19. Joan Turner Beifuss, *At the River I Stand* (Memphis: St. Luke's Press, 1990), p. 180.

CHAPTER 19

1. Lawrence to SAC, "Communist and Black Power Infiltration, Poverty Program, Memphis Area Project–South (MAPS), Memphis, Tennessee, RM; IS-C," September 21, 1967.
2. "Charles Laverne Cabbage," FBI case file, March 25, 1968, p. 22.
3. Lawrence to SAC, "Palmer Watson Gunter, aka Watson Gunter, SM-C," October 12, 1967.
4. "Commissioner Loeb's Grave Blunder," *Tri-State Defender*, March 15, 1958, p. 1.
5. "Evers and Willis Clash on Air . . . The Winner??" *Memphis World*, October 21, 1967, p. 1.
6. Lawrence to SAC Memphis, "COMINFIL of SNCC," November 17, 1967.
7. "Charles Laverne Cabbage," FBI case file, p. 10.
8. Jesse H. Turner, "Jesse Turner's Analysis of City Election," *Memphis World*, November 25, 1967, p. 1.
9. "Charles Laverne Cabbage," FBI case file, p. 9.
10. Lawrence to SAC, "COMINFIL of Student Nonviolent Coordinating Committee (SNCC) IS-C; RM," December 4, 1967, p. 4.
11. Ibid., p. 1.
12. Lawrence to SAC, "COMINFIL of SNCC, IS-SNCC; RM," January 25, 1968.
13. Lawrence to SAC, "COMINFIL of SNCC, IS-SNCC; RM," January 5, 1968.
14. FBI interview report of Charles Cabbage and Clifford Taylor, January 5, 1968, included in "Charles Laverne Cabbage," FBI case file, pp. 36–37.
15. Lawrence to SAC, "COMINFIL of SNCC, IS-SNCC; RM," January 25, 1968.

CHAPTER 20

1. Frank Holloman to J. Edgar Hoover, January 6, 1959, Frank Holloman Collection, Memphis Public Library.
2. Cartha "Deke" DeLoach to Frank C. "Preacher" Holloman, January 4, 1960, Holloman Collection.
3. Holloman to Edward L. Boyle, February 15, 1960; and Holloman to Lee Teague, January 26, 1960, both in Holloman Collection.
4. Holloman to J. Edgar Hoover, March 2, 1960, Holloman Collection.
5. Holloman to Teague, January 26, 1960, and Jack Carley to Hoover, April 25, 1960, both in Holloman Collection.
6. Holloman to Hoover, September 21, 1960.
7. Frank Holloman to department heads, January 22, 1968, Frank Holloman Collection.
8. William H. Lawrence, testimony to the House Select Committee on Assassinations, November 21, 1978, HSCA, MLK Appendix, vol. 6, p. 546.

CHAPTER 21

1. Joan Turner Beifuss, *At the River I Stand* (Memphis: St. Luke's Press, 1990), p. 49.
2. Frank Holloman, interview by David Yellin and Joan Beifuss, May 9, 1973, transcript in Crossroads to Freedom Archive, Rhodes College, Memphis.
3. Director FBI to SAC Memphis, "The Invaders," January 15, 1968.
4. Beifuss, *At the River I Stand*, p. 108.
5. Holloman interview by Yellin and Beifuss, May 9, 1973.
6. Whittier Sengstacke, Jr., and Ed Harris, "Strikers Mauled by Cops," *Tri-State Defender*, March 2, 1968, p. 12. Holloman quotes are from Yellin and Beifuss interview.
7. "RE: Sanitation Workers Strike, Memphis, Tennessee" (LHM), February 24, 1968, p. 3.
8. Dorothy Withers, interview by Jack Hurley, 1999; Jack Hurley, "Bearing Witness to Change: Ernest Withers and the Civil Rights Movement," unpublished essay, Hurley's possession.
9. Ernest C. Withers, *Pictures Tell the Story* (Norfolk, Va.: Chrysler Museum of Art, 2000), p. 82.
10. This account comes from Memphis Police Department intelligence chief, Lieutenant Eli H. Arkin, "Civil Disorders, Memphis, Tennessee (February 12–April 16, 1968)," p. 13, Frank Holloman Collection. The document seems to have been produced from MPD informant reports made during the sanitation strike, for internal use rather than for public circulation.
11. Beifuss, *At the River I Stand*, p. 129.
12. Lawrence to SAC, "COMINFIL of SNCC, IS-SNCC; RM," February 14, 1968, pp. 1–3.
13. SAC Memphis to Director FBI, "Sanitation Workers Strike, Memphis, Tennessee, RM" (LHM), February 27, 1968.
14. Capt. Earl J. Clark to Asst. Chief W. W. Wilkinson, February 27, 1968, Holloman Collection, Memphis Public Library.
15. Michael Honey, *Going Down Jericho Road* (New York: W.W. Norton, 2011), p. 405.

CHAPTER 22

1. Director FBI to SAC Albany, "Counterintelligence Program, Black Nationalist-Hate Groups, Racial Intelligence" (FBI airtel), March 4, 1968.
2. SAC Memphis to Director FBI, "Sanitation Workers Strike, Memphis, Tennessee, RM" (LHM), March 6, 1968, p. 4.
3. "Strike Supporters Told, 'Clear Out of Here or Go to Jail,'" *Memphis Press-Scimitar*, March 6, 1968, p. 37.
4. Ibid.
5. Marrell McCullough, testimony to the House Select Committee on Assassinations, November 20, 1978, HSCA, MLK Appendix, vol. 6, p. 415.

6. The first draft of these events was memorialized in SAC Memphis to Director FBI, "Sanitation Workers Strike, Memphis, Tennessee, RM," March 7, 1968. The "put-up" characterization and Withers's and Black's regrets appear in Lawrence to SAC, "COMINFIL of SNCC, IS-SNCC; RM," March 25, 1968.

CHAPTER 23

1. "Re: Sanitation Workers Strike, Memphis, Tennessee, Racial Matters" (FBI report), March 9, 1968, p. 6.
2. William H. Lawrence, testimony to House Select Committee on Assassinations, November 21, 1978, HSCA, MLK Appendix, volume 6, p. 553.
3. Frank Holloman, interview by David Yellin, May 9, 1973, transcript in Crossroads to Freedom Archive, Rhodes College, Memphis.
4. Martin Luther King, Jr., address at Bishop Charles Mason Temple, March 18, 1968, http://kingencyclopedia.stanford.edu/encyclopedia/documentsentry/address_at_mass_meeting_at_the_bishop_charles_mason_temple.1.html.
5. K. W. Cook, "King Urges Work Stoppage by Negroes to Back Strike," *Memphis Commercial Appeal*, March 19, 1968, p. 1. For Lawson and Young's discussion of King's return engagement, see James Lawson, interview by David Yellin and Bill Thomas, July 1, 1968, transcript in Crossroads to Freedom Archive, Rhodes College, Memphis.
6. James Lawson, interview by Joan Beifuss and David Yellin, July 8, 1970, transcript in Crossroads to Freedom Archive, Rhodes College, Memphis.
7. Memphis to Director and Jackson, "Sanitation Workers Strike, Memphis, Tenn.; RM" (teletype), March 19, 1968.

CHAPTER 24

1. SAC Memphis to Director FBI, "Sanitation Workers Strike, Memphis, Tennessee, RM" (LHM), March 26, 1968; and Memphis to Director, "Sanitation Workers Strike, Memphis, Tenn.; RM" (teletype), March 26, 1968.
2. George C. Moore, testimony to House Select Committee on Assassinations, November 17, 1978, HSCA, MLK Appendix, vol. 6, p. 366.
3. "Martin Luther King, Jr.: A Current Analysis," FBI monograph, March 12, 1968.
4. David J. Garrow, *The FBI and Martin Luther King, Jr.* (New York: Penguin Books, 1983), p. 186.
5. Section Chief George C. Moore, Racial Intelligence, SOG, to SAC Jackson, "Washington Spring Project, RM," March 11, 1968.
6. Lawrence to SAC Memphis, "COMINFIL of SNCC, 157-1092-128," March 21, 1968,

7. Inspector G. P. Tines to Chief J. C. MacDonald, "Departmental Communication: Activities Planned During the March, March 27, 1968," Frank Holloman Collection, Memphis Public Library.

8. Ernest C. Withers, *Pictures Tell the Story* (Norfolk, Va.: Chrysler Museum of Art, 2000), p. 84.

9. Ibid.

CHAPTER 25

1. This conclusion according to anecdotal observations of march participants, including James Lawson, as well as statements of police director Holloman, and the March 28 police roll call, Frank Holloman Collection, Memphis Public Library.

2. "Students Hurl Rocks at Police," *Memphis Press-Scimitar*, March 28, 1968, p. 1.

3. Joan Turner Beifuss, *At the River I Stand* (Memphis: St. Luke's Press, 1990), p. 289.

4. SAC Memphis (probably written by William Lawrence, signed off on by Memphis SAC Robert Jensen) to Director "Black Organizing Project" (FBI airtel), May 6, 1968, p. 40.

5. Ralph David Abernathy, *And the Walls Came Tumbling Down* (New York: Harper & Row, 1989), p. 417.

6. James Lawson, interview by Joan Beifuss and David Yellin, July 8, 1970, transcript in Crossroads to Freedom Archive, Rhodes College, Memphis.

7. SAC Memphis (apparently written by William Lawrence and signed off on by Memphis SAC Robert Jensen) to Director and Washington Field Office (FBI teletype), March 28, 1968, p. 3.

8. Ibid.

9. "Day's Log of Police Calls Traces Racial Disturbance Shock Waves," *Memphis Commercial Appeal*, March 29, 1968, p. 25.

10. "One Boy Started It, Minister Says," *Memphis Commercial Appeal*, March 29, 1968, p. 9.

11. E. E. Redditt and W. B. Richmond to Graydon P. Tines, "RE: Information Re: Garbage Strike and Garbage Strike Sympathizers," Memphis Police Department, Inspectional Bureau memo, April 1, 1968, Frank Holloman Collection, Memphis Public Library.

12. Ralph Abernathy, *And the Walls Came Tumbling Down* (New York: Harper & Row, 1989), p. 418.

13. Thomas BeVier, "Widow's Wreath Is Bright Spot in Riot Rubble," *Memphis Commercial Appeal*, March 29, 1968, p. 25.

14. "One Fatality During a Storm of Rioting," *Memphis Press-Scimitar*, March 29, 1968, p. 11.

15. The local black press and white press, respectively, published drastically different accounts of the slaying. The black *Tri-State Defender* quoted Patrolman Jones as saying to Payne, "Come out nigger, or I'm going to shoot." In the white *Memphis Press-Scimitar*, Fowler Homes residents surrounded and intimidated the two officers. According to Patrolman Williams, "They were calling us every dirty name in the book, and shouting 'Kill the white ——.'" The *Defender* story described Payne's mother witnessing the shooting and crying, "You killed my son!" This, according to the *Defender*, prompted Jones to swing the shotgun toward her and say, "If you don't get back nigger, I'll kill you," at which point she fainted. But Payne's mother does not appear in the *Press-Scimitar* account. The *Press-Scimitar* described Patrolman Jones as staying with Payne and urging him to keep breathing and stay calm until an ambulance arrived, while in the *Defender* version, Payne was instantly killed. In the *Defender*, Jones kicked the boy's dead body, while in the *Press-Scimitar*, Jones repeated, "I'm sorry it happened. I didn't want to kill him."

16. "Downtown Area Left Scarred as Violence Erupts," *Memphis Press-Scimitar*, March 28, 1968, p. 6-X.

17. "Guardsmen Back Riot Curfew," *Memphis Commercial Appeal*, March 29, 1968, p. 1.

18. FBI Memphis to Director and WFO, "114PM URGENT," March 28, 1968, p. 1.

19. "Guard Arrives in City," *Memphis Press-Scimitar*, March 28, 1968, p. 1.

20. Mary George Beggs, "Curfew Streamlines Swinging Loeb Party," *Memphis Commercial Appeal*, March 29, 1968, p. 18.

CHAPTER 26

1. David J. Garrow, *The FBI and Martin Luther King, Jr.* (New York: Penguin Books, 1983), p. 194.

2. SAC Memphis to Director FBI, "Sanitation Workers Strike, Memphis, Tennessee, RM" (LHM), March 29, 1968, p. 3.

3. Ibid., p. 4.

4. Ibid., p. 13.

5. Lawrence's handwritten notes, obtained by *Memphis Commercial Appeal* reporter Marc Perrusquia.

6. House Select Committee on Assassinations, *Report*, 95th Cong., 2nd sess. (Washington, D.C.: Government Printing Office, 1979), pp. 411–13.

7. SAC Memphis to Director FBI, "Black Organizing Project," May 6, 1968, p. 42.

8. Ibid., p. 36.

9. Ibid., pp. 41–42.

10. Lawrence to SAC, "Sanitation Workers Strike, Memphis, Tenn., RM," April 2, 1968, p. 2.
11. Director FBI to SAC Memphis, teletype, April 2, 1968, in "FBI Sanitation Workers Strike, Memphis, Tennessee" file.

CHAPTER 27

1. James Lawson, interview by David Yellin and Joan Beifuss, July 8, 1970, transcript in Crossroads to Freedom Archive, Rhodes College, Memphis.
2. "2 Senators Ask That U.S. Block King" (UPI), *Memphis Press-Scimitar*, March 28, 1968, p. 1.
3. G. C. Moore to Mr. Sullivan, "Sanitation Workers Strike, Memphis, Tennessee, Racial Matters" (LHM), March 28, 1968.
4. David Garrow, *The FBI and Martin Luther King, Jr.* (New York: Penguin Books, 1983), p. 196.
5. FBI Memphis to Director, "Sanitation Workers Strike, Memphis, Tenn., RM" (teletype), March 28, 1968, p. 3.
6. Moore to Sullivan, "Counterintelligence Program, Black Nationalist-Hate Groups, Racial Intelligence (Martin Luther King)," March 29, 1968.
7. "King's Credibility Gap," *Memphis Commercial Appeal*, March 30, 1968, p. 6.
8. SAC Memphis to Director FBI, "Sanitation Workers Strike, Memphis, Tennessee, RM" (LHM), April 6, 1968, pp. 1–6.

CHAPTER 28

1. Howard Teten, interview by Stanley Pimentel, November 19, 2004, Society of Former Special Agents of the FBI, Oral History Project.
2. Ernestine Cofield, "S. African Student Photographer Gets Assassination Shots," *Chicago Daily Defender*, April 8, 1968, p. 29.
3. Ernest C. Withers, *Pictures Tell the Story* (Norfolk, Va.: Chrysler Museum of Art, 2000), p. 95.
4. Eliza Berman, "The Photograph That Captured the Horror of MLK's Assassination," *Time*, April 3, 2015.
5. Frank Holloman, interview by David Yellin, August 14, 1973, transcript in Crossroads to Freedom Archive, Rhodes College, Memphis.

AFTERWORD

1. Jim Balentine, "Withers Tells About Role in Pardon-for-Pay Deal," *Memphis Press-Scimitar*, April 7, 1981, p. 1.
2. Clayborne Carson, ed., *The Autobiography of Martin Luther King, Jr.* (New York: Warner Books, 1998), p. 358.

INDEX

Page numbers in *italics* refer to illustrations. Page numbers after 305 refer to endnotes.